CATHOLIC LANCASHIRE
From Reformation to Renewal
1559 -1991

Ladywell, Fernyhalgh. By permission of his Lordship the Bishop of Lancaster.

CATHOLIC LANCASHIRE
From Reformation to Renewal
1559 -1991

J. A. Hilton

Phillimore

1994

Published by
PHILIMORE & CO. LTD.
Shopwyke Manor Barn, Chichester, Sussex

© J. A. Hilton, 1994

ISBN 0 85033 893 X

Printed and bound in Great Britain by
THE BATH PRESS

To
A. M. C.

Contents

List of Illustrations

Frontispiece: Ladywell, Fernyhalgh. By permission of His Lordship the
Bishop of Lancaster

List of Maps

Preface

Since the Reformation, Lancashire has been the centre of English Catholicism, its Sacred Heartland. In the 16th century the Protestant Reformation turned Catholicism, which had previously commanded universal assent in Western Europe, into a minority in England. The largest concentration of the English Catholic minority was in Lancashire, where, under the impact of the Catholic Counter-Reformation, it survived and expanded. The influence of Catholic foreign powers and the attachment of Catholic Lancashire to the royal house of Stuart made a great noise until the final defeat of the Jacobites in the middle of the 18th century. With the Industrial Revolution, Catholic Lancashire grew even stronger, especially as it was reinforced by Irish immigrants. Halévy, in his *History of the English People in the Nineteenth Century*, described Catholics as 'emigrés de l'intérieur'—emigrants of the interior—but they had to make a living, and in doing so they made a contribution to the wider community. However, for Catholics the interior life of the soul, the eternal drama of salvation, remained ultimately more important. Meanwhile, the progress of secularisation placed these supernatural concerns in increasing doubt, and, despite the recent Catholic Renewal, the survival of Catholic Lancashire is once more at risk.

In writing this history of Catholic Lancashire, my debt to the historians whose work I have used is acknowledged in the notes. When I have already published work, I have cited my publication rather than the original sources. I am grateful for the help of the House of Lords Record Office, the Lancashire Record Office, the Cheshire Record Office, the Catholic Central Library, Liverpool City Library, Manchester Central Library, Wigan Library, the St John Rigby College Library, the Gradwell Library of Upholland College, and the Talbot Library at Preston. I am also grateful to Graphic Design Ltd. (Wigan) for drawing the maps. I am specially grateful to Dr. Gordon Blackwood, Mr. John McDermott, Mr. Brian Plumb, Mr. Leo Warren, and Dr. Maurice Whitehead for their comments on drafts of this book.

J. A. HILTON

Wigan 1994

xi

Super flumina Babylonis, illic sedimus et flevimus: cum recordaremur Sion.

Upon the rivers of Babylon, there we sat and wept: when we remembered Sion.

(Psalm136,1)

Chapter I

Reformation, 1559-1603

The Lancashire Catholic community was the local product of the opposing pressures of the Protestant Reformation and the Catholic Counter-Reformation. The study of Catholicism in Elizabethan Lancashire was pioneered by Leatherbarrow, and has been surveyed by Bossy, detailed by Haigh, and summarised by Walton.[1]

For a thousand years or more—since long before the county had been organised—the people of Lancashire, the region between the Pennines and the Irish Sea, had been members of the Roman Catholic Church. Untroubled by heresy or schism (Lancashire was virtually untouched by Lollardy), they had lived together as part of Western Christendom. According to the tradition of the Church, the Catholic faith had been taught by Jesus Christ to His apostles, and handed down by them to their successors, the bishops. The faith was identical with this tradition. Adumbrated in the Old Testament, and enshrined in the New Testament, it was was clarified and elaborated by the teaching of the Fathers and Doctors of the Church, pre-eminently, St Augustine and St Thomas Aquinas. That faith was that mankind, created by God for paradise, had fallen into Original Sin, inherited from Adam, but that God incarnate as man, Jesus Christ, had made atonement for this sin by His death, and demonstrated His divinity by His resurrection and ascension. He would return to judge all men according to their works. He had left the Holy Spirit to guide the Church He had founded, ruled by His apostles, and headed by St Peter, succeeded by the bishops and the pope. The Church not only taught the faith but also made available to the faithful the grace of God through the sacraments administered by bishops and priests. The faithful responded by prayer, penance, and, above all, by charity. Individuals might doubt and disbelieve. They might fall short in charity and commit actual sin, but the Church existed to call sinners to repentance. It joined its members together as the body of Christ, and called upon them and helped them to practise good neighbourliness.[2]

The sacraments included the rites of passage: baptism at birth, confirmation at adulthood, matrimony at marriage, ordination for the priesthood, and extreme unction, the viaticum, and burial at death. They also included the sacrament of penance or confession or reconciliation to mark repentance for sin. And they also included the Mass, which re-enacted the sacrifice of Calvary, made present the body of Christ, and joined the faithful in communion. Every priest was obliged to say Mass daily,

1

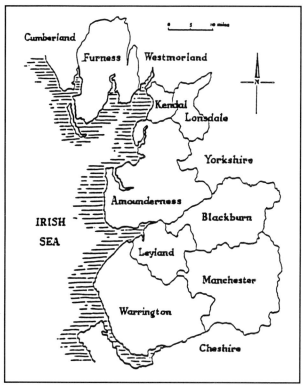

I   The Lancashire Deaneries, 1559

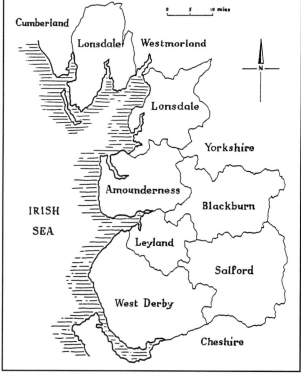

II   The Lancashire Hundreds, 1559

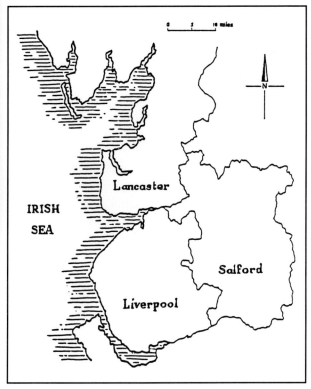

III   The Lancashire Catholic Dioceses, 1991

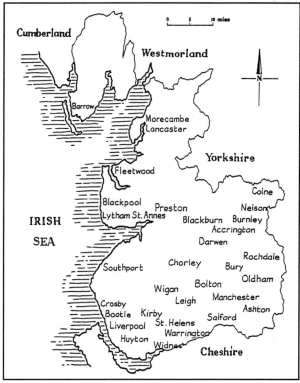

IV   The Lancashire Towns, 1991

and the faithful were obliged to attend every Sunday and on the numerous feast days throughout the year. Preparation for the feasts involved frequent, lengthy, and rigorous fasts.

The sacraments were celebrated in Latin, the universal language of the Western Church, according to the immemorial Latin rite. In England it combined the noble simplicity of the Roman rite with the elaborate ceremonial of the Gallican rite of the French Church. To the south of the Ribble, which was part of the diocese of Coventry and Lichfield, the Church followed the Sarum use. To the north of the Ribble, which was part of the archdiocese of York, it followed the similar use of York.[3]

In addition to administering the sacraments, the clergy and all members of religious orders, whether priests or not, were obliged to recite or sing the divine office. This consisted of seven hours or services of prayer, praise, psalms, lessons, and hymns. The liturgy was surrounded by sacramentals, the sign of the cross, holy water, candles, incense, and images, and devotions, such as the Little Office of Our Lady, the Rosary, the Jesus Psalter, the Angelus, and a whole host of practices which the devout clergy and laity might observe.

Lancashire had long been a poor and backward county. It was distant from the south-eastern centres of commerce, government, and learning, and on the edge of two large dioceses. It was a sparsely populated land of moors to the east—proverbially 'If thou canst see Pendle Hill, it is going to rain, and if thou cannot, it is raining'—and mosses to the west—proverbially 'God's grace and Pilling Moss are endless'. It was divided into 60 large parishes, grouped into eight deaneries. It had only a few abbeys and priories—Furness, Whalley, Cockersand, Cartmel, Lancaster, Burscough, Upholland, Penwortham, and Lytham—and friaries—Preston, Lancaster, and Warrington—and no convents.[4]

However, in Lancashire the Tudor Reformation in religion overtook a Church that was undergoing a belated efflorescence. Between 1470 and 1548 nearly fifty new chapels were added to the existing 58 parish churches and fifty-odd chapels. This late flowering of medieval Lancastrian Catholicism was personified by Lady Margaret Beaufort. The daughter of John Beaufort, Marquess of Somerset (a son of John of Gaunt, Duke of Lancaster), she married Edmund Tudor, Earl of Richmond, son of Owen Tudor and Queen Katherine, the widow of Henry V. Her son became King Henry VII. Her third marriage was to Thomas Stanley, first Earl of Derby, the greatest landowner in Lancashire. She was a devout Catholic and a patron of religion and learning. She was a penitent of John Fisher, and finally took monastic vows. She translated Thomas a Kempis's *Imitation of Christ* into English, and was the patron of Caxton and Wynkyn de Worde, the pioneers of printing in England. She established chairs at Oxford and Cambridge, and endowed St John's College, Cambridge and Westminster Abbey, and financed the completion of King's College, Cambridge. She also supported the re-building of Manchester collegiate church (now the Anglican cathedral), and drew many of her household from Manchester. In 1509 she was buried in Westminster Abbey under a gilded bronze Renaissance effigy. An alabaster effigy was erected next to that of Lord Derby at Burscough Priory, and after the Dissolution both were removed to Ormskirk parish church where they remain as a monument to the art and piety of the early 16th century.[5]

Religious change was imposed on Lancashire from above by the English Reformation. The Henrician Reformation embodied in the Act of Supremacy of 1535 replaced the pope with the king as the head of the Church of England, but otherwise made no change in Catholic teaching and practice. However, between 1536 and 1539, the monasteries were dissolved in the teeth of active opposition, but, otherwise, the ordinary Catholic in his parish church saw little if any change. Moreover, in 1541 the new diocese of Chester—its cathedral the former monastery—was created from parts of the dioceses of Lichfield and York and included Lancashire and Cheshire, together with parts of Cumberland, Westmorland, and Yorkshire. The Edwardian Reformation began with the dissolution of the chantries in 1547 and continued with the Acts of Uniformity of 1547 and 1552 which replaced the Roman liturgy with successively more Protestant English Books of Common Prayer. The Marian Counter-Reformation repealed the Act of Uniformity in 1553 and the Act of Supremacy in 1554. The Elizabethan Reformation in 1559 restored the Act of Supremacy and by the Act of Uniformity imposed a new Book of Common Prayer, which was in effect a compromise between the first and second Edwardian Prayer Books.

Protestantism was a dynamic and complex religious movement dedicated to the reformation of Christianity. Originating in Germany with Luther, it spread into the rest of northern Europe in the first half of the 16th century, and was developed further by Calvin. It exalted the authority of Scripture but limited the authority of the Church, and denied the authority of the papacy. It emphasised divine grace, and denied that good works effected salvation. It retained baptism and holy communion, but denied the other sacraments, together with the sacrifice of the Mass and the doctrine of transubstantiation, and it denounced devotion to the saints.[6]

The Protestant Reformation was opposed by the Catholic or Counter-Reformation. The papacy, episcopate, priesthood, and religious orders underwent moral reform. New, active religious orders, pre-eminently the Jesuits, were organised to evangelise the faithful. The Council of Trent (1545-1563) codified these reforms, and defined as essential Catholic beliefs the very doctrines controverted by the Protestants.[7]

The Elizabethan religious settlement survived a series of attempts to overthrow it. The Northern Rising of 1569, which received no active support from Lancashire, was defeated. The papal bull, *Regnans in excelsis* of 1570, declaring Elizabeth deposed and her subjects absolved of obedience, intensified the religious and political crisis still further, and was followed by increasingly harsh anti-Catholic legislation and by Catholic plots, resulting in the execution of Mary Queen of Scots in 1587 and culminating in the defeat of the Spanish Armada in 1588.

By the end of the reign a whole battery of anti-Catholic penal legislation was in place. Attendance at the Sunday services of the Established Church of England was compulsory on pain of heavy fines backed by imprisonment, whilst attendance at Catholic rites was banned under similar penalties. The presence of a Catholic priest on English soil was treason punishable by death, and harbouring a priest incurred outlawry and forfeiture.

Despite conservative resistance, the royal Reformation produced conformity. The bulk of the clergy accepted the changes. The parish church or chapel was the centre of communal life, and to opt out of the Established Church was to withdraw from the local community. An increasingly severe range of penalties inflicted not only formal exclusion from government and society but also fines and imprisonment on those who did withdraw. These penalties were not consistently applied, and, therefore, Catholicism survived, but they were sufficient, when combined with the other motives to conform, to reduce it to a very small minority even in Lancashire.

Nevertheless, a Catholic minority did survive and was at its strongest in Lancashire. In 1578 the convicted recusants, that is those found guilty of refusing to attend the services of the Church of England, numbered 304 in Lancashire, and there were 29 non-communicants, that is those who attended the Anglican services weekly but refused to receive the Anglican communion at least once a year. By 1601 the number of recusants had more than doubled to 754, and the number of non-communicants had increased by more than ten-fold to three hundred and forty-nine. Nevertheless, the recusants constituted a mere 0.4 per cent of an estimated population of about 100,000, though convicted recusants may only have been the tip of the Catholic iceberg, which included unconvicted recusants and Church-Papists, that is those who outwardly conformed to the Church of England whilst remaining inwardly Catholics. There was nothing like even this amount of resistance elsewhere, but the attention it attracted as the last English outpost of the great Roman Catholic Church, which retained its hold on southern Europe and reached across the Atlantic to the New World, must not blind us, especially those inside it, to the fact that the Lancastrian Catholic community was a pathetic remnant.[8]

That it survived at all remains something of a mystery, though the reason has been attributed to the geography and social structure of the county and to the failings and the zeal of individuals. Lancashire was distant from the centre of government and inaccessible behind its moors and mosses, but the even more distant and inaccessible Lake counties were lost to Catholicism. Lancashire was a backward county characterised by its conservatism which made its local administration reluctant to enforce the new religious regime. The first Elizabethan bishop of Chester, William Downham, was notorious for his weakness. The lords lieutenant, the earls of Derby, were hardly zealous persecutors of Catholics. The justices of the peace were notoriously lax in their enforcement of the religious laws. These Catholic or quasi-Catholic magistrates and their subordinates were part of the problem, for Catholicism obviously exerted an attraction on a minority of the Lancashire gentry and yeomanry. This attachment helped and antedated the work of the seminary priests.[9]

A significant factor was the number of recusant clergy, that is priests ordained in England as Catholics who refused to accept the Elizabethan Protestant Settlement. About 1570 there were at least 56 working in the county. The impact of the Jesuit Edmund Campion who came late and briefly to the county has certainly been over-estimated, but the influence of Lawrence Vaux and William Allen has, if anything, been under-estimated.[10]

In 1559 Vaux (born at Blackrod, educated at Manchester Grammar School and at Oxford), as warden of the collegiate church of Manchester—his choir-stall is still there—was the pre-eminent ecclesiastic in the county. His refusal to conform in 1559 and his circulation of letters in 1566 to gentry like Molyneux and Norris, conveying the papal ruling that conformity to the Church of England was the sin of schism from the Catholic Church, took the lead in creating Lancastrian recusancy:

> I am charged to make a definitive sentence, that all such as offer children to the baptism now used or be present at the communion or service now used in churches in England, as well the laity as the clergy, do not walk in the state of salvation; neither may we not communicate nor sociate ourselves in company with schismatic or heretic in divine things; there is no exception nor dispensation can be had for any of the laity if they will stand in the state of salvation. Ye must not think this be any severity or rigorousness of the Pope, Pius V, that now is God's Vicar in earth, to whom at this present God hath appointed the government of His Church in earth ... If ye associate yourselves at sacraments or service that is contrary to the unity of Christ His Church ye fall into schism, that is to say, ye be separated from Christ His Church, and living in that state (as saith St Augustine) although you lead never so good a life in the sight of the world, the wrath of God hangeth over you, and dying in that state shall lose the everlasting life in Heaven ... I pray you the comfortable promise of our Saviour Christ in His Gospel, Whosoever will confess Christ and the faith of His spouse of the Catholic Church before men, He will confess Him before His Father in Heaven ...

His *Catechism*, first published at Louvain in 1567, became one of the principal means of formation for his co-religionists. It was 'an Instruction, what all people ought to believe and do, if they will be saved', and expounded the creed, the commandments, and the sacraments. It insisted that 'the Church is a visible company of people, first gathered together of Christ and His disciples, continued unto this day in a perpetual succession in one Apostolic faith, living under Christ the head: and in earth, under his Vicar, Pastor and chief Bishop', and, therefore, that 'a man ought to forsake all new doctrines, and constantly to cleave to the ancient religion and doctrine, universally and openly professed in England, by all the ancient kings and peoples of this island, ever since the first receiving of Christian religion there'. He worked in Lancashire, sheltered by the gentry, but was captured in 1580, and died in prison in 1585.[11]

William Allen (born at Rossall and educated at Oxford) preached the same message as Vaux, and by his foundation of the English seminary at Douay in 1568 ensured that there would be a future supply of priests to preach that message: 'Our aim is and has always been, to train Catholics to be plainly and openly Catholics; to be men who will always refuse any kind of spiritual commerce with heretics'. Made a cardinal in 1587, he was to all intents and purposes the leader of the English Catholics until his death in 1594. Lancastrian Catholicism was to a certain degree the

1 *William Allen. From a print in the possession of the author.*

extended family of Vaux and Allen, what Rowse calls 'the social bonds, the intricate threads of interest and affection, that kept the Catholic minority together'.[12]

The recusant priests like Vaux were followed by the seminary priests trained by Allen. Between 1582 and 1592 their local leader, known as 'bishop of Chester', was Thomas Bell. Born in Yorkshire in 1551 he had been ordained for the Church of England, but went to Rome and was ordained a Catholic priest in 1579. He was sent to England in 1582, and went first to York, and then to Lancashire, working mainly in the Wigan district, based in the house of Miles Gerard of Ince. However, he was arrested in 1592 and conformed. He provided the government with a list of a network, which he had helped to set up, of 93 households which harboured priests, and he was sent back to Lancashire to assist Lord Derby in arresting those whom he had betrayed. Some of the gentry were imprisoned, but many of the intended victims, both gentry and priests, were forewarned by Bell's conformity, and had fled. As a result, the Catholic Lancashire community survived what might have been a major blow.[13]

The Lancashire Catholics responded by sending more recruits to the seminaries, a total of 60 out of 815 in Elizabeth's reign, a number only exceeded by the 79 from the much larger county of Yorkshire. Despite the fact that it was made illegal, they went abroad to prepare for ordination at the English continental colleges: Douay (Douai) founded in 1568, Rome in 1579, Valladolid in 1589, and Seville in 1592. They received their initial schooling at home or in grammar schools, like Blackburn, still under local Catholic influence, or in clandestine Catholic schools, such as that at Ormskirk, which amounted on and off to as many as 32 before the end of the century.[14]

There were no Catholic bishops at liberty in England. The only acknowledged leader of English Catholics was Cardinal Allen in exile on the continent, and he died in 1594. This lack of leadership and organisation led to difficulties and disputes, like that in 1595 amongst the priests imprisoned at Wisbech. In an attempt to remedy the problem, two leading secular priests, John Mush (of the diocese of Chester) and John Colleton, proposed that the secular clergy establish a congregation or fraternity with common rules, and divided into branches, each with its own elected officers, one centred on London, and the other on Lancashire. Meanwhile, the secular clergy also applied to the holy see for the appointment of English bishops. In 1598 at the suggestion of the Jesuit Robert Persons, Cardinal Cajetan, the Cardinal Protector of England, decided to appoint an archpriest, George Blackwell, to act as superior of the secular clergy, and ordered him to consult the English Jesuit superior. The secular clergy protested, and so the holy see confirmed the appointment of the archpriest but forbade him to consult the Jesuit superior. Meanwhile, the archpriest divided the country into districts, each under an assistant appointed by himself. In Lancashire the assistant was John Mitchell, a Yorkshireman educated at Oxford and Douay, who had been at work here since coming on the English mission in 1578.[15]

At the same time, a Lancastrian, Thomas Worthington, was appointed president of Douay, and managed to bring the college into disrepute with the English secular clergy. The son of Peter Worthington of Blainscough, Standish, he was born about 1550 and educated at Oxford and Douay. He served on the English mission, and as chaplain to the English Catholic troops in Spanish service in the Netherlands. He was appointed vice-president of Douay in 1598, and president in 1599. He was believed to be under the influence of Persons, and was accused of sending too many insufficiently trained priests to England. However, in 1611 he did come to an agreement with the archpriest to regulate the flow of priests from Douay to England. Nevertheless, in 1613 he was removed from the presidency by the cardinal protector, and returned to England where he became Catholic archdeacon of Nottinghamshire and Derbyshire. When he died about 1626 he was reported to have become either an Oratorian or a Jesuit, rumours which display the suspicions of the secular clergy.[16]

From their first participation in the English mission at the instance of William Allen, the Jesuits brought discipline and an increasing organisation. On its foundation in 1579 the English College at Rome was placed under a Jesuit rector. In 1580 the Jesuits Campion and Persons were sent to England and worked for a time in Lancashire. Thereafter Jesuits came in increasing numbers, whilst Persons exercised an inordinate influence over the entire English mission until his death in 1610.[17]

Eight Lancastrians joined the Jesuits before the end of Elizabeth's reign: John Gerard, Thomas Lister, John Nelson, Richard Singleton, Thomas Talbot, John Worthington, Lawrence Worthington, and Peter Worthington. John and Lawrence Worthington were brothers, the sons of Richard Worthington esquire of Blainscough, Standish, and the nephews of Thomas Worthington, president of Douay. Their eldest brother, Thomas, married a niece of Cardinal Allen. John was born in 1573, and educated at Eu, Rheims, Valladolid, Seville, and Rome. He joined the Jesuits in 1598, was the first Jesuit to work in Lancashire, and became Jesuit superior of the Lancashire district in 1622. He died in 1652. Lawrence was born about 1576, educated at Douay, and joined the Jesuits in 1599. He taught for a time in Spain, and was sent on the English mission in 1612, arrested in 1615, banished in 1618, and returned in 1621. He died in Lorraine in 1637.[18]

The Jesuits and the seminary priests brought the revived Catholicism of the Counter-Reformation, its doctrine defined and its discipline renewed by the Council of Trent. Trained in the new seminaries, they carried with them the systematic spirituality of the Spanish mystics.[19]

Although in the north the Catholics reached up into the Ribble valley, they were concentrated on the coastal plain, in the deaneries of Warrington, Leyland, and Amounderness, and, to an extent, in Blackburn, that is the hundreds of West Derby, Leyland, Amounderness, and Blackburn.[20]

This Lancastrian Catholic enclave was almost surrounded by hostile or indifferent territory. To the north lay Cumberland and Westmorland where Catholicism virtually withered away. To the north-east beyond Ribblesdale it just touched the Catholic districts of Yorkshire. To the south-east and the south were Protestant Manchester and Cheshire.[21]

The religious frontier between Catholic and Protestant was finely drawn. It ran from Lancaster in the north, along the edge of the moorland into Ribblesdale, and then south of the Ribble betweeen Wigan and Bolton to the Mersey. There were a few recusants in the Manchester deanery, especially in the border parishes of Eccles and Dean, the debatable land close to the safe Catholic areas. There was also the mixed deanery of Blackburn where recusants clustered round the estates of the Catholic squires.[22]

Allen had remarked enviously on the geographical toleration in some religiously divided countries like Germany and Switzerland, where 'if they cannot have the exercise of their profession in one territory, canton, town, church, or parish, yet they may have it in another'.[23]

The geography of religion in Lancashire was influenced not so much by agriculture as by industry. The arable region was shared, at least south of the Ribble, between Catholic and Protestant zones. The pastoral Protestant area centred on Manchester was dominated by woollen-weaving and linked with the Protestant West Riding of Yorkshire, East Anglia, and London. The Catholic area was dominated by linen-weaving and had links with Ireland. The Catholic area was characterised by its isolation from the rest of England, by its numerous gentry, and by its addiction to country sports and pleasures. As the old rhyme (quoted by Collins) has it:

> When all England is aloft
> Where so safe as in Christ's croft?
> Where do you think that Christ's croft to be
> But between Ribble and Mersey? [24]

The old Roman road ran along the eastern edge of the Catholic area from Warrington through Wigan and Preston to Lancaster, and an old track-way ran south from Morecambe Bay at Heysham through Lancaster and Preston and then southwards through Ormskirk to Liverpool and Chester. The Catholic part of Lancashire lay along the Irish Sea, part of the Atlantic zone, with the Protestant area in the inland moorland part of the Highland zone.[25]

However, the career of Henry Fitzsimon illustrates the connection with the Irish colony in Manchester whither linen yarn was imported from Ireland. He was born in 1566, the son of Sir Nicholas Fitzsimon of Dublin. He was educated at Manchester Grammar School and Oxford, and then went to Pont à Mousson and Douay. He joined the Jesuits at Tournay in 1592, and went on to Louvain. He was sent to Dublin in 1597, arrested in 1598, and banished in 1603. He later returned to Ireland, and died at Kilkenny in the 1640s.[26]

Looked at another way, Catholicism was stonger where Protestantism, radiating out from Manchester, became weaker. The Catholics lay roughly outside a fifteen-mile radius or a day's journey round Manchester. Again it must be emphasised that, even in the so-called Catholic areas, Catholics were in a minority. The relative success of Catholicism in Lancashire should not blind us to the overwhelming success of Protestantism, nor to the continued existence of an alternative religion, witchraft, or to the even more widespread religious apathy and indifference amounting to atheism.[27]

The distribution of Catholic recusancy casts light on its growth. The number of recusants detected in the Catholic areas reflects, in Haigh's view, 'not so much the incidence of recusancy but the efforts put into finding them'. Zealous Protestant clergy in Catholic parishes like Prescot greatly increased the number of recusants detected. For much of Elizabeth's reign sympathetic local officials protected Catholics in the Catholic areas. In these large scattered parishes amateur and incompetent, as well as sympathetic, local officials found it difficult to enforce the law. Nevertheless, the total population was small—the average population of each parish was 1,500—and could be known to those officials. Moreover, the myth of the Catholic family, generation succeeding to generation in unbroken devotion to the Catholic faith, hides the truth that families are made up of individuals whose religious views and behaviour might differ from one another, and indeed might change. An individual, like John Rigby of Harrock Hall, Wrightington, Eccleston, might be brought up a Catholic, then abandon the practice of his faith, and then might recover it, with, in Rigby's case, fatal consequences: he was hanged, drawn, and quartered at Southwark on 21 June 1600 for being reconciled to Catholicism. The fact that the number of recusants reported in Catholic areas depended on the zeal of local officials does not lead to the absurd conclusion that the fewer the number of recusants reported the more Catholic the district was. Nobody claims that Manchester was a hotbed of secret Catholicism. Nevertheless, it is sometimes implied that Catholicism was much stronger than indicated by the figures cited above, that throughout the reign of Elizabeth it constituted the majority of the population, and that it only declined into a small minority in the 18th century. Whatever went on in the minds and hearts of men and women, practising Catholics, which in the 16th and 17th centuries meant recusants, were a small but growing minority responding to the call of their priests 'to be plainly and openly Catholics'.[28]

The Catholic recusants were led by the gentry, though in Lancashire there was an unusually large number of recusant yeomen and farmers, but the overwhelming majority of recusants in all classes were women. The recusant gentry set an example for their servants and neighbours and used their influence to protect them. In Blackburn and Burnley they ensured a Catholic influence in the local grammar schools. Pre-eminent amongst the Lancashire Catholic gentry was John Towneley of Towneley, Burnley. He was one of the richest gentlemen in the county, and certainly the richest of the Catholic gentry. With his large household and his collection of Duchy of Lancaster stewardships, he exercised great patronage and influence. Towneley was prepared to conform but not to communicate, and accordingly from 1568 onwards spent most of his time in prison until his death in 1608. The gentry made up a large proportion of the total recusants. In 1596, 149 (20 per cent) of the 724 Lancashire recusants were gentry. In Lancashire the recusants formed a disproportionately large fraction of the gentry. In 1590 41 (30 per cent) of the 129 gentry families were recusant, and an even larger number, 74, had Catholic sympathies. The Catholic gentry were even more significant in the Protestant areas. In 1596, 10 of the 16 recusants in Manchester deanery were gentry, compared with 71 gentry out of 443 recusants in Warrington deanery. Not only were the great majority of recusants women, but even more significantly, many of the conformist gentry had recusant wives and, therefore, recusant children. The Elizabethan Catholic family was matri-archal.[29]

A detailed official survey of recusancy in the province of York in 1596 provides a clear picture of the Lancashire Catholic community, though the details may reflect enforcement as much as real numbers.[30]

Catholics were thin on the ground in the sparsely populated northern deaneries: there were only three in Furness, 16 in Kendal, and 25 in Lonsdale. They were also rare, a mere 16, in the Protestant stronghold of Manchester deanery. They were stronger in the deaneries of Leyland with 45 recusants and Blackburn with 61, and stronger still in Amounderness with its total of a hundred and forty. However, the real Catholic heartland appeared to be the south-western deanery of Warrington with 465 recusants, more than in all the other deaneries put together.

There were a few large concentrations of recusants. The recusants of Manchester deanery were a few gentry, apparently isolated within their families, such as Eliza-beth Barlow, sister of Alexander Barlow of Barlow, Cuthbert Hulton, the son of William Hulton of Hulton, and Mary Orrell, wife of William Orrell of Turton. Blackburn deanery included Robert Towneley, son of Henry Towneley, and small concentrations of a dozen or so at Whalley, Burnley, and Blackburn. Similarly, Leyland deanery included amongst a scattering of recusants two concentrations: 10 at Leyland and 22 at Standish, led by such gentlemen as Thomas Worthington of Blainscough. Lonsdale, Kendal, and Furness deaneries also included a few recusant gentry here and there, and a number of poor vagrants. The distribution of recusants in Amounderness deanery was apparently haphazard, ranging from three in Cockerham to 32 in Garstang and 47 in Kirkham. In Warrington deanery most parishes, except Liverpool with one, Aughton with five, and Halsall with eight, had concentrations in double figures, but by far the largest group was the 126 in Wigan.

The rural townships of the parish of Wigan demonstrated the typical pattern of gentry households, like the Langtons of Lowe, Hindley, and the Bradshaighs of Haigh, and a few plebeians. However, the borough of Wigan contained 71 recusants, 59 of them women, and nearly all of them craftsmen and shopkeepers or rather their wives, widows, and daughters. Wigan with its Catholic butchers' wives, such as Eleanor Grange and Alice Almond, looks very much like York, where another butcher's wife, Margaret Clitheroe, was executed for maintaining priests, and where Thomas Bell had begun his missionary career. Within the seigneurial rural Catholicism of the county as a whole there lurked the urban Catholicism of Wigan, not unlike the urban centres of Irish and French Catholicism.[31]

By the end of the reign of Elizabeth I Lancastrian Catholicism had not only survived but was increasing in numbers. There were 498 detected recusants in 1598, 754 in 1601, and nearly 2,000 in 1603, a fourfold increase in the last five years of the reign. It was, in Rowse's words, 'a self-contained minority with its affiliations abroad'.[32]

The strongest Catholic community in England, Catholic Lancashire looked foward to the reign of a new king and the rule of a new dynasty and even to the prospect of toleration.

Notes

1. J. S. Leatherbarrow, *The Lancashire Elizabethan Recusants* (Chetham Society (hereafter CS), new series, vol.90, 1947); J. Bossy, *The English Catholic Community 1570-1850* (1975)(hereafter Bossy, *Community*), pp.91-5; C. Haigh, *Reformation and Resistance in Tudor Lancashire* (1975)(hereafter Haigh); J. K. Walton, *Lancashire: A Social History, 1558-1939* (1987)(hereafter Walton).

2. Bossy, *Christianity in the West* (1985); E. Duffy, *The Stripping of the Altars, Traditional Religion in England, c.1400-c.1580* (1992); Haigh, pp.76-85.

3. *Catholic Encyclopedia* (hereafter *CE*)(15 vols, 1907-12), vol.13, pp.155-6, vol.15, p.735.

4. *Victoria County History of Lancaster* (hereafter *VCH Lancs*)(8 vols, 1906-14), vol.2, pp.104-67.

5. Walton, p.37; *Dictionary of National Biography* (hereafter *DNB*)(21 vols, 1907-17), vol.2, pp.48-9; M. Jones and M. G. Underwood, *The King's Mother: Lady Margaret Beaufort, Countess of Richmond and Derby* (1992), pp.149-53.

6. J. J. Scarisbrick, *The Reformation and the English People* (1984); A. G. Dickens, *The English Reformation* (1967).

7. N. S. Davidson, *The Counter-Reformation* (1987).

8. Walton, pp.25,45; A. L. Rowse, *The England of Elizabeth* (1950), p.449.

9. Walton, p.47; J. A. Hilton, 'The Cumbrian Catholics', *Northern History* (hereafter *NH*) vol.16 (1980).

10. Haigh, p.249; Walton, p.46.

11. Haigh, pp.203-4; P. Hughes, *The Reformation in England* (3 vols, 1963)(hereafter Hughes), vol.3, pp.248-50, 425; T. G. Law (ed.), *A Catechisme or Christian Doctrine by Laurence Vaux* (CS, new series vol.4, 1885), pp.xxxiii-xxxiv, lxxxvii, 5, 15, 95, passim.

12. Hughes, vol.3, pp.282-302; G. Anstruther, *The Seminary Priests* (4 vols, 1968-77)(hereafter Anstruther), vol.1, pp.4-5; F. J. Singleton, 'Recusancy in the Fylde', *North West Catholic History* (hereafter *NWCH*), vol.13 (1986); Rowse, p.451.

13. Haigh, pp.280,289; Anstruther, vol.1,pp. 29-30.

14. Anstruther, vol.1, pp.x-xii, 395: A. C. F. Beales, *Education Under Penalty* (1961)(hereafter Beales), pp.74-83; P. W. Armitage, 'Catholicism and Educational Control in North-East Lancashire in the Reign of Elizabeth', *NWCH*, vol.13 (1986).

15. Hughes, *Rome and the Counter-Reformation in England* (1941)(hereafter Hughes, *Rome*), pp.278-306; M. A. Tierney (ed.), *Dodd's Church History of England* (5 vols, 1839-49)(hereafter Tierney), vol.3, pp.36-56; Anstruther, vol.1, p.229.

16. Anstruther, vol.1, p.387; Tierney, vol.5, pp.4-7,28-30.

17. D. A. Bellenger, *English and Welsh Priests 1558-1800* (1984)(hereafter Bellenger, *Priests*), p.17; M. E. Williams, *The Venerable English College Rome* (London,1979); H. Foley, *Records of the English Province of the Society of Jesus* (7 vols, London, 1877-83)(hereafter Foley), vol.7, pp.571-4.

18. Bellenger, *Priests*, pp.150-63; Foley, vol.7, pp.864-6.

19. Davidson, *Counter Reformation*.

20. Bossy, *Community*, p.92; Haigh, p.316.
21. Bossy, *Community*, pp.80-93; Hilton, *NH*, vol.16; H. Aveling, 'The Catholic Recusants of the West Riding of Yorkshire', *Proceedings of the Leeds Philosophical and Literary Society, Literary and Historical Section*, vol.10 (6) (1963), pp.190-306; Hilton,'Post-Reformation Catholicism in Cheshire ', *NWCH*, vol.9 (1982); K. R. Wark, *Elizabethan Recusancy in Cheshire* (CS, 3rd series, vol.19 1971).
22. Bossy, *Community*, p.92; Haigh, pp.316-7.
23. Tierney, vol.3, p.3.
24. Bossy, *Community*, p.93; Haigh, pp.324-6; H. C. Collins, *Lancashire Plain and Seaboard* (1953), p.53.
25. Collins, pp.1-9, 122-8 ; C. Fox, *The Personality of Britain* (1959); M. J. Wise, *Ordnance Survey Atlas of Great Britain* (1982), p.10.
26. Walton, pp.21,26; Foley, vol.7, 260.
27. Haigh, p.325; Walton, pp.36-39; K. Thomas, *Religion and the Decline of Magic* (1978); C. Hole, *Witchcraft in Britain* (1980).
28. Haigh, pp.273-78; P. Laslett, *The World we have lost* (1979); J. Cartmell, *Blessed John Rigby* (1958); L. Brooks, *Faith Never Lost* (1982); Haigh, 'The Continuity of Catholicism in the English Reformation', *Past and Present*, vol.93 (1981).
29. Walton, pp.46; Haigh, pp.260-1,281-5; Armitage, *NWCH*, vol.13 ; *VCH Lancs*, vol.6, pp.459-60; Bossy, *Community*, pp.153-8.
30. *Miscellanea* (Catholic Record Society [henceforth CRS], vol.53, 1960), pp.74-87, 101-7.
31. Aveling, *Catholic Recusancy in York* (CRS monograph vol.2, London, 1970), pp.45-76; Rowse, *The Expansion of Elizabethan England* (1955); J. H. Elliott, *Europe Divided, 1559-1598* (1968), pp.324-9.
32. Haigh, p.33; Rowse, *England of Elizabeth*, p.451.

Chapter II

The Consolidation of the Catholic Community, 1603-42

Between the accession of James I in 1603 and the outbreak of the Civil War in 1642, the Lancashire Catholics, who were concentrated in the west and north of the county, grew in numbers, received a formal ecclesiastical organisation, and adopted their contemplative spirituality.

In 1603 Lancashire possessed the largest Catholic community in England. As the King himself (quoted by Haigh) wrote in 1617, 'At our first entering to this Crown and Kingdom we were informed, and that too truly, that our county of Lancaster abounded more in popish recusants than any other country of England'. A return of 1603 estimated that a quarter of the English and Welsh recusants was contained by the diocese of Chester (the counties of Lancashire and Cheshire, and there were few in Cheshire). In 1641, Richard Heyrick, warden of Manchester collegiate church (quoted by Richardson), complained that 'Popery has multiplied abundantly. In Lancashire it has superabounded above an hyperbole; the mass has outfaced our Christian meetings, Jesuits have jeered our ministers, confronted and abused authority'.[1]

However, despite an increase in recusants, they were still only a minority, as the vicar of Prescot pointed out in 1604:

> I see no cause of any danger from such simple recusants, whom though popish priests inveigle what they can, yet the governors of the country being sound and loyal, the most populous part thereof zealously disposed in religion, ever able to suppress their insolence, and Cheshire confining upon them being exceedingly well affected, there is no fear of attempts by such weak means, whose malice is more happily than their might. There is of my knowledge in one parish of Lancashire, viz Manchester, 16,000 communicants able to encounter all the known recusants in the North part of England.[2]

James's rule (1603-25) was relatively tolerant. As the son of the Catholic Mary, Queen of Scots, and as a king of Scotland who was lenient towards Scottish Catholics, James aroused unrealistic Catholic hopes of toleration. When these hopes were dashed the extremists turned to the Bye Plot of 1604 and the Gunpowder Plot of 1605. Although these plots resulted in intensified penal legislation, in practice James did not apply the full rigour of the penal laws, partly because he was tolerant by nature and partly because he was involved in long marriage negotiations, first with Catholic Spain and then with Catholic France.[3]

As a result, recusancy increased considerably in Lancashire. The increase was specially marked in the first year of the reign. When toleration was not granted there was some decline in recusancy with an increase in the number of non-communicants, but overall there was a considerable increase in recusancy. The number of non-communicants almost doubled from 349 to 521 between 1601 and 1604, but the number of recusants increased more than four-fold from 754 in 1601 to 3,516 in 1604. The diocesan visitation of 1604 was careful to distinguish between old and new recusants. By 1613 the number of recusants had fallen to 2,075, but this was still twice as large as the number in 1601. Meanwhile, the number of non-communicants had risen to two thousand three hundred and ninety-two. Nevertheless, by 1630 the number of recusants had risen again to 3,433, and by 1641 of the 15,000 recusants on the subsidy roll 9,000 were in Lancashire. Catholics slipped back and forth between recusancy and non-communicating conformity.[4]

The number of recusants fell back after the initial increase at the start of James's reign, because the expected toleration was not forthcoming. When the secular priest Thomas Briscow or Burscough was taken in Lancashire when about to say Mass in 1605, 26 of the 29 taken with him promptly submitted and conformed. Similarly, of 56 Lancashire recusants who appeared before the judges in 1605, 52, including Thomas and Henry Clifton, gentlemen, conformed. In 1604 the vicar of Prescot diagnosed the cause of recusancy and prescribed its cure in his parish and the county as a whole. Even though Prescot was:

> one of the most infected parishes in Lancashire and most haunted by seditious priests where of late years the Queen's messengers were slain and wounded.

> The persons named in this presentment are of mean reputation and of no force or ability of themselves and may for the most part easily by authority be reclaimed when their hopes are at an end.

> There is in this parish planted a bachelor of divinity, a diligent preacher, but the persuasion of priests and backwood landlords are the chief cause of the people's inconstancy and unsettled disposition in religion.

The Puritan White came to the same conclusion (quoted by Richardson): 'I speak not of simple recusants but of fugitive Jesuits and seminarists ... for many Papists when their seducers are removed shall come home to obedience, and repenting then of their idolatry and superstition embrace ... the religion established'. Writing in 1609 from within the Catholic community, the Jesuit John Gerard came to the same conclusion:

> when a large number of the people are Catholics and nearly all have leanings towards Catholicism, it is easy to make many converts and to have large congregations at sermons. For instance, in Lancashire, I have seen myself more than two hundred present at Mass and sermon. People of this kind come into the Church without difficulty but they fall away the moment persecution blows up. When the alarm is over, they come back again.[5]

Despite Charles I's marriage to the French Catholic Princess Henrietta Maria, his Catholic subjects fared little better, for the marriage incurred Protestant suspicions of Catholic influence at Court, and so the King sought to distance himself from Catholicism by upholding the penal laws. Thus Edmund Arrowsmith, born in Lancashire in 1585, ordained in 1605, and admitted to the Jesuits in 1613, was captured at work in his native county, and hanged at Lancaster in 1628. At least after 1626 Catholics were allowed to compound for the recusancy fines, and a total of 316 Lancastrians did so in 1629 and 1630.[6]

The recusants in Jacobean Lancashire were still concentrated in the western deaneries of Amounderness, Leyland, and Warrington. In 1604 they were one in nine of the population in Amounderness, one in 26 in Leyland, and one in 13 in Warrington, compared with one in 72 in Blackburn, and one in 2,479 in Manchester. In 1604, 2,661 out of 3,222 recusants were from only 13 parishes: Garstang, Poulton, Kirkham, Preston, Ribchester, Chipping, Standish, Wigan, Eccleston, Prescot, Sefton, Huyton, and Childwall. These were all densely populated and divided into several townships, and were all led by significant numbers of recusant gentry. They were all also on the routes which ran through the coastal plain north and south between Morecambe Bay and the River Mersey.[7]

A detailed account of a typical Catholic centre is provided by a reliable document. On 17 May 1604, the curate and churchwardens of Farnworth reported on recusancy in their chapelry, which was part of the parish of Prescot. In 1592 only six recusants had been presented in Prescot, but, at the instance of Bishop Chadderton, the Protestant clergy and churchwardens made a census of the parish and kept a strict check of church attendance. As a result, the presentation of recusants increased considerably from 18 in 1598 to 184 in 1602 and 569 in 1604, far higher than for the rest of the deanery of Warrington. In Prescot, therefore, the detection of recusants became vigorous and the concealment of recusancy ceased, so that this survey of 1604 may be considered reliable. The survey was particularly concerned with those who had become recusants or non-communicants since the death of Elizabeth. The return lists and totals the recusants and non-communicants, though the lists and the totals do not always tally.[8]

Farnworth chapelry consisted of seven townships that stretched along the marshy plain beside the Mersey below Warrington: Great Sankey, Bold, Penketh, Widnes (which included Farnworth itself with its chapel and where there was a crossing over the Mersey to Runcorn), Cuerdley, Ditton, and Cronton. They extended for six miles from Warrington with its bridge to the estuary of the Mersey, and they were all within three miles of the river, that is they were all within an hour or two's walk of each other.[9]

They had all seen a massive increase in recusancy since the death of Elizabeth I. There had been a total of 29 'obstinate recusants in the late Queen's time' and the total number of 'revolters since the Queen's death' was 95, bringing the full total to 124, an increase of 77 per cent. There was also a large number of non-communicants, a total of eighty-three.[10]

Women Catholics heavily outnumbered men. Eighty women recusants outnumbered 44 men by nearly two to one. This imbalance may be the obverse of a male-dominated society. This domination may be reflected in the way in which the return seems to count a man and wife as one. The reluctance of men to become recusants may have been motivated by a desire to avoid penalties so as to protect property. The conformity of the male head of a household allowed the females the luxury of recusancy. This supposition is borne out to some extent by the number of non-communicants, where the imbalance between 37 males (44 per cent) and 46 females (55 per cent) was not as great. Nevertheless, the women were still in a majority which reflects the apparently greater attraction of Catholicism for women than for men.

The local recusants were led by the gentry and yeomanry. They included Nicholas Penketh gent of Great Sankey, who together with his wife, daughter, and maid-servant, had emerged as a recusant since James's accession, and was suspected of having Masses said in his house. There were also three obstinate recusant wives of conformist gentry: Jane, the wife of Thomas Whittle gent of Widnes, Elizabeth, the wife of William Ditchfield gent of Ditton, and Margaret, the wife of John Ditchfield gent of Ditton. Other householders who were suspected of having Masses in their houses were Francis Worsley of Bold, John Windle of Cronton, and William Smith, Thomas Harrison, and John Linacre of Widnes, the last of whom was said to have had a congregation of a hundred and to have had as many wax candles as a man could carry burned in his house on Candlemas Day (the Purification of the Blessed Virgin Mary, 2 February) 1604. Francis Worsley of Bold, whose entire household had become recusants in the new reign, was suspected of harbouring his brother, a seminary priest, who was also harboured by a milliner and a tailor in Golborne, six miles to the north-east. William Tarbuck, yeoman, formerly of Ditton but then of Burtonwood, six miles to the north-east, Thomas Linacre of Ditton, Alexander Denton of Ditton, John Linacre of Widnes, John Windle of Cronton, and John Forest of Cronton were all suspected of being married before Catholic priests. These people were not merely recusants who refused to attend the Protestant Church but also Catholics who received the sacraments from their own priests and kept the feasts of their Church with some ceremony.

Throughout the county Catholicism exerted a tight hold over the gentry. In 1613 out of 129 gentry families 65, that is 50 per cent, were Catholic. The gentry as the natural leaders of local society exercised considerable influence which extended outwards from the seigneurial household into the community. As Richard Heyrick, the warden of Manchester College (quoted by Richardson), put it: 'Great men have followers of their vices, as of their persons, and when they please to be idolatrous, their children, servants, tenants, their poor kindred and idolising neighbours will to the mass with them'. John Gee (quoted by Richardson) explained that 'there is not a Popish gentleman in all the country but there is a priest to his steward and disposer of household revenues; neither does the owner let or sell land without the approbation and consent of these pretended spiritual guides'. Thus in 1639 out of 82 mass-centres in Lancashire 75 were provided by the gentry. Moreover, marriages, like that between a Blundell of Crosby and a Haggerston of Haggerston, linked Lancashire and the North-East as what Bossy calls 'ill-assorted yoke-fellows to the English Catholic community'.[11]

Nevertheless, the Catholic gentry were heavily outnumbered by the commons. In 1641, the 616 recusant gentry made up only seven per cent of the total Lancashire Catholic community of over 8,000, whilst over 2,000 husbandmen made up nearly 24 per cent. Moreover, over 5,000 women (62 per cent) remained in a majority over men. The proportion of the gentry within the Catholic community was highest where Catholicism was weakest. Thus in 1641 the proportion of gentry to other recusants was over one to 64 in Warrington deanery, and one to 38 in Amounderness deanery, but only one to five in Manchester deanery.[12]

Pre-eminent amongst the Catholic gentry in early Stuart Lancashire were the Gerards of Bryn, who held the manors of Ashton, Garswood, and Windle in Lancashire, a cluster of estates five miles to the south of Wigan, and Etwall and Hardwick in Derbyshire. Thomas Gerard succeeded his father Sir Thomas Gerard in 1603. The father had been sent to the Tower in 1571 as sympathiser with Mary Stuart and again in 1586 as a sympathiser with Spain. After his release he conformed but remained suspect as a Catholic. The son was also suspect in his religion, and his first wife Cecily, the daughter of Sir Thomas Maney, was a recusant. His second wife was Mary, daughter of Sir Thomas Hawes, Lord Mayor of London, and widow of Sir Robert Lee, Lord Mayor of London. His third wife was Mary, the daughter of Sir William Dormer, another Catholic. His younger brother John was a Jesuit who worked in England, was implicated in the Gunpowder Plot, wrote his autobiography in 1609, was the first rector of the English Jesuit College at Liège from 1614 to 1621, and died in Rome in 1637. Thomas's daughter Frances married Ralph Standish of Standish, a member of another Catholic family. Thomas was elected M.P. for Liverpool in 1597, for Lancashire in 1614, and for Wigan in 1621. He was knighted in 1603, and received a baronetcy, on the first institution of the order in 1611, an honour which cost him £1,000, at that time a considerable sum, which is said to have been returned to him in consideration of the sufferings of his father on behalf of Mary, Queen of Scots: in 1603 the new King en route to London at York said to him 'I am particularly bound to love your blood on account of the persecution you have borne for me'. He died in 1621, and was succeeded by his only son, Sir Thomas Gerard, second baronet. This Sir Thomas Gerard married Frances, daughter of Sir Richard Molyneux, first baronet, of Sefton, and sister of the first Viscount Molyneux. Sir Thomas was elected M.P. for Liverpool in 1624. He died in 1631, and was succeeded by his elder son Sir Wiliam Gerard, third baronet. Sir William married Elizabeth, daughter of Sir Cuthbert Clifton of Lytham and Westby. Well-connected, politically active, and loyal to the Stuarts, the Gerards were typical members of the Lancashire Catholic gentry.[13]

As the centre of English Catholicism, Lancashire contributed its share to the priesthood: 117 were ordained seminary priests in the period 1603-59, the largest number of any county (Yorkshire came second with a hundred and seven). Clandestine schools, like that at Scarisbrick, continued to flourish, as many as 75 during the early 17th century, and Catholics continued to exert influence on some grammar schools, such as Kirkham. Students left the country illegally to train as priests in the English seminaries abroad scattered throughout Belgium, France, Italy, Spain, and Portugal. Most of them returned to work on the English mission, many of them in Lancashire.[14]

Christopher Lister was typical of the Lancashire seminary priests. He was the son of Richard Lister of Widnes in Farnworth chapelry, Prescot, who together with the spinsters Marie and Mildred, either his sisters or more probably his daughters, was listed as an obstinate recusant in 1604. Christopher went to St Omers (St Omer), a Jesuit boarding school, for three years, and then in 1600 with three other students set out by sea for Spain. They were captured at sea and taken to Plymouth. They refused the oath of supremacy, and were imprisoned until their parents paid the costs involved. Richard Lister was remiss in paying, and died, and was buried at Farnworth in 1604. Meanwhile, Christopher was released, and set out for Spain again. He was ordained at Seville, and then in 1605 went via Douay to the English mission, and was at work in Staffordshire in 1627.[15]

John Thules was a Lancastrian seminary priest who suffered martyrdom. Born in 1568, he was the son of William and Anne Thules of Whalley, and the brother of another priest, Christopher. He went to the English college at Rheims in 1583 and on to Rome in 1590, where he was ordained in 1592, when he left for the English mission, having foretold his martyrdom. He was captured in Northumberland in 1593, but escaped. Rather mysteriously he signed the appeal against the archpriest at Wisbech, although he was not a prisoner there. In 1605 he was in Essex, but in 1610 he was back in Lancashire, where he was captured in 1615. He was imprisoned in Lancaster with a Catholic weaver Roger Wrenno, more probably Wrennall, a common Lancashire name. There was a mass escape, but the two wandered about in the dark, and were captured not far away. They were sentenced to death, and offered their lives if they would take the oath of allegiance, but they refused. Thules had opposed the Jesuits, but as a sign of reconciliation he sent a gold angel (a coin worth ten shillings) to every Jesuit he knew. On the way to execution they were compelled to enter a Protestant church. Both struggled, and Thules was dragged in with a broken head, though Wrennall won his fight. Both were hanged, the priest being quartered.[16]

The first half of the 17th century saw the remarkable expansion of the Jesuits in Lancashire. In 1600 there were 12 Jesuits in England, and by 1620 there were 100, 16 of them in the Lancashire district. By 1630 the Jesuits in Lancashire had increased to 20 and by 1639 to twenty-one. During James's reign some 30 Lancastrians joined the Jesuits, including some who had been ordained as secular priests. Another 27 joined between 1625 and 1642. In the haphazard circumstances of the English mission, the Society of Jesus offered the virtues of discipline and organisation, the methodical self-programming of the *Spiritual Exercises*, and a record of missionary success from China to Peru.[17]

Apart from the fact that all four of them joined the Jesuits, the brothers Laithwaite were typical of their background and career. They belonged to the class of well-to-do yeomanry who might be considered gentry. They were the sons of Henry Laithwaite yeoman of the Meadows, an estate on the banks of the River Douglas in Pemberton near Wigan. Henry Laithwaite and his brother John were imprisoned for their religion in 1577, and Henry harboured seminary priests, John Lowe in 1579 and Alexander Markland, another Wiganer, in 1585-88. In 1595 Henry's widow and daughter Anne were both recusants. The sons began their education at Blackrod Grammar School, but as the master was a Protestant they were removed and received instruction from a Catholic neighbour and then in schools in Wigan. The eldest son, Thomas, born in 1576, was trained at Douay and Seville, ordained priest, and sent on the English mission in 1604. He was arrested at Plymouth and banished, but his ship was driven back by a storm, and he escaped. He went to find Henry Garnet, the English Jesuit superior, with the aim of joining the Society, but in the uproar of the Gunpowder Plot he was captured, escaped again, and was re-captured. He was again banished, and joined the Jesuits at Louvain in 1607. He returned to the English mission, and died in London in 1655. The second son, Edward, born in 1582, while in London awaiting an opportunity to get a passage to Douay, was persuaded to become apprentice to an apothecary and was converted to Protestantism. Visiting his brother Thomas in Exeter gaol in the hope of persuading him to abandon his Catholicism, he was himself converted by his brother. He went to Douay, then to Rome, was ordained in 1612, and became a Jesuit in 1616. He went to work on the English mission, and became the Jesuit superior in Devon where he died in 1643. The third son, John, born in 1585, was trained at Rome and joined the Jesuits in 1604, but then disappears from the records. The fourth son, Francis, born in 1589, was trained at Douay and Rome, joined the Jesuits in 1607 and was sent to Ingoldstadt in Bavaria. In 1624 he was the Jesuit procurator in Brussels. The brothers had two sisters who entered English continental convents.[18]

The career of William Malone or Moloney illustrates the Manchester Irish connection. He was born in either Dublin or Manchester in 1585. He was a Protestant, but was converted to Catholicism by some Irish merchants in Manchester, and joined the Jesuits in Rome in 1606. He was sent to Ireland, and in 1635 was recalled to Rome to become rector of the Irish College. In 1647 he was appointed superior of the Irish Jesuits, but was taken prisoner at Waterford, and was banished. In 1651 he became rector of St Gregory's College, Seville and died there in 1655.[19]

The Benedictines had almost as much attraction for the Lancastrian Catholics as the Jesuits. Forty Lancastrians, including a few already ordained as seminary priests, had joined the Benedictines by 1642. The active life of the English mission rather than the contemplative life of the continental monasteries was the destiny of most English Benedictines. Nevertheless, the Benedictine rule, like that of the Jesuits, offered discipline and organisation. At the same time, the Benedictine vocation carried with it the guarantee of continuity and the promise of the restoration of the Ecclesia Anglicana, the English Catholic Church.[20]

Pre-eminent amongst the missionary monks was Robert Haydock. He was born at Brunton, Lancashire, in 1582, the son of William Haydock of Cottam. He was converted by his uncle, the seminary priest Robert Woodruff, and was educated at St Omers and Valladolid, where he became a Benedictine. In 1607 he went on the English mission, and became superior of the Anglo-Spanish Benedictine mission. After the foundation of the English Benedictine congregation he was appointed provincial of York. He was at work in Lancashire in 1631, and died in Staffordshire in 1650.[21]

Unlike his missionary brother Ambrose, William Rudesind Barlow lived a more monastic life. Born in Manchester in 1585, he was the son of Sir Alexander Barlow of Barlow Hall. He went to Douay in 1602, and joined the Benedictines at Cella Nuovo in Galicia, Spain, in 1606, was ordained in 1616, and obtained a doctorate of divinity at Salamanca. He removed to Douay in 1611, where he obtained another D.D. He was prior of St Gregory's, Douay, from 1614 to 1620 and again from 1625 to 1629. He died at Douay in 1656.[22]

The religious life also appealed to an increasing number of Lancastrian women. In addition to its intrinsic attractions, the spiritual appeal of a life of prayer under the vows of poverty, chastity, and obedience, it gave to women, in the patriarchal society of the 17th century, a life free, to a certain extent, from male company and male domination, and offered, instead of marriage, the alternative of the only real, quasi-professional, career open to women. That the numbers of female religious were not proportionate to the numbers of female Catholics is explained partly by its limited appeal and partly by the difficulties in their way. Apart from the renunciations required by the vows, there was the difficulty of going abroad in a period of persecution and once there the problem of financing the religious life. The rich had to provide their own income in the form of a dowry, which depended on the goodwill of their families and was difficult to transfer under persecution. The poor might enter convents as lay-sisters, that is as religious domestic servants, but they were even more dependent on the convents' having sufficient funds. Fortunately, convents were also the recipients of alms from pious benefactors, like Thomas Worthington gent of Blainscough, Standish, Lancashire, who guaranteed the finances of the English Augustinian convent at Louvain when it was founded in 1609.[23]

At least 32 Lancastrian women entered English religious houses on the continent between 1603 and 1642. They were divided amongst seven communities, but were concentrated in two, nine with the Augustinian canonesses at Louvain and 11 with the Poor Clares at Gravelines. There was a tendency for them to concentrate in family groups. Thus the four Clopton girls entered the convent at Louvain in 1622, and the two Bradshaigh girls who entered Gravelines in 1630 were followed by another two in 1640.[24]

2 *Ambrose Barlow. From a print in the possession of the author.*

The English colleges and religious houses on the Continent formed a Catholic England in exile and within it a little Catholic Lancashire overseas with the same attitudes and responses. There were 5,000 Catholic emigrants to the continent between 1598 and 1642 compared with the 20,000 English who emigrated to America and the West Indies during the same period. Thomas Low, a Lancastrian, became the steward of the English college at Douay. He married a Fleming and four of their sons became priests. Thomas Worthington gent of Blainscough, Standish, lived in exile at Louvain, and died in exemplary piety in 1619.[25]

There was another career abroad open to Lancashire Catholics: a soldier in the Spanish army of Flanders which from 1618 was engaged in the Thirty Years War against the Dutch and German Protestants. William Singleton, born at the Lodge in Prescot, after serving as butler to Robert Hindley of Hindley, Wigan, went abroad about 1616, and served as a soldier in the Low Countries.[26]

The continental houses and the English mission were connected by a secret network of communications, which sometimes emerges into the light of discovery. William Singleton was taken at Durham in 1626 en route between Yarmouth and Berwick. He carried a letter that made it clear that he had conducted students to the seminaries and priests to England. He admitted to being a Catholic and indeed a Benedictine lay brother, but denied that he was in holy orders, though much of this, including his name, as the Archbishop of Canterbury pointed out, could have been what is now called disinformation.[27]

The English mission received increasing organisation and this led to conflict which was only partly resolved. The secular clergy received their own organisation but were involved in conflict with the regular clergy, both the Jesuits and the Benedictines. However, the appointment of a vicar apostolic led to a compromise between the seculars and the Benedictines. The clerical divisions may have been detrimental to the laity but they were more than counterbalanced by a more efficient organisation. The number of priests in Lancashire had peaked in 1590 at 29 and then declined to 16 in 1605, but had risen again to 28 by 1610.[28]

Since 1598 the secular clergy had been under the control of the archpriest. In 1611 Archpriest Birkhead came to an agreement with the president of Douay to regulate the flow of priests to England. At the same time he organised a petition to Rome for a bishop, and his successor, William Harris, continued the campaign. As a result in 1623 William Bishop was appointed vicar apostolic to act as bishop in England. He divided the country into five vicariates, subdivided into archdeaconries with a rural dean in each county. John Mitchell was appointed a member of the bishop's chapter and archdeacon of the Lancashire district.[29]

From 1580 the Jesuits in England were always provided with a superior and in 1623 the English Jesuit province was erected, and divided into colleges, which included that of St Aloysius covering Lancashire, Cheshire, Staffordshire (until 1660), and Westmorland. By 1620 there were a dozen Jesuits at work in Lancashire and these had increased to 26 by 1642.[30]

The permanent Jesuit mission in Lancashire was founded in 1622 by John Worthington. He was succeeded by Laurence Anderton. Born in 1576, he was probably the son of Christopher Anderton esq. of Lostock. He was educated at Blackburn Grammar School, which was under Catholic influence, and Christ's College, Cambridge, where he became known as 'the golden-mouthed Anderton'. He was ordained a Protestant, but was converted by reading controversial literature, and went to Rome where he joined the Jesuits in 1605. After teaching in the continental colleges he went on the English mission, and worked mainly in Lancashire as chaplain to the Cliftons of Lytham, and was appointed Jesuit superior in Lancashire in 1621. After a period working in London, he returned to Lancashire where he died in 1643.[31]

The Benedictine presence in England owed much to two Lancastrians: Edward (or Edmund) Augustine Smith and Anselm Beech. Smith was born near Manchester in 1565 and was educated at St John's College, Cambridge, and Rome, where he was ordained in 1591. He entered the monastery of Monte Cassino, the mother house of the Italian Cassinese Benedictine Congregation, in 1592. Smith came on the English mission in 1605, and acted as superior of the Anglo-Italian monks until he was succeeded by Beech in 1613. Beech was born in Manchester in 1568, went to Rome, where he was ordained in 1594, and then joined the monastery of St Justina, Padua, a house of the Cassinese Congregation, in 1596. Beech was instrumental in persuading the Holy See to allow English Benedictines to go on the English mission, and he himself went in 1603 together with Roland Thomas Preston, O.S.B., alias Roger Widdrington, who was born in Shropshire but was a descendant of the Prestons of Furness in Lancashire. In England they sought out Dom Sigebert Buckley, the last surviving member of the old English Benedictine Congregation, a monk of the community of Westminster Abbey which had been restored by Queen Mary. In 1607 they arranged for Buckley to receive two new novices in his cell at the Gatehouse Prison in London, and thus to ensure the survival of the English Benedictine Congregation.[32]

Meanwhile, more Englishmen had joined the Spanish Valladolid Benedictine Congregation, and gone on the English mission, founding new houses on the continent to act as bases. In 1619 the English and Anglo-Spanish monks united to form the restored English Benedictine Congregation, committed to the English mission. However, Beech and the few Anglo-Cassinese monks were committed to the ideal of the enclosed monastic observance, and they refused to join the restored English Congregation, Beech returning to Padua where he died in 1634.[33]

Under the early Stuarts, therefore, the English Catholic clergy were divided into at least three increasingly organised but also increasingly competing orders: the seculars, the Jesuits, and the Benedictines. At least the appointment of William Bishop led to an agreement in 1623 between the seculars and the Benedictines, but he died in 1624 before he could reach an agreement with the Jesuits.[34]

Bishop was succeeeded as vicar apostolic by Richard Smith. He arrived in England in 1625, and proceeded to make a visitation of the whole country, administering the sacrament of confirmation. However, his authority was challenged by the regulars, supported by their patrons amongst the laity, and he was obliged to retire to France in 1631. Nevertheless, the organisation of the secular clergy into districts under a chapter survived the collapse of episcopal authority.[35]

A picture of the Lancashire mission in 1639 is provided by a list of the Catholic gentry and clergy compiled for the collection of a subsidy for the King's campaign against the Scots rebels. The list was compiled under the superiors of the clergy assisted by the local gentry, three of whom—Charles Towneley junior, William Gerard, and Roger Bradshaigh—acted as agents for the county. Although produced under government pressure, it was compiled by the Catholics themselves, and is, therefore, that rare and useful thing—an internal Lancashire Catholic document of the period.[36]

The missions were listed roughly according to their hundreds. Lonsdale hundred was ignored, which implies not only that the government found it hard to list Catholics there but that there were few Catholics to list. It was noted that, except for Sir Cecil Trafford, Salford hundred contained few Catholics. Blackburn hundred contained one Catholic gentry household in Chipping, four in Whalley, five in Blackburn, and two in Ribchester. Amounderness hundred contained two Catholic gentry households in Poulton and Bispham, two in Garstang, three in Goosnargh and St Michael's-on-Wyre, three in Kirkham and Lytham, and two in Preston. Leyland hundred contained three Catholic gentry households in Leyland, two in Brindle and Penwortham, five in Croston and Chorley, and five in Standish and Eccleston. West Derby hundred contained few, if any, poor Catholics in North Meols, but three Catholic gentry households in Ormskirk, three in Warrington, six in Wigan, two in Walton, two in Childwall, two in Huyton, three in Winwick, six in Prescot, three in Sefton, three in Leigh, four in Halsall and Altcar, and four in Aughton. In all, 79 gentlemen were listed and 41 priests, including 27 seculars, 15 Jesuits, and nine Benedictines, many, like Barlow, circulating around several houses.

Increasing in strength and confidence, and adopting their own ecclesiastical structures, the Catholics of early Stuart Lancashire developed into a separate community with its own peculiar characteristics. As Mathew puts it, 'Socially they were inextricably mingled with their Protestant fellow countrymen but in devotional and doctrinal matters they had developed their own special ethos'.[37]

Lancashire was to gain, in Walton's phrase, 'a reputation for intransigent and enduring religious extremism', because the Catholics in the west were challenged by the Puritans in the south-east. As Dean Heyrick of Manchester (quoted by Richardson) explained in 1641, 'I was but lately removed into these parts, and one of special note forewarned me I should be crucified as Christ was between two thieves: the Papist [and] the Puritan'. However, even in the so-called Catholic area, Catholics were in a minority and, as Mathew writes, 'The Catholic community was constantly dissolving at the edges'. Nevertheless, the Catholics were stronger here than in any other part of England, kept to their faith by what Mathew calls 'the point of honour which has done so much to keep minorities faithful to their traditions'.[38]

Gradually the Catholics withdrew from the parish and county community but reluctantly and under protest. As the Puritan White (quoted by Richardson) put it in 1624, 'in all excess of sin, Papists have been the ringleaders, in riotous companies, in drunken meetings, in seditious assemblies and practices, and in profaning the Sabbath, in quarrels and brawls, in stage plays, greens, ales, and all heathenish customs'. In 1631 Sir William Norris of Speke (quoted by Blundell) complained that a local magistrate 'had been too precise in examining the church-wardens touching his, Sir William's, not coming to church and that it was ungentlemanly dealing', and struck the magistrate with his sword. In 1632 the Catholic Mary Abram, widow of Thomas Abram of Abram, near Wigan, founded Hindley and Abram Grammar School for the benefit of the local community. In 1630 Thomas Melling, a secular priest, and Elizabeth Tarleton, his housekeeper, (quoted by Alger) left their goods 'for a beginning of a religious house of women in Catholic times'.[39]

The pain of schism, of separation from the parish and county communities, of the breakdown of good neighbourliness, as well as the exclusion from office and the subjection to penalties was expressed by William Blundell gent of Crosby:

> The time hath been we had one faith
> And strode aright one ancient path.
> The time is now that each man may
> See new religions coined each day.[40]

Catholic confidence in their faith was expressed in the ballad 'True Christian hearts, cease to lament', in which the following words (quoted by Mathew) were attributed to John Thules at his trial:

> Christ's passion oft before your face,
> I have declared plain;
> How for our sins he suffered death,
> And how he rose again;
> And how the twelve apostles, eke,
> Were put to death for preaching
> The Catholic faith which Christ did teach.
> Christ send us happy rising.

The same attitude was expressed by Sir Alexander Barlow of Barlow Hall, Manchester, who declared himself in his will in 1620 (quoted by Blundell) to be 'a true perfect Recusant Catholic'. Similarly in 1605 John Ashton gent (quoted by Tait) declared that he was 'a recusant and so hath been all his lifetime and ... he is not minded to reform himself as yet because his conscience will not suffer him ...'. This faith resulted in proselytising. In 1605 Janet Middleton, widow, and Alice Hayhurst, spinster, of Aighton, Mitton, were not only absent from the parish church themselves but also persuaded several young folk not to go. In 1616 John Birtwisle and his wife Dorothy of Huncote, Clitheroe, were accused not only of recusancy and harbouring seminary priests and Jesuits but also of attempting to convert Elizabeth Morcroft, the wife of the curate of Clitheroe, and even Peter Ormerod, the vicar of Whalley.[41]

Despite the apparent pacifism and subsequent royalism of the Lancashire Catholics, their religion initially led some of them into hostility to the Stuarts. After the proclamation of the accession of James I at Ormskirk in 1603, Humphrey Horton, butcher, of Upholland, Wigan, declared (quoted by Tait) that 'The King cannot be crowned till he be anointed with an old priest'. At the same time some recusants were buying arms, and in 1604 a few seminary priests in Lancashire even proposed to raise a revolt and to seize Chester.[42]

Nevertheless, the Lancashire Catholics became increasingly overtly loyal to the Stuart kings. When in 1605 at the Quarter Sessions in Wigan, John Ashton gent (quoted by Tait) declared himself to be a determined recusant, he went on to say 'that he doth think in his conscience that the King's majesty hath authority in all causes in this realm as well ecclesiastical as temporal, and sithas God shall save him he doth not think the King is an heretic'. In 1606 in the aftermath of the Bye and Gunpowder Plots, parliament imposed a new oath of allegiance on recusants and on non-communicant Church papists. The oath not only acknowledged James as their rightful king, and denied the right of the pope to depose him, but also condemned as heretical the doctrine that the pope had that power. Despite papal condemnation of the oath, some of the clergy, led by Thomas Preston, O.S.B., alias Roger Widdrington, and even Archpriest Blackwell argued that Catholics could in conscience take the oath.[43]

Catholics were defined negatively as recusants by their refusal to attend the services of the Established Protestant Church of England as the law required, but their religion centred on their rituals. Pre-eminent was the Mass which on great feast-days might be celebrated with more ceremony. Baptism could be administered in private by laymen, and Catholics were married before Catholic priests. The parochial graveyards and church-vaults were in Protestant hands so that in 1620 Sir Alexander Barlow was buried secretly by torchlight in Manchester collegiate church. However, in 1611 William Blundell esq. of Little Crosby established a Catholic burial ground on his estate at Harkirk. Meanwhile, early Stuart Catholics were increasingly influenced by a Counter-Reformation spirituality which was monastic, contemplative, and quietistic.[44]

This Catholicism involved an active belief in the supernatural. When Thomas Worthington died at Louvain in 1619 a red cross appeared on his forehead, and his back was covered with red marks as though he had been scourged. In a county notorious for its witches, the Catholic priest was revered as a wonder-worker and a shield against witchcraft. A Jesuit imprisoned at Lancaster in 1619-20 had brought to him for healing those who were sick or poisoned or possessed by the devil.[45]

The tradition of pilgrimage, especially to the shrine of St Winefride at Holywell in North Wales, continued to be observed. A spy reported that on the feast of St Winefride in 1629 the shrine was attended by 'knights, ladies, gentlemen, and gentlewomen of divers countries to the number of fourteen or fifteen hundred: and the general estimation about a hundred and fifty more priests', including at least 13 members of the Lancashire gentry: Sir Thomas Gerard, Sir William Norris, Sir

Cuthbert Clifton, Sir John Talbot, Preston of Furness, Anderton of Clayton, Anderton of Ford, Gerard of Ince, Bradshaigh of Haigh, Harrington of Huyton, Blundell of Crosby, Scarisbrick of Scarisbrick, and Lathom of Mossborough.[46]

The ancient Catholic cult of the martyrs had its contemporary equivalent. Thus the clothes of the martyred Edmund Arrowsmith and the knife used to quarter him were kept at Sir Cuthbert Clifton's house.[47]

Catholic folk religion was supplemented by the literate religion of the Counter-Reformation, and a secret printing-press was established in Lancashire at Birchley Hall, Billinge, near Wigan. Roger Anderton of Birchley sheltered his cousin Laurence Anderton, the Jesuit superior, who set up the press in 1615. It was raided in 1621 but was re-established in the 1640s. Meanwhile it had printed 16 books, seven of them in 1620. They included controversial books like Thomas Worthington's *Whyte dyed Black* (1615) and *An anker of Christian doctrine* (1618), and liturgical and devotional works like *The liturgy of the masse* (1620) by John Brerely (the pseudonym of James or Laurence Anderton) and *A Manual of godly prayers* (1620). When Catholic prisoners were released in 1622, those responsible for printing books remained in prison at Lancaster.[48]

Birchley Hall with its printing-press, its chapel built in 1618, and its Jesuit chaplains, was an outstanding example of the seigneurial household Catholicism of the gentry, like the Blundells of Little Crosby. These rural Catholic congregations, led by the gentry, were typical of English Catholicism as a whole.[49]

However, Lancastrian Catholicism was also an urban phenomenon. As early as 1605 there was a secret Catholic chapel in Preston in Chapel Yard off Friargate, serving 68 recusants in the town and another 19 in the surrounding rural parish. Here and in Wigan, urban Catholic congregations were quick to develop, though they remained conspicuous by their absence in other towns like Liverpool and Manchester.[50]

This early Stuart Lancastrian Catholicism was best represented, as it wished to be known, in the life of Ambrose Barlow, recorded in a work of hagiography by one of his penitents and ostensibly for his brother.[51] Born Edward Barlow in Manchester, he joined the Benedictines in 1615, taking the name Ambrose. He was ordained in 1617, and sent on the English mission, declaring that 'he must not go out of Lancashire'. Thomas Tyldesley of Myerscough provided him with a base at Morleys Hall, Leigh, some twelve miles west of Manchester, and Tyldesley's grandmother left him an income of £8 per annum to 'take charge of these poor neighbouring Catholics'. Barlow kept a servant, but lived as a lodger with a poor couple who kept house for him. He spent three weeks of every month there, keeping open house for the poor and for his penitents of all ranks: to the gentry he would say "You must not be offended at our clownishness for we are all clowns". His preaching on Sundays and holidays was 'brief, plain, and pithy'. He learnt to paint so as to provide a picture of Christ crowned with thorns for his altar. On the solemn days of Christmas, Easter, and Whitsun he served a meal of boiled beef, pottage, mince pies, goose, and groates (meal-puddings) to the poor, waiting at table himself, and provided them all with grey coats. He protested to Tyldesley about the rack-renting lessee of the Morleys estate, and secured a reduction of rents. One week in four he set out in his grey frieze jerkin, doublet, breeches, and hat, with a long staff in his hand to walk the twenty miles to the house of a widow at Sefton via Winwick, Warrington, Ormskirk, and Aughton, hearing confessions and saying Mass on the way. He was an admirer of the mysticism of Augustine Baker, and 'so mild, witty, and cheerful ... that ... he seemed ... to represent the spirit of Sir Thomas More', and though he ate no red meat he said that 'if God should send a venison pastie, he would not refuse to eat it'.

Barlow and his biographer, like the early 17th century, seem suspended between the old belief in magic represented by King James and the new belief in science represented by Francis Bacon. Called upon to exorcise a man possessed by the devil, Barlow doubted whether it were not so much a case of demon-possession as possession by some vice such as avarice. The man admitted this, and Barlow asked to see his treasure. He 'found a thing in shape most like a toad, having down upon its back like to a gosling', and cast it into the fire where it exploded.

Barlow embodied the militant Counter-Reformation. He demanded unconditional adherence to the Catholic faith—'I like not those that will be peeping at God'—but thought, 'As concerning the conversion of England indeed it must be by the sword'. He knew that he incurred the risk of martyrdom—'I have bidden as fair for it as another'—and on Easter Sunday 1641 he was arrested whilst saying Mass. He was hanged at Lancaster on 18 September 1641.

By the outbreak of the Civil War in 1642 Catholic Lancashire had grown much stronger. It had increased in numbers, developed its organisation, and, above all, strengthened in self-confidence. It was to have need of its strength.

Notes
1. Haigh, p.275; Bossy, *Community*, p.92; R. C. Richardson, *Puritanism in North-West England* (1972)(hereafter Richardson), pp.6-7.
2. *Miscellanea* (CRS vol.53), pp.146-47.
3. S. J. Houston, *James I* (1973), p.66.
4. Haigh, pp.277, 330; Walton, p.45; Cheshire Record Office, Chester, Visitation Correction Book 1604, EDV 1/13.
5. Tierney, vol.4, xcv; *Miscellanea* (CRS vol.53), pp.146-7; Richardson, p.155; C. P. Caraman (ed.), *The Hunted Priest: The Autobiography of John Gerard* (1959), p.50.
6. M. J. Havran, *The Catholics in Caroline England* (1962); Anstruther, vol.2, p.9; *Miscellanea* (CRS vol.53), pp. 291-307, 322-332, 347-51.
7. Walton, p.46; Haigh, pp.294, 317-18.
8. *Miscellanea* (CRS vol.53), pp.147-50; Haigh, p.273.
9. *VCH Lancs*, vol.3, pp.341, 386.
10. *Miscellanea* (CRS vol.53), pp.147-50.
11. Haigh, pp.281-5; Richardson, pp.5-7; B. G. Blackwood, 'Plebeian Catholics in the 1640s and 1650s', RH, vol.18(1) (1986), p.50; Bossy, *Community*, p.95.
12. Haigh, p.283; Blackwood, RH, vol.17, p.52.

13.   Caraman, *Hunted Priest*, p.213; *VCH Lancs*, vol.4, pp.144-5; *Burke's Peerage and Baronetage* (London, 1980), p.1085; D. Mathew, *The Jacobean Age* (1938), p.248; Hilton, 'Post-Reformation Catholicism in Derbyshire', *Derbyshire Miscellany*, vol.11 (3) (1987); J. F. Giblin, 'The Gerard Family', *NWCH*, vol.17 (1990).

14.   Anstruther, vol.2, pp.395-405; Beales, pp.201-15.

15.   Anstruther, vol.2, pp.200-1; *Miscellanea* (CRS vol.53), p.149.

16.   Anstruther, vol.1, p.355.

17.   Bossy, 'The English Catholic Community 1603-1625' in A. G. R. Smith (ed.), *The Reign of James VI and I* (1973), p.98; Foley, vol.7, p.clxviii.

18.   F. O. Blundell, *Old Catholic Lancashire* (3 vols, 1925-39) (hereafter Blundell), vol.2, pp.53-6; Foley, vol.7, pp.428-9; Anstruther, vol.2, p.187.

19.   Foley, vol.7, pp.481-2.

20.   H. N. Birt, *Obit Book of the English Benedictines* (1913)(hereafter Birt).

21.   Anstruther, vol.1, p.385; Birt, p.31.

22.   Birt, p.36.

23.   Aveling, p.91; Tierney, vol.4, pp.106-7.

24.   Blundell, vol.3, pp.199-209.

25.   Aveling, p.98; Anstruther, vol.2, pp.203-204; *Dominicana* (CRS vol.25, 1925), pp.96-101.

26.   *Miscellanea* (CRS vol.53), pp.287-88.

27.   *Miscellanea* (CRS vol.53), pp.287-91.

28.   *VCH Lancs*, vol.2, pp.59-60; Haigh pp.279-80.

29.   Tierney, vol.4, p.cclxxxiv, vol.5, pp.clxxiii-clxxv, 48-51, 92-9; Anstruther, vol.1, p.229.

30.   Foley, vol.5, p.987, vol.7, p.lxxi.

31.   Foley, vol.7, pp.864-5; Armitage, *NWCH*, vol.13, pp.1-9, Blundell, vol.1, p.123; Foley, vol.7, p.11.

32.   Birt, pp.xvi-xxiv, 13, 16, 21; Anstruther, vol.1, pp.28, 320; Lunn, D., *The English Benedictines 1540-1688* (1980)(hereafter Lunn), pp.25-6.

33.   Lunn, pp.107-8.

34.   Hughes, *Rome*.

35.   Hughes, *Rome*, pp.329-408; Anstruther, vol.2, pp.321-2.

36.   Anstruther, 'Lancashire Clergy in 1639', *RH*, vol.4 (1) (1957).

37.   Mathew, *Jacobean Age*, p.230

38.   Walton, pp.36-7; Richardson, p.153; Mathew, *Jacobean Age*, pp.230, 241.

39.   Richardson, p.157; Blundell, vol.1, pp.77-8; Jordan, W. K., *The Social Institutions of Lancashire* (CS, 3rd series, vol.11, 1962), p.61; B. Alger, 'An Optimist's Will and Convent Life', *NWCH*, vol.2 (1) (1970).

40.   Gibson, T. E. (ed.), *Crosby Records* (1888), p.28.

41.   Mathew, *Jacobean Age*, p.232; Blundell, vol.2, pp.14-5; Tait, J. (ed.), *Lancashire Quarter Sessions Rolls* (CS, new series, vol.77, 1917).

42.   Tait, pp.167-8; Haigh, pp.329-30.

43.   Tait, pp.282-3; Tierney, vol.4, p.73; Hughes, *Rome*, pp.306-11; Smith, p.93.

44.   *Miscellanea* (CRS vol.53), pp.147-50; Blundell, vol.1, pp.34-6, vol.2, p.15; Smith, pp.104-5.

45.   *Dominicana* (CRS vol.25, 1925), pp.96-8; Smith, p.104; Foley, vol.5, p.993; Thomas, K., *Religion and the Decline of Magic* (1978), pp.569-88.

46.   Miscellanea (CRS vol.3, 1906), p.108.

47.   Miscellanea (CRS vol.3), p.108.

48.   Giblin, 'The History of Birchley Hall', *NWCH*, vol.4 (1972); Milward, P., *Religious Controversies of the Jacobean Age* (1978), passim.

49.   Blundell, vol.1, pp.1-2; Giblin, *NWCH*, vol.4, pp.11-12; Bossy, *Reign of James VI and I*, p.103.

50.   Blundell, vol.2, p.137.

51.   Rhodes, W. E. (ed.), 'The Apostolical Life of Ambrose Barlow', *Chetham Miscellanies* (CS new series, vol.2, 1909).

Chapter III

The Catholic Cavaliers, 1642-88

From the beginning of the Great Rebellion in 1642 to the Glorious Revolution of 1688, Catholic Lancashire was associated with the Stuart cause. It shared therefore in the unhappy fortunes of the Stuart kings. It rallied to the royal standard in the Civil War, it bore the defeat of Charles I, it survived the Interregnum, it rejoiced in the Restoration, it suffered the anti-Catholicism of Charles II's parliaments, it was exalted to ascendancy with the Catholic King James II, and it was overthrown with him in the Revolution. Meanwhile, it continued to develop its own characteristics, to grow in numbers, and to develop its organisation. The constitution of the Catholic community in later Stuart Lancashire has been analysed in depth by Dr. Blackwood.[1]

The Scots rebellion of 1639 was followed by the Irish rebellion of 1641, and both precipitated the Great Rebellion in England in 1642. On the one side was the king, supported by the Anglicans and the Catholics, and on the other side was parliament supported by the Puritans. The war became a struggle for the king to consolidate his support in the North, in Wales, and in the West, and to use it to conquer the South-East and the centre of parliamentary power in London. In 1642 his advance on London was contested at Edgehill. In 1644 he lost control of the North at Marston Moor, and in 1645 he was finally defeated at Naseby. The king then came to an agreement with the Scots, who invaded England but were defeated at Preston in 1648. As a result the king was executed in 1649. Then in 1651 the Scots again invaded England on behalf of Charles II but were defeated at Worcester.[2]

In Lancashire, as elsewhere, there was a war within the war. In 1642 Lord Strange, the eldest son of Lord Derby who succeeded his father that year, assembled a royalist army, and advanced on Manchester only to be repulsed. He then detached part of his army to join the king at Edgehill. In 1643 the war in Lancashire developed into a struggle to control the main north-south road by capturing the main towns along it at Lancaster, Preston, Wigan, and Warrington, but, after the royalist defeat at Whalley, this struggle was won by the parliamentarians. Only Greenhalgh Castle, near Garstang, and the Derby stronghold of Lathom House remained in royalist hands. Then in 1644 the royal army under Prince Rupert entered Lancashire, capturing Bolton, Wigan, and Liverpool, and relieving Lathom House. Rupert's defeat at Marston Moor undid his work in Lancashire and Lathom House fell in 1645. The Scottish defeat at Preston in 1648 involved virtually no royalist Lancastrian forces, but during the Scottish invasion of 1651 Lord Derby entered Lancashire from the Isle of Man, but was defeated at Wigan.[3]

On the eve of the war in 1642 parliament ordered all adult males to take a protestation of loyalty to king and parliament and the Protestant religion. The numbers of refusals indicated the strength of Catholicism. The returns for the hundreds of Amounderness, Blackburn, Leyland, Salford, and West Derby list the names of some 30,611 who took the protestation, and some 4,031 who did not, 11.7 per cent out of a total of 34,442. In Amounderness, where some 4,615 took the protestation, only some 588 (8.4 per cent) refused, but 1,752 were ambiguously listed as not taking the protestation so that it is not clear whether they refused or were merely absent. The main centres of opposition were Broughton where 136 (43 per cent) refused, St Michael's where 266 (28.9 per cent) refused, and Woodplumpton where 101 (19.5 per cent) refused. In Blackburn Hundred 7,121 took the protestation, 509 (6.6 per cent) refused, and seventeen were absent. Here the main centres were Blackburn where 225 (9.5 per cent) refused, and Chipping where 121 (16.8 per cent) refused. In Leyland hundred 3,652 took the protestation, 945 (20.5 per cent) refused, and nine were absent. Here there were places where the majority refused: Brindle where 88 (53.6 per cent) out of 164 refused; Mawdesley and Rufford where 125 (66.8 per cent) out of 187 refused; and Bispham and Croston where 44 (68.7 per cent) out of 64 refused. In West Derby hundred at least 2,486 took the protestation, and 154 (5.8 per cent) refused. Here the main centre was Wigan where 103 (14 per cent) refused. In Salford hundred 12,747 took the protestation and a mere 57 (0.4 per cent) refused.[4]

Bossy has painted an idyllic picture of the pacifist Caroline Catholics, only fighting in the Civil War as loyal subjects of the King and in defence of their own territory. However, Blackwood concludes that 'Lancashire was more sharply divided in religion than any other English county'. It was, according to the contemporary historian Thomas Fuller, 'the cockpit of conscience', a kind of English Ulster.[5]

Contemporary Puritan opinion presented Manchester as in danger from bloodthirsty Papists. They pointed to the strength and growth of Catholic Lancashire: 'in Lancashire and Yorkshire there are more Papists than in all England besides'; 'there appears by record to be in Lancashire 1,800 recusants; of these there were not above eight or nine hundred in the Queen's time' (quoted in F.Walker's *Historical Geography of South West Lancashire*); 'being seated in the mouth of danger ... where the number of Popish recusants and the opportunity of landing may invite an invasion'; 'the Papists are upon Lancashire and threaten some heavy doom to befall the Protestants in these parts' (quoted by Gratton); 'we daily expect and fear great insurrections of Popish Protestant professors, Papists and other malignant persons'; 'the town of Manchester having ... multitudes of Papists near unto it, and being reputed a religious and rich town, hath been much envied and often threatened by the Popish and malignant party'. Looking back in 1650 the Lancashire committee pointed out that, 'In the beginning of the war this county was looked upon by parliament as one of the most dangerous, in respect of the interest which some great men had in it that went with the king's party, and of the many Papists that abound in parts of it' (quoted by Gratton).[6]

The Catholics felt themselves at the mercy of both parliament and king. Already they had been warned by the collectors of the contribution of 1639 that their condition would 'much alter ... either to the better or the worse, according as we shall express ourselves affectionate or cold' (quoted in Anstruther's *Vaux of Harrowden*), and 'the urgent occasions now required and the imminent danger as we are informed (we doubt) too certainly may happen unto us all if we show not ourselves free upon this occasion to the uttermost of our power' (quoted by Hibberd). They knew only too well what to expect from a parliamentary and Puritan victory. The Puritan Heyrick (quoted by Richardson) fulminated: 'The quarrel betwixt Rome and us is not like Caesar and Pompey, which should be chief, but like that betwixt Rome and Carthage, which should not be. If Rome prevail we shall not stand; and if we prevail they should not stay long'.[7]

In this atmosphere of mutual fear and hatred, both sides regarded attack as the best form of defence:

> They (the Papists) had a good ground to have been neuter in this war had not their spirits and malice against the Protestant religion provoked them to it ... Therefore they thrust themselves in to the war ... and so have brought upon them a greater burden of evil than they needed ... upon the meaner sort it lies heavy ... They thought they could have done all by their multitude. And it may be they were conceited that if the king had prevailed through their assistance they could have forced him to set up their religion.[8]

The king appeared reluctant to employ Catholics if only because it justified parliamentary propaganda, but he needed all the help he could get. When, therefore, the Lancashire Catholic gentry petitioned for the right to bear arms they were allowed to do so for the defence of king and country.[9]

These Lancashire Catholic gentry entered the war with enthusiasm and out of all proportion to their numbers. Two hundred and twenty-one (28.6 per cent) out of 774 gentry families in Lancashire were Catholics, but out of 177 royalist families 116 (65.5 per cent) were Catholics. Out of 272 individual royalists 157 (57 per cent) were Catholics. Out of 42 royalist gentlemen killed in the war, 30 (71 per cent) were Catholics.[10]

The royalist army commanded by Lord Derby at the start of the war in Lancashire was known with some justification as 'the Catholic army': 'There is now at present great preparation among the papists for [raising] of companies my lord [Strange] having some companies already in a body at Wigan, and about Lathom and Ormskirk, as is related to us, which we feared were daily increased in strength and arms both horse and foot, and besides that, some papists have commission to raise volunteers ... this country and especially this hundred ... was never in greater fear nor more danger than now it is' (quoted by Gratton). Thirty-nine (44 per cent) out of 88 officers in this army were Catholics, though only 21 per cent amongst the rank and file can be identified as Catholics. The Catholic royalist recruiting grounds were the Fylde in Amounderness and West Derby hundred, the main centres of Catholic Lancashire. When it attacked Manchester in 1642 this army numbered some 3,000 but 1,600, the regiments of Sir Gilbert Gerard and Lord Molyneux, went to join the king at Edgehill. And all this out of an estimated 13,500 Lancashire Catholics out of a Lancashire population of a hundred and fifty thousand. The return of Molyneux and Tyldesley after Edgehill led to the further recruitment of Catholics. Although this army was virtually destroyed at Whalley in 1643, even more of the Catholic gentry rallied to the royalist cause when Rupert's army entered the county in 1644 only to be scattered at Marston Moor.[11]

At the start of the war the Lancashire Catholic leader was Lord Molyneux. Richard Molyneux, second viscount Maryborough, born about 1623, was second only to the Earl of Derby in the ranks of the county. He owned considerable property around Liverpool and in Sussex, the latter inherited through his mother Mary Caryll, giving him an income of over £4,000 per annum, compared with Derby's income of £6,000. In 1642 he raised a regiment of foot and led them against Manchester. He then took his regiment to fight at Edgehill. He left his regiment with Sir Gilbert Gerard's at Brill on the Hill, one of the forts defending Oxford, and returned to Lancashire. He threw himself into recruiting more men, raising a regiment of horse, and was present at the royalist capture of Lancaster and Preston and in the defeat at Whalley. He eventually withdrew to re-join the main royalist army in the south. He and his troops fought at Bristol, Gloucester, and Chipping Camden, and they returned north with Byron and joined Rupert's army for the attacks on Bolton and Liverpool. He followed Rupert to defeat at Marston Moor, and retreated to Lancashire where his force was defeated at Ormskirk. He then made for Chester, where he rejoined the royal army, and was present at Naseby. He made his way to Ludlow where he surrendered in 1646. He subsequently took part in a plot to free the king, but after repeated arrests and releases he died in 1654.[12]

Despite his noble status, Molyneux was outshone as a royalist commander by his co-religionist Sir Thomas Tyldesley. As a parliamentarian (quoted by Newman) put it, Tyldesley 'doth more harm than any man I know'. Born in 1596, Sir Thomas was the eldest son of Edward Tyldesley of Morleys Hall, Astley, but he let Morleys to Ambrose Barlow, and resided at Myerscough Lodge near Garstang. He was a professional soldier who had served in the Thirty Years War in Germany, and on the outbreak of the English Civil War he immediately joined the royalist army in Lancashire, raising regiments of horse, foot, and dragoons. He was present at Manchester in 1642, and then accompanied the Lancashire force which marched to Edgehill. He returned with Molyneux to Lancashire, and after the defeat at Whalley led his forces into Yorkshire to join the queen and the earl of Newcastle. He marched south with the queen, and was knighted and promoted to brigadier for his dashing storm of the bridge at Burton-upon-Trent. He was sent north again with Molyneux

3 *Thomas Tyldesley. From a print in the possession of the author.*

under Byron, and joined forces with Rupert for the capture of Bolton and Liverpool. He was with Rupert and Molyneux at Marston Moor. After this defeat, he was made governor of Lichfield in 1645, but was obliged to surrender it in 1646. He withdrew into Lancashire and then retreated to Appleby where he surrendered in 1648. He then went to Ireland, then to the Isle of Man, then to Scotland, and then back to the Isle of Man, where he joined Lord Derby for his invasion of Lancashire in 1651. They landed at the mouth of the Wyre and moved south across the Ribble to Lathom House, recruiting a force of 1,500 men. They moved south to Warrington and then moved north through Wigan to Preston where they turned back to Wigan. There they were ambushed in Wigan Lane by parliamentary troops on 25 August 1651. Derby escaped to join the Scots at Worcester but was captured and executed at Bolton. Tyldesley was killed in the battle at Wigan. The monument erected to his memory after the Restoration by his cornet Alexander Rigby still stands in Wigan Lane.[13]

Richard Gerard was another Lancastrian Catholic professional soldier who embodied the personal devotion of the cavaliers to the house of Stuart. Born in 1613, he was the younger son of Sir Thomas Gerard of Bryn by Frances, daughter of Sir Richard Molyneux, and was therefore the cousin of the second viscount. He went to the new Catholic American settlement of Maryland in 1634, but returned in 1635. He then raised a troop of foot which he led in the Spanish service in the Netherlands from 1638. On the outbreak of the English Civil War, he entered the service of Queen Henrietta Maria at the Hague, and returned with her to England, taking command of her bodyguard, and fighting with Tyldesley at Burton-upon-Trent and at the second battle of Newbury. After the Restoration he was appointed cup-bearer to Henrietta Maria, and retired to Ince near Wigan where he died in 1686.[14]

The defeat of the king left the Lancashire Catholics at the mercy of the triumphant Puritans. The end of the first Civil War was marked by the execution of three priests at Lancaster. Edward Bamber was born at Carlton, Blackpool, educated at St Omer and Seville, and ordained in 1626. Captured on landing at Plymouth in 1626, he conformed and was pardoned, but reverted to Catholicism and went back to Lancashire to work as priest at Leigh and Wigan. In 1643 he was captured but not executed until 1646. John Woodcock was born at Clayton-le-Woods, Leyland, in 1603 and educated at Rome. He became a Franciscan and was ordained in 1634. He went on the English mission in 1643 and worked in Lancashire, but was arrested at Bamber Bridge in 1642 and executed with Bamber. Thomas Whitaker was born at Burnley in 1611, was educated at Valladolid, ordained in 1638, and sent to England to work at Goosnargh, Kirkham, and St Michael's. He was arrested, escaped, and was re-captured at Goosnargh. He too was hanged with Bamber. Nevertheless, the war in Lancashire was not marked by massacres and the sectional hatred appealed to in the propaganda must not be exaggerated.[15]

At the start of the war in 1642, parliament had declared that the cost of raising its forces should be borne by delinquents and malignants, that is by the royalists, and that parliament's creditors would be repaid out of their estates, in effect amounting to the expropriation of the royalists. Moreover, a new oath was devised in 1643, renouncing characteristically Catholic doctrines such as papal supremacy, transubstantiation, and purgatory, to be tendered to suspected Catholics on pain of the confiscation of two-thirds of their estates for refusing to take it, though recusants were allowed to compound for their forfeitures.[16]

The parliamentary committee for compounding estimated that there were 12,000 Catholic families in Lancashire. In 1655, 739 recusants were listed as under sequestration, including 181 (24 per cent) delinquents, that is active royalists. In addition, there were 40 Protestant delinquents so that Catholics consitituted 81.9 per cent of 221 delinquents. Some sought to escape the penalties by conforming, some in the indistinguishable accents of conversion or hypocrisy, using the formulae of the victors. William Blackburn yeoman of Walton-le-Dale told the committee that 'God by his marvellous light hath discovered unto your petitioner the dark and erroneous ways of the popish religion wherein he was bred', and William Sharrock, also of Walton-le-Dale, outdid him in declaring that:

> God by his marvellous light hath discovered unto your petitioner the dark and erroneous ways of the popish religion wherein he was bred. Out of a sense thereof and in testimony of his conforming to the Protestant religion your petitioner doth frequent the church and doth partake of the ordinances of God there, and hath solemnly and sincerely taken the oath of abjuration.

Some tried to avoid sequestration by the old trick of conveying their estate to a sympathetic Protestant relation. As the commissioners remarked in the case of the Shireburns of Stonyhurst, 'There was some indirect dealing to avoid sequestration', but they were unable to discover it. Some were downright defiant. Lawrence Ireland of Lydiate, a minor, was overseas being educated as a Catholic. When the commissioners advised his widowed mother to have him educated as a Protestant to escape sequestration, she replied that he 'had rather see him hanged'.[17]

Fortunately for the Catholics, the Puritans divided between the Presbyterians, supported by the Scots, who wanted an established Presbyterian Church in place of the Church of England, and the Independents, supported by the English parliamentary army led by Cromwell, which wanted toleration, and the Independents were victorious. In 1650 the Commonwealth, which replaced the monarchy after the execution of the king, granted toleration to all forms of Christianity, except to popery and prelacy, that is Catholicism and Anglicanism. In practice, Catholics like others were no longer fined for recusancy, that is for failure to attend their parish church. When in 1655 the anti-Catholic penal laws were re-enacted, the test was not recusancy but refusal to take the oath of 1643, and the law was not enforced by Cromwell, who became Lord Protector in 1653. The execution in 1654 of John Southworth, a Lancashire-born priest who had long worked in London, was an exception.[18]

An influential group of secular clergy, Blacklo's cabal, sought an accommodation with the Commonwealth, and one of their leading spokesmen was the Lancastrian Henry Holden. Thomas White alias Blacklo, a member of the chapter, a thinker who was read with approval by Descartes and was a friend of Hobbes, argued that Catholics had a duty of passive obedience to any de facto government. His supporters included John Sergeant, the secretary to the chapter from 1655 to 1667, Sir Kenelm Digby, a former courtier, and Holden. According to Birrell the great liberal Catholic historian Lord Acton placed the cabal amongst the 'original thinkers among the English Catholics'. Born in 1597, Holden was the son of Richard Holden of Chaigley Manor, Mitton, Lancashire, and his wife Eleanor, a daughter of Miles Gerard of Ince. He was ordained in 1622, and obtained a doctorate of divinity at the Sorbonne. He became a member of the chapter but spent most of his time in Paris where he was vicar general. He did return to Lancashire in 1661, but fell ill on his way back to Paris where he died.[19]

Holden was not only prepared to come to an accommodation with the Commonwealth but, in his Anglo-Gallican zeal for the restoration of the English Catholic episcopate, was also prepared to try to obtain that restoration without papal permission by seeking consecration from the French or Irish bishops: 'If the pope will not send us bishops it must be done without him'. He argued:

> These bishops will be (as all other ordinary bishops are) in the belief of all Catholics successors to the apostles, having authority immediately from Christ Jesus himself, and consequently independent of all other spiritual power, even of the Pope himself. For though all bishops are bound to acknowledge the Pope their head or the chief pastor, yet he cannot impose any special command upon them of what nature soever unless both they, and the commonwealth in which they live do think it fit, and this hath been the practice heretofore in Catholic times in England, is now in France, and in all other Catholic states and kingdoms.

Holden was only stating the English version of the Gallican tradition that the national churches were autonomous, but he did so with a theologian's venom and a Lancastrian's bluntness: his opponents would 'never dare to go to the close-stool without a breve from Rome'.[20]

However, Cromwell was not prepared to accept the restoration of the English Catholic hierarchy and the scheme came to nothing. Cromwell died in 1658, and in 1660 the monarchy was restored in the person of Charles II.

Despite the attempts of the Blackloists to abandon the Stuart cause, the Catholic royalists of Lancashire hoped for the reward of their loyalty in some measure of toleration, and, indeed, Charles II promised as much in the declaration of Breda in 1660. However, the Church of England was also restored by the Act of Uniformity of 1662, and the penal laws against Catholics were re-enacted together with new measures directed against the Protestant Nonconformists.

Nevertheless, the anti-Catholic penal laws were not rigorously enforced, but when the king issued the declaration of indulgence of 1672, granting religious toleration, parliament forced him to withdraw it. Anti-Catholic feeling culminated in the agitation which followed Titus Oates's so-called discovery of the Popish Plot in 1678, but once the excitement was over the application of the penal laws was again relaxed.

In 1683, out of 80 prisoners at Lancaster there were two priests and only eight lay recusants, and the laymen were not kept in the castle but lodged in the town.[21]

Not that the Catholics were passive under persecution or without sympathisers. When the bailiffs tried to distrain the property of Ann Pennington widow of Wigan in 1681 for non-payment of her recusancy fines, there was a riot, and the bailiffs barely escaped and without any property. When the bailiffs tried to distrain the property of Margery Tickle widow and John Sutton yeoman at Altcar in 1682 there was another riot. It was reported that the Protestant community in Altcar was 'so slender that they dare not deny the Roman whatsoever he is pleased to call neighbourly civility'.[22]

The Lancashire Catholic community was the largest in the country. Indeed, it dwarfed the next largest. A return of 1671 put the recusant population of England at 10,236, and that of Lancashire at 5,496, that is 53 per cent, and the returns indicate that it was growing. It numbered 5,216 in 1667-8, 5,782 in 1678-9, and 6,206 in 1682.[23]

It remained concentrated in the coastal plain. West Derby hundred had the largest Catholic population in Lancashire, about 2,000, then came Amounderness with about 1,500, then Blackburn with about 1,000, then Leyland with over 500, then Lonsdale with about 300, and lastly Salford with about two hundred.[24]

It remained a predominantly female community, whose viewpoint was carved in stone at Aldcliffe (the stone was later removed to Thurnham Hall) for the daughters of Robert Dalton : 'Catholicae Virgines nos sumus: Mutare vel tempore Spernimus Ano Dni 1674—We are Catholic virgins who scorn to change with the times'. It also remained dominated by the gentry but with a considerable proportion of husbandmen-farmers, and within the county Catholic community there were local plebeian Catholic communities independent of the gentry, such as those at Brindle, Burscough, and Lathom.[25]

Its clandestine Catholic schools, such as Scarisbrick, continued to function, the celebrated school at Fernyhalgh was established by 1650, and 21 such schools were in operation under Charles II.[26]

Brindle, like Fernyhalgh, cherished an ancient holy well whose origins lay beyond the Reformation and probably beyond Christianity. It was described in 1675 as:

> a spring of very clear water, rushing straight upward into the midst of a fair
> fountain, walled square about in stone, and flagged in the bottom, very transparent
> to be seen and a strong stream issuing out of the same. This fountain is called
> St Ellen's Well, to which place the vulgar neighbouring people of the Red Letter
> do much resort with pretended devotion on each year upon St Ellen's day.

The well had its hereditary guardians, the Gerards of the Well, who lived in a house which contained a chapel. In 1767 Alice Gerard built a new chapel and a permanent residence for the priest.[27]

The parish of Broughton and its dependent chapelry of Barton just north of Preston are illustrated by the survival of the Compton census ordered by the archbishop of Canterbury in 1676. The curate and churchwardens numbered the inhabitants at 636, the Catholic recusants at 192 (198 are listed), and the Protestant Nonconformists at nil. The list of recusants reveals not only a majority of women but also a significant proportion of households, 29 (30 per cent) out of 96, headed by widows. Seventeenth-century society was in theory patriarchal but widows were left as the heads of households. Moreover, the list does not sustain the image of separate Catholic and Protestant households. There was the classic seigneurial household of Nicholas Wadsworth esquire and his Catholic family and servants, and small households of a husband and wife or a widow and child tended to be wholly Catholic or Protestant, but larger households tended to contain a mixture; thus the Catholic Thomas Kitchin, goldsmith, had a Catholic wife, two Catholic children, and two Catholic servants, but also one Protestant servant, whilst the Protestant household of William Leyton esquire contained his Protestant wife and three children and three Protestant servants, but also one Catholic servant. Here, at least, the household united individuals of different religions.[28]

The religion of the Catholic gentry is illustrated in the papers of William Blundell of Crosby. In 1635 at the age of 15 he married Anna Haggerston of Haggerston, Northumberland: 'You will remember,' he wrote (in *Cavalier*) to his mother-in-law in 1651, 'what a pretty, straight young thing, all dashing in scarlet, I came to Haggerston'. He joined the royal army with a troop of dragons in Tyldesley's regiment, and was wounded at Lancaster in 1642, his house was plundered by parliamentary troops, and his property was sequestrated in 1643, so that he was (according to *Crosby Records*) 'overcloyed with care, debts, business, and imprisonments'. However, he did take a share in the *Antelope*, which was sent to Barbados in 1660, probably the first Liverpool ship to cross the Atlantic for sugar, and made 100 per cent profit. He could boast (according to *Crosby Records*) that Crosby 'had not a beggar ... an alehouse ... a Protestant'. He was philosophical about persecution but a convinced royalist as well as a Catholic. In 1673 after the failure of the declaration of indulgence he wrote (in *Cavalier*):

> I think that none but madmen can execute these cruel things that are threatened against His Majesty's Catholic subjects. And if men be really mad, there is not defence against them by paper walls ... I knew no leading rebel ... who was not ... a notable taker or tenderer of the oath of allegiance, nor any one Catholic refuser who proved disloyal to the king ... If we must therefore beg or pay I pray God bless the King, and the will of God be done.

Thus he wrote (in *Crosby Records*) on the sacrament of confession that 'when God forgiveth us our sins He scourgeth us roundly (notwithstanding though with worldly afflictions) both to punish what is past and to teach us to mend for the future. And the less we have of those the more we have of Purgatory in another world'.[29]

He describes (in *Crosby Records*) the regime of fasts and feasts, which ordered a Catholic's life:

> AD 1683 Christmas began on Tuesday, so that we had eight holy days together ... immediately before that Christmas we had six days ... whereof five were

fasting-days, one holyday, and one Sunday, so that here at that time fourteen days togethere which were all of them either holydays or fasting-days.

He also describes (in *Crosby Records*) the devotions of the devout:

> Upon the eve of the Conception of Our Lady, I being of the sodality with others of my family proposed to our spiritual director that we might all together say the rosary upon the said feast day.

The priest declined on the grounds of ill health but then spent the afternoon playing at table and shovel-board.[30] His essential Christianity he summed up thus:

> And will Faith, Hope, and Charity bring us to Heaven too? ... Aye, they will bring us to Heaven's gates, but Faith and Hope must go back again, and only Charity must enter into Heaven.[31]

His brother Richard wrote an English epitome of Sir Kenelm Digby's scientific works, and wrote one himself in Latin on meteors, for natural science was the new interest of the Catholic gentry. Christopher Towneley (1604-1674), a younger son of Richard Towneley of Towneley, was a friend of the Lancashire astronomers Horrocks and Crabtree, and preserved their papers, as well as serving in the royalist army. His nephew Richard Towneley (1629-1707) of Towneley was an outstanding scientist. He was at the centre of the Towneley circle, which included his brothers, Charles, John, and Francis, other local Catholic gentry, like Sir Nicholas Sherburn of Stonyhurst and Richard Walmesley of Dunkenhalgh, and the astronomer Flamsteed, who visited Towneley in 1671 and 1672. Towneley was a Cartesian who made a number of observations with a variety of instruments, including a series of experiments with barometers which he carried up Pendle Hill and down mines. As a result, he discovered the relationship between the pressure and the density of air, which was made known by Boyle in 1662, and has since been called Boyle's Law but was called 'Mr Towneley's hypothesis' by Boyle.[32]

Engrossed in their families and their estates, devoted to religion and learning as gentlemanly pursuits—William Blundell would have his son 'to dance and fence, to speak Latin and French readily and to see the world ... You may find us now and then up to our ears in Plutarch' —the Restoration Catholic gentry seemed resigned to their lot as a persecuted minority—as Halifax put it, 'The laws have made them men of pleasure, by excluding them from public business'—but they were soon caught up again in the fortunes of the house of Stuart.[33]

In 1685 Charles II died, having become a Catholic on his death-bed, and was succeeded by his brother, the duke of York, already a Catholic convert, who came to the throne as King James II. He was determined to secure toleration for his co-religionists, and, indeed, to embark upon the conversion of England. He always insisted that he wanted toleration for all religions but Protestants suspected that this was only a pretence, and that he intended eventually to impose Catholicism by persecuting Protestantism, especially as in 1685 King Louis XIV of France revoked the toleration of French Protestants. James proceeded to effect his policies by the exercise of the royal prerogative, and, though he declared that he desired the consent of parliament, his activities seemed to threaten parliamentary liberty. He began by abandoning the application of the penal laws and by using his dispensing power to permit an increasing number of Catholics to hold public office, and then in 1687 he issued a declaration of indulgence suspending all the penal laws.[34]

In Lancashire a Catholic ascendancy was established. The Catholic Lord Molyneux replaced Lord Derby as the lord lieutenant, and an increasing number of Catholics, including William Blundell and Richard Towneley, were appointed justices of the peace, a total of 27, 55 per cent of the magistrates but 76 per cent of the active magistrates.[35]

Moreover the king proceeded to regulate the boroughs so as to place urban local government under Catholic and Nonconformist control and to secure the election of sympathetic members of parliament. Liverpool proved defiant. A Presbyterian was appointed mayor of Lancaster. The regulation of Preston was supervised by Molyneux who appointed a local regulator John Scarsfield, who was decribed as a 'Quaker ... and not without some suspicion of being a Jesuit'. At Wigan the Catholic Thomas Gerard esquire of Ince was appointed mayor and publicly attended Catholic worship in the town.[36]

The king also secured the appointment in 1685 of a vicar apostolic, John Leyburn, who set out on a visitation of his flock to administer confirmation. He admitted to the sacrament 20,859 people, 7,217 (34 per cent) in Lancashire, including 158 at Thurnham, 1,105 at Nateby, 397 at Lytham, 1,143 at Preston and Tulketh, 216 at Towneley, 1,047 at Euxton, 464 at Wrightington, 1,333 (the largest single congregation in England) at Wigan, 306 at Lostock, and 1,048 at Croxteth.[37]

In 1688 England was divided into four districts or vicariates, each with its own vicar apostolic, including the Northern district, which covered Lancashire, under Bishop James Smith.[38]

The Lancashire Catholics continued to worship in their secret private chapels, like that at Birchley Hall where Roger Anderton, the archdeacon of Lancashire and Westmorland, was resident priest. They also opened public chapels in the towns, such as Lancaster, Preston, and Wigan, where the Jesuits also opened a school. Chapels were also opened elsewhere, notably at Ladywell, Fernyhalgh, an ancient place of pilgrimage—one descends by steps into a narrow stone-walled pit and there in the flagged floor the holy water brims into its square basin—and Euxton, built by Molyneux. However, when Bartholomew Walmesley of Dunkenhalgh seized the Anglican chapel of Langho for Catholic worship the government ordered him to desist.[39]

This Catholic ascendancy looked like being made permanent by the birth of a Catholic heir to the throne, James, Prince of Wales, in 1688. However, the royal policies had aroused so much resistance that the king began to give way, replacing Molyneux with Derby as lord lieutenant of Lancashire. It was too late and in November William of Orange, the king's son-in-law, invaded England to defend parliament and

Protestantism, and King James fled. The Catholic ascendancy collapsed, and the public Catholic chapels were looted and destroyed.

The Catholic alliances with the Anglicans and the Nonconformists had both collapsed, leaving the Catholics isolated. Nevertheless, the re-organised structure of the English mission under vicars apostolic survived to provide the Lancashire Catholics with some form of episcopal government. They remained committed to the cause of the exiled King James. Catholic and Jacobite became synonymous. It was to take the Lancashire Catholics nearly a century to abandon this commitment to a lost cause.[40]

Notes

1. B. G. Blackwood, *The Lancashire Gentry and the Great Rebellion* (hereafter *Lancs Gentry & Gt Rebellion*) (CS, 3rd series, vol.25, 1978); Blackwood, 'Parties and issues in the Civil War in Lancashire', *Transactions of the Historic Society of Lancashire and Cheshire* (henceforth THSLC), vol.132 (1982); Blackwood, 'Plebeian Catholics in Later Stuart Lancashire', *NH*, vol.25 (1989).
2. J. P. Kenyon, *Stuart England* (1978); G. Davies, *The Early Stuarts* (1959); R. Ashton, *The English Civil War* (1978).
3. J. J. Bagley, *A History of Lancashire* (1961) (hereafter Bagley), pp.34-35; Bagley and A. S. Lewis, *Lancashire at War: Cavaliers and Roundheads 1642-1651* (1977); S. Bull, *The Civil War in Lancashire* (1991); E. Broxap, *The Great Civil War in Lancashire* (1910).
4. House of Lords Record Office, Westminster, Protestation Returns for the Hundreds of Amounderness, Blackburn, Leyland, Salford, and West Derby, 1642.
5. Bossy, *Community*, pp.94-95; Blackwood, *Lancs Gentry & Gt Rebellion*, p.27; Haigh, p.332.
6. G. Ormerod (ed.), *Tracts relating to the Military Proceedings in Lancashire during the Great Civil War* (CS, vol.2, 1844), pp.3-4, 49, 101-2; F. Walker, *Historical Geography of South West Lancashire before the Industrial Revolution* (CS, new series, vol.103, 1939), p.78; J. M. Gratton, 'The Earl of Derby's Catholic Army', *THSLC*, vol.137 (1988), pp.28, 32.
7. Anstruther, *Vaux of Harrowden* (1953), p.464; C. Hibbard, 'The Contribution of 1639: Court and Country Catholicism', *RH*, vol.16 (1) (1982), p.49; Richardson, p.154.
8. Beaumont, W.(ed.), *A Discourse of the War in Lancashire* (CS, new series vol.62, 1864), pp.14-15.
9. Ormerod, pp.38-40, Gratton, *THSLC*, vol.137, pp.31-2.
10. Blackwood, *Lancs Gentry & Gt Rebellion*, pp.20, 64-5.
11. Gratton, *THSLC*, vol.137, p.33; Gratton, 'The Military Career of Richard, Lord Molyneux, c.1623-54', *THSLC*, vol.134 (1985), pp.26-28.
12. Gratton, *THSLC*, vol.134 , pp.17-38.
13. P. R. Newman, 'Catholic Royalist Activists in the North, 1642-46', *RH*, vol.14 (1) (1977), p.30; *DNB*, vol.19, pp.1344-5; S. Reid, *The Finest Knight in England* (1979).
14. *DNB*, vol.7, p.1103.
15. Anstruther, vol.2, pp.13-14, 346-7; B. Foley, *The Eighty-Five Blessed Martyrs* (1987), pp.20-21; Newman, 'Aspects of the Civil War in Lancashire', *TLCAS*, vol.72 (1983).
16. *Royalist Composition Papers* (Record Society of Lancashire and Cheshire (hereafter RSLC) , vol.115, 1941, vol.6(1), pp.2-11.
17. *Royalist Composition Papers* (RSLC, vol.24, 1891, vol.36, 1898, vol.115, 1941, vol.116, 1942) vol.1, pp.191-3, vol.4, pp.14-23, vol.6 (1), pp.21-2,69-78,99-100, (2), pp.405-6.
18. Davies, pp.198-99, 210-3; Anstruther, vol.2, pp.306-8.
19. T. A. Birrell (ed.), 'Introduction' to R. Pugh, *Blacklo's Cabal* (1978); Anstruther, vol.2, pp.158-9, 280-9, 349-55; Bossy, *Community*, pp.60-9.

20. Anstruther, vol.2, p.158; Pugh, pp. 27, 33; Bossy, *Community*, p.66.
21. *HMC Kenyon*, p.159.
22. *HMC Kenyon*, pp.137-38.
23. *Miscellanea 6* (CRS vol.6, 1909) p.77; Blackwood, *NH*, vol.25, p.160.
24. Blackwood, *NH*, vol.25, pp.162-64.
25. Blundell, vol.3, pp.13-14; N. Pevsner, *Lancashire: The Rural North* (henceforth *Lancs:North*)(1969), p. 247; Blackwood, NH, vol.25, pp. 158-70.
26. Beales, pp.223-30.
27. Blundell, vol.1, pp.135-6.
28. J. H. Adamson, 'Popish Recusants at Broughton, Lancashire, 1676', *RH*, vol.15 (3).
29. T. E. Gibson (ed.), *Crosby Records* (CS, new series, vol.12, 1887)(hereafter Gibson), pp.2, 33-4, 54; M. Blundell (ed.), *Cavalier: Letters of William Blundell to his Friends, 1620-1695* (London, 1934), pp.10-13, 304-12.
30. Gibson, pp.122, 133.
31. Gibson, pp.304-12.
32. Gibson, p.174; C. Webster, 'Richard Towneley, 1629-1707, and the Towneley Group', *THSLC*, vol.118.
33. Gibson, p.61; Halifax, *Complete Works* (1969) p.83.
34. Kenyon, J. Miller, *Popery and Politics in England 1660-1688* (1973).
35. G. A. Fallon, 'The Catholic Justices of Lancashire under James II', *NWCH*, vol.8 (1981).
36. M. Mullett. '"To Dwell Together in Unity": the Search for Agreement in Preston Politics, 1660-1690', *THSLC*, vol.135 (1974), p.77; Hilton, 'Wigan Catholics and the Policies of James II', *NWCH*, vol.1(3)(1969).
37. F. J. Vaughan, 'Bishop Leyburn and His Confirmation Register of 1687', *Northern Catholic History*, vol.12 (1980).
38. B. Hemphill, *The Early Vicars Apostolic of England* (1954)(hereafter Hemphill), pp.16-26.
39. Hilton, 'The Catholic Ascendancy in the North, 1685-88', *NWCH*, vol.5 (1978).
40. Walker, pp.116-20; Fallon, *NWCH*, vol.8, pp.8-10.

Chapter IV

The Jacobite Catholics, 1688-1746

Between the Glorious Revolution in 1688 and the defeat of Prince Charles Edward at Culloden in 1746 the Lancashire Catholics remained associated with the Jacobite cause. A few were active in the Jacobite revolts, though the majority got on with trying to lead normal lives while still subject to penalties. The system of ecclesiastical government under vicars apostolic continued to function, but the secular clergy remained desirous of the restoration of a national episcopate, a view to which a Lancastrian gave expression in one of the classics of Anglo-Gallicanism.

Despite his overthrow in 1688, James II's supporters, the Jacobites, remained optimistic that he would be restored as his brother had been before him. The Catholics were natural supporters of a Catholic king who had been overthrown while trying to secure toleration for his co-religionists. Moreover, the Anglicans, having committed themselves to the doctrines of the divine right of kings, non-resistance, and passive obedience, were inclined to the Jacobite cause. A few, including Achbishop Sancroft of Canterbury, who in defence of the Church of England had stood up to James, could not take the oath of allegiance to William and Mary and went into schism as the Non-Jurors in 1691. High Church Anglicans in general, who consolidated their position under Queen Anne, remained sympathetic to the Jacobite cause, especially after the accession of the Hanoverian George I in 1714.[1]

In 1689 a fracas involving Philip Langton of Lowe, the Catholic squire of Hindley near Wigan, demonstrated the Catholic view of William of Orange and his local supporter the Earl of Derby. As one of the magistrates reported:

> There was two men with me, the one lives in Bolton, the other on Tonge Moor, that were but a few days since at the ale-house on Hindley Common, when Mr Langton of Lowe being gone to look on the wall, the landlord began the Earl of Derby's health, which Mr Langton hearing, broke the landlord's head with his cane and threw him on the fire. One of the witnesses blaming of him for his abuse, he fell upon him, who threw Mr Langton in the fire; but Mr Langton goes and fetched four more, so they being but two, thought it convenient to march off.

Another magistrate noted that:

> It is talked here that the Papists in our country are inquiring who those were that pulled down or defaced their chapels. I can scarce believe they would be so silly at this time to act so impudently

and again he reported that:

> The papists and others as disaffected as themselves are very high in your parts
> as though they had something in prospect.[2]

The something in prospect was James's landing in Ireland in 1689 and the possibility that, having won control there, he would invade Lancashire. As Lord Derby put it, 'the Papists were in great expectation of the late king's and their great master's coming into Lancashire'. However, James was defeated at the battle of the Boyne in 1690 and returned to France. With the surrender of Limerick in 1691, Ireland was once again under British Protestant domination.[3]

Then in 1694 the leading Lancashire Catholics were put on trial at Manchester for their part in the Lancashire plot. Lord Molyneux, Sir William Gerard of Bryn, Sir Thomas Clifton of Lytham, William Dicconson esq. of Wrightington, Philip Langton esq. of Hindley, Bartholomew Walmesley esq. of Dunkenhalgh, William Blundell gent of Crosby, and Sir Roland Stanley, the leading Catholic in Cheshire, were accused of treason, of conspiring to rebel so as to restore James II to the throne. The evidence of the prosecution witnesses was so obviously faulty that the accused were acquitted, and successfully prosecuted these witnesses for perjury.[4]

And there apparently the matter rested. In 1757 workmen engaged in alterations at Standish Hall discovered in a wall some papers in cipher. However, they remained unintelligible until they were deciphered by Porteus in 1927. Then it was revealed that there had been a real Jacobite Lancashire plot. The papers include correspondence from James II, his secretary of state, Lord Melfort, the Benedictine priest Henry Joseph Johnston alias Harrison, and a Colonel John Parker, to whom the bulk of the correspondence belonged. The papers include commissions from James II, a declaration of loyalty to him, and accounts of weapons. The declaration of loyalty was signed by, amongst others, William Standish and Charles Towneley.[5]

The enduring loyalty of the Lancashire Catholic gentry to the Jacobite cause was personified in William Dicconson of Wrightington Hall (now the site of Wrightington Hospital), who joined the court of James II at St Germain in France in 1694 and became governor of the young James, the Jacobite Prince of Wales. He was also the author of a life of James II. He died at St Germain in 1743.[6]

The death of William III's successor, Queen Anne, in 1714, and the accession of the German George I as king of England led to renewed activity on behalf of James III, the Jacobite Pretender, who had succeeded to his father's claims in 1701. There were Jacobite riots throughout the county, including Manchester, Warrington, and Wigan.[7]

In 1715 a Jacobite revolt began in the Highlands of Scotland and was joined by a force from Northumberland. The bulk of the Scottish Jacobites remained in their own country, but a few followed the English Jacobites, led by Derwentwater and Forster, through Cumberland and Westmorland into Lancashire, where they hoped to raise the Lancashire Jacobites and to capture Liverpool. On 9 November 1715 they entered Preston. They had lost five or six hundred men by desertion, but they were joined by about sixteen hundred new but poorly armed and undisciplined recruits. These included a number of the Lancashire Catholic gentry: Richard Towneley of Towneley, Shuttleworth of Shuttleworth, Sir Fancis Anderton of Lostock, Richard Chorley of Chorley, Gabriel Hesketh of St Michael's-on-Wyre, John Leyburn of Nateby, Ralph Standish of Standish, Albert Hodgson of Leighton, John Dalton of Thurnham, Edward Tyldesley of Myerscough, Henry Butler of Rawcliffe, and Walton of Cartmel.[8]

However, they were soon surrounded in Preston by Hanoverian forces, and by 14 November Forster had decided to surrender. On the same day, the Scottish Jacobites were defeated at Sheriffmuir. Many of the Lancashiremen at Preston were able to escape, but over a thousand Jacobites were captured. Shuttleworth and Chorley were tried at Liverpool and executed at Preston, but Standish, Anderton, Dalton, Tyldesley, and Towneley were sent to London and pardoned. In the aftermath of the revolt Catholic missions like that at Fernyhalgh were attacked and looted.[9]

In 1745 there was another Jacobite revolt in the Scottish Highlands led by Prince Charles Edward, the Young Pretender, acting on behalf of his father, James III, the Old Pretender. The Jacobite army again invaded England by way of Cumberland and Westmorland and entered Lancashire. They marched south through Lancaster, Preston, Chorley, Manchester, and Stockport. The Rev. John Sergeant arrived on the mission just in time to meet the Jacobite army at Preston. As a result he was subsequently imprisoned but was eventually released. On the way the Jacobites were joined by some three hundred Lancastrians formed into the so-called Manchester regiment commanded by Colonel Charles Towneley, a figure from the shady world of Jacobite adventurers described in Robert Louis Stevenson's *The Master of Ballantrae*.[10]

Towneley was born in 1709, the fifth son of Charles Towneley of Towneley and the brother of Richard who had fought at Preston. Like some other English Catholics, he had followed a military career in the French service from 1728, serving at the siege of Philipsburg in 1733 during the War of the Polish Succession. After the war he had gone to live quietly in Wales, but on the outbreak of the Jacobite revolt the King of France had sent him a colonel's commission, and he went to Manchester to take command of the Lancashire Jacobites. He proved a professional, veteran, hard-swearing, popular commander, and he led his men as part of the Jacobite army south to Derby.[11]

Faced with overwhelming odds, Charles Edward decided to retreat, marching through Stockport, Manchester, Wigan, Preston, and Lancaster. He left Towneley with the Manchester regiment to hold Carlisle, and continued his retreat into Scotland, where he was finally defeated at Culloden in 1746. Meanwhile on 30 December 1745 Towneley surrendered. He and his troops were sent to Newgate Gaol, and on Kennington Common on 30 July 1746 Towneley and eight other officers were executed. Towneley's body was buried at St Pancras' church, London, but his head, exposed on Temple Bar, was recovered and buried in Towneley chapel.

After the rebellion there were attacks on Catholics chapels. That at Liverpool was destroyed. At Lee House, Chipping, the Franciscan Father Germanus Helme or Holmes was seized, and imprisoned in Lancaster Castle where he died, probably the last priest to die in such circumstances.[12]

By the time the exiled Charles Edward succeeded his father as Charles III in 1766 the Jacobite cause was already dead. The anti-climax of Scott's *Redgauntlet*, set in 1765, when the Jacobite gentry refuse to answer Charles Edward's renewed call to revolt, portrays their disillusion. Jacobitism, however, did linger on as a sentimental attachment to a lost cause.

Despite their Jacobitism and their religion, the Lancashire Catholic gentry survived, primarily because of their considerable landed wealth. About 1694 there were 43 Catholic gentry with estates worth more than a hundred pounds. They were headed by Lord Molyneux worth £3,000, and there were six others worth more than £1,000: Sir Charles Anderton of Lostock, Sir Thomas Clifton of Lytham, Richard Sherborne of Stonyhurst, Lady Tyldesley of Astley, and Edward Trafford of Trafford. When the government ordered Catholic estates to be registered in the aftermath of the 1715 rebellion they were still headed by Viscount Molyneux with his estates around Liverpool, centred on the great house at Croxteth built in 1702, worth £3,500 per annum. Sir Thomas Clifton of Lytham with £1,500 per annum dominated the Fylde. Sir William Gerard of Garswood had estates to the south of Wigan which brought him £1,200 per annum. Sir Nicholas Shireburn of Stonyhurst worth £1,200 dominated the upper Ribble valley. Richard Towneley of Towneley near Blackburn had £900 per annum. Edward Tyldesley of Myerscough in the Fylde had £700 per annum. Sir Laurence Anderton of Lostock, who was a priest, had estates between Bolton, Wigan, and Preston worth £600 per annum. John Brockholes of Claughton on the edge of Bowland Forest was worth £500 per annum.[13]

The wealth of the gentry was the financial mainstay of the mission. Thus in 1700 Sir Nicholas Shireburn of Stonyhurst had given £140 to poor Catholics over the previous years, £100 towards defraying the debts of the Lancashire Jesuits, £100 towards the English Franciscan house at Douay, £23 towards vestments and altar hangings, a guinea towards the release from prison of a convert, a guinea to a poor travelling priest, and a guinea for the requiem mass of one of his servants.[14]

The tenor of their days is revealed in the diaries of Thomas Tyldesley of Myerscough and Nicholas Blundell of Crosby. The two men were acquainted, inhabited the same society, and shared the same concerns. The opening entry of Tyldesley's diary sets the tone, the country pursuits they shared with the rest of the gentry and their Catholicism:

> 25 March 1712
> Went with Mrs to Brooke, to prayers, and home to dinner. Afterwards went a fowling to Lancaster and Aldcliffe marshes and to see Ashton gardens; thence home.[15]

The source of their income and their main concern was the management of
their estates and their expansion by good marriages, but along with this went the
usual sports of the country landowner: hunting, shooting, and fishing. Fish—pike,
carp, tench, and eels—were an important part of their diet, especially for Catholics
with their days of abstinence from meat on every Friday of the year and every day
in Lent, and were stocked in special ponds or pits, which explains some at least of
the many which are scattered about Lancashire. They also followed horse-racing and
those typical 18th-century sports, cock-fighting and smuggling. Moreover, they were
also actively engaged in trade with the West Indies and North America, Tyldesley
through Lancaster and Blundell through Liverpool—Blundell's brother was a factor
in Virginia—whilst they both took an interest in coal-mining, an enterprise shown
also by their counterparts in the North-East.[16]

The Blundells maintained a priest who acted not only as chaplain to the family
but also as pastor to their Catholic tenants. He said Mass and vespers, administered
such sacraments as baptism, matrimony, and extreme unction, and catechised the
children. Until 1720 the family chapel served both family and tenants, but sometimes
on occasions like a baptism the congregation overflowed onto the stairs.[17]

The chaplain was also expected to participate in the social activities of the
gentry including such sports as fishing. Thus Blundell exercised his seigneurial right
in specifying to the Jesuit superior exactly what he wanted in a chaplain:

> a man of wit and conversation, one that can preach well and is willing to take
> pains amongst the poor Catholics, of which we have a great many, and one that
> is of a good humor and will easily be contented with tolerable good fare.

Therefore he asked the superior to permit the chaplain to join company which
included the Anglican parson who 'desired their company for they find them men
of parts, good company and conversation and free from all manner of vice'.[18]

The Jesuit superior obliged by appointing Robert Aldred in 1707. In 1720
Father Aldred took up residence at West Lane House (which became the chapel of
Little Crosby until 1847 when it became a school), a move which marked the
beginning of clerical independence.[19]

The Blundells' Catholicism stretched outside Lancashire to Holywell in North
Wales, whither they frequently went on pilgrimage, and to the convent of the Poor
Clares at Gravelines which contained no fewer than four Blundells—Alice, Anne,
Mary, and Margaret—at the beginning of the 18th century. Their Catholicism also
maintained its local connections with the old folk religion, the Blundells, their chil-
dren, and their servants decorating with flowers the crosses at Ince Blundell and
Great Crosby at Midsummer.[20]

By 1715 Thomas Tyldesley was dead, but his son Edward joined the Jacobite
rebellion, though at his trial he claimed that he was forced to join, a plea that was
accepted by the jury. The Jacobite plots and revolts caused the Blundells considerable difficulties, though Nicholas Blundell avoided rather than sought trouble. His

house was searched in 1705, 1708, and 1715, when he took refuge in a hide, 'a strait place' he remarked 'for a fat man'. In 1716 and 1717 the family sought safety in Flanders. Even in his diary Blundell maintained a neutral objectivity about the Jacobite cause as two entries for 1715 on the death of the Jacobite leaders illustrate:

> Feb 24th. Lords Derwentwater and Kenmure were executed.
>
> Feb 27th. There was High Mass for Lord Derwentwater at the French Envoy's. Several persons of note were there.

His resigned patience was probably more typical of the Catholic community as a whole than was the enthusiasm of Jacobite activists such as Charles Towneley.[21]

The letters of Ralph Howard Standish provide an insight into the local patriotism of the Lancashire Catholic gentry. He was born Ralph Howard Standish in 1700, the son of Ralph Standish of Standish and Borwick, Lancashire, and Lady Philippa Howard, the daughter of the sixth Duke of Norfolk, but changed his name to Ralph Standish Howard on inheriting the Howard property in Glossop. His parents were naturally anxious that he should marry well, and he spent the winter of 1727-8 in the south of England in pursuit of pleasure and a wife. As he wrote to his mother:

> I am so pestered with wives since I have been here that I don't know what to think. It's thought here that I am about matrimony, but they don't know.
>
> I am sorry to find your Ladyship can't think of my coming down, as I came up, single.[22]

In particular he set his cap at Lady Catherine Petre. She was born in 1698, the daughter of Bartholomew Walmesley esquire of Dunkenhalgh, Lancashire, and she inherited his fortune of £25,000 and property worth an income of £5,000 per annum. In 1712, aged fourteen, she married Robert, seventh Lord Petre, then aged twenty-two, whose earlier flirtation with Arabella Fermor had occasioned Pope's *Rape of the Lock*. The Walmesley family chaplain, who accompanied the new Lady Petre to her husband's home at Ingatestone, Essex, was the Jesuit Gilbert Talbot who succeeded as thirteenth Earl of Shrewsbury in 1718. The young couple were members of a house-party, joined by Thomas Tyldesley the diarist, at the Cliftons of Lytham (Lord Petre's mother was the daughter of Sir Thomas Clifton). However, Lord Petre died within a year, leaving his widow pregnant with the eighth Lord Petre.[23]

Young Ralph Howard Standish courted her in London and at Ingatestone, but she gave him to understand that he was not to 'lose my time by thinking of a person that I have no hopes of obtaining'. Accordingly he gave up his hopes in that direction and in 1730 married Mary Butler of Kilkenny, but died in 1735.[24]

His own love of Lancashire, especially of Standish, and its country pleasures is a recurring theme of his letters:

> I long mightily to be in Lancashire again, ballet [he wrote it 'bally'] and operas and plays afford me no sort of pleasure in comparison with hunting and shooting ... I am overjoyed to hear Mama's so much better, and able to tip a glass of

Catharine Walmesley.
Widow of Robert.
Lord Petre

4   *Catherine Walmesley. From a print provided by the Essex Record Office from a portrait at Ingatestone Hall, Essex, and by permission of the Right Honourable Lord Petre.*

champagne which by the by, I believe, would do her more good at old Standish than at Borwick when the weather is so frosty, now the south country at Standish there's such sunshining weather that, barely living there without champagne or burgundy would cure any body.[25]

In 1733 Catherine Petre married Charles Stourton, who became the fifteenth Baron Stourton and died in 1753, leaving Catherine a widow for the second time. In 1733 commenting on the rumours that Lady Petre was to re-marry, Howard remarked on 'her zeal to establish another Catholic family in Lancashire, which certainly is a very pious desire'. Although Lord Petre was her only child, she succeeded in this ambition by leaving Dunkenhalgh to her grandson, Lord Petre's younger son, George William Petre. Handsome and alert, the young widow in her mourning still stares out from her portrait. She died aged 85 in 1785.[26]

The size of the Lancashire Catholic community is problematic. Catholic writers like Berington in 1781 and Newman in 1857 believed that the 18th century was a period of numerical as well as political decline for Catholics, but modern historians, notably Bossy, agree with 18th-century Anglican observers that Catholics, especially in Lancashire, were increasing in numbers. Basing himself on the fact that Leyburn confirmed 8,900 Catholics in Lancashire in 1687, and that the local Jesuits put the number of adult Catholics in their care in 1710 at 4,420, Bossy estimates that the Lancashire Catholics about 1700 numbered sixteen to eighteen thousand. However, the incomplete return of 1705, made in response to Protestant fears of Catholic growth, lists only 2,861 Catholics concentrated in the coastal plain with much the largest group, 499 including the Blundells clustered in Sefton parish around Lord Molyneux. The returns for the parish of Deane for both 1705 and 1706 survive. The former lists 41 Catholics and the latter 34 but only 20 appear to be common to both lists. This suggests that these lists need to be treated with caution. Lancashire almost certainly contained the largest Catholic community in England. In 1728 Bishop Williams administered confirmation to 3,386 Catholics in Lancashire, more than the 2,827 in the rest of the Northern district.[27]

The registers of estates, which, of course, ignore the propertyless, reveal a community dominated by the nobility and gentry but solidly based on yeomen, husbandmen, and tradesmen. Nevertheless, the return of 1705 noted that 'Very few of these in the said parish of Sefton exceed £30 or £40 per annum, many have much to do [to] live and pay taxes and their dues, and not a few are so poor that they live by their neighbours' charity', but this was typical of society as a whole as described in Gregory King's national survey of 1688.[28]

The strength of the Lancashire Catholic community was analysed in 1714 by the vicar of Preston, Samuel Peploe, who in 1715 defied the Jacobite who threatened to kill him unless he ceased to pray for George I with his 'Soldier, I am doing my duty; do you do yours', and earned George I's 'Peep-low, Peep-low is he called? But he shall peep high; I will make him a bishop'. He blamed the strength of Catholicism on the lack of Anglican preachers, the poverty of the Anglican clergy, the size of the

Anglican parishes, the consequent lack of Anglican churches, and the sympathy of Tory magistrates. The county still had its 'dark parts', and he described in detail the activities of the Catholics:

> We have five or six houses in this town where the Papists meet, sometimes at one, sometimes at another, and pretty often in two or three at once: in these houses they have chapels decked with all the Popish trinkets. They go as publicly to their meetings as we go to church, and on Sabbath days they go by our bells. One Knight is the only priest that lives in the town, ... There are others who come in to officiate every Sunday and holy day. In the county part of this town ... there [are] several priests ... There is a great number of Popish priests who meet in this town, on market days, to consult together. There are several good estates ... which serve superstitious uses ... in so large a parish ... and among so many Papists ... there are some who shift side in religion: we both get and lose... they brought a corpse ... and ... kneeled at the Market cross to say their prayers ... The best estates in this country are in the hands of Papists. Their priests swarm in it, and the Romish Party is of late very uppish ...[29]

The parish of Standish to the north of Wigan on the little hills on the right bank of the River Douglas had long been a centre of recusancy. Two hundred and thirty-three Catholics were listed there in 1705, but servants were excluded from the list. The Catholics were headed by Ralph Standish esquire of Standish but there were a number of other Catholic gentry in the parish including Edward Standish, Emer Grymbalson, Thomas Hatton, Thomas Worthington, and William Houghton. The rest included yeomen, farmers, and labourers, together with shopkeepers and crafts-men, such as carpenters, and, mainly, linen-weavers. In 1746 another survey made by the rector put the total population at 3,524, including 2,881 (79.4 per cent) Anglicans, 133 (3.6 per cent) Dissenters, probably Presbyterians, twenty-nine (0.8 per cent) Quakers, and 571 (15.7 per cent) Catholics.[30]

The essentially seigneurial structure of the mission is described in a list made about 1705 of Catholic families, arranged according to social rank, which maintained priests. However, it goes on to explain how:

> In several parts of England where the Catholics of the lower rank are numerous, and are taken care of by the clergy ... there are funds established by the priests who have died there, to help the poor that cannot contribute towards a priest's maintenance. The same is done in many parts of Lancashire where Catholics are more numerous ...[31]

The evidence of the apostate priest and informer Hitchmough specifies some of the priests working in Lancashire and the funds available to them, for example William Moore, a secular priest who had left £100 in trust to Richard Golden gent of Winwick to help maintain a priest at Winwick. It also describes their altar plate, for example, the silver and gilt chalices and patens in the chapel of the Gerards of Garswood.[32]

The difficulties under which the mission was conducted are illustrated in the letters of Thomas Roydon who was vicar general for Lancashire and the other western counties of the Northern district in the first half of the 18th century as well as the riding-priest based at Dodding Green, Westmorland, and covering a circuit which extended through northern Lancashire, Yorkshire, Cumberland, and Westmorland:

> In the late years of trouble and plunder there was little convenience and much hazard ... What a number of miles was I obliged to travel! What a fatigue of riding... When I reached home (if I may call it home, where, God be my comfort, I scarce ever rested three nights successively in the same bed) I had but a scantling of time ... (quoted by Bishop B. C. Foley)
>
> As to myself I live among rocks. Some of my horses have perished, some half-killed are lamed upon them. My debtors defraud me. My relatives lay waste what I dare not spend. My nephew must be educated. A combination of exigencies have drained my purse. (quoted by Foley)
>
> The consideration of their great hardships amongst the gentry who have been generally sufferers, chiefly on the north of the Ribble... (quoted by Hemphill)
>
> The necessities of our brethren can scarcely be imagined. These poor, but zealous labourers, live on a mite, and have not a mite to spare. (quoted by Hemphill)

Nevertheless, (as Foley records) he managed to make collections to relieve the English college at Lisbon and Bishop Dominic Williams.[33]

The first three vicars apostolic of the North—James Smith (1688-1711), George Witham (1716-1725), and Dominic Williams (1726-1740)—resided on the eastern side of the Pennines, but in 1740 a new vicar apostolic took up residence in his native county of Lancashire. Edward Dicconson was born in 1670, the fourth son of Hugh Dicconson of Wrightington, Lancashire. He was educated at Douay and Paris, was ordained in 1701, and returned to Douay as a teacher, becoming vice president. Despite his wish for a benefice in Belgium, in 1720 he was sent on the English mission, and became vicar general of the Midland district. He was then sent to Rome as assistant to the agent of the English secular clergy. While there this reluctant misssioner, who was afflicted with a stammer but had won the regard of his fellow-priests, was appointed vicar apostolic of the North in 1741. He took up residence at Finch Mill, Appley Bridge, Shevington, a family property—Finch Mill Farm survives—which led to his being known as the auditor of the rota (rota is Latin for a mill, and the auditor of the rota was the head of one of the ecclesiastical courts in Rome). He died in 1752, and, since his family had burial rights there, he was buried in Standish Anglican parish church with a memorial tablet in the chancel, which gives him his full Roman Catholic episcopal style together with his arms, crozier, and mitre.[34]

Lancashire continued to contribute the major share of candidates to the priest-hood, 481 (25.6 per cent) out of 1,878 in the 18th century. They included Thomas Worthington, a Worthington of Blainscough, Standish, who joined the Dominicans, and became prior of Bornhem, and provincial of the order. Between 1708 and 1710 he made a visitation of the Dominican English mission, arriving in Lancashire in time to administer extreme unction to his dying father in the bitter winter of 1708-9.[35]

A steady stream of Lancashirewomen joined the English convents abroad, about a hundred and fifty during this period. The most popular community for Lancastrians was the house of the Poor Clares at Gravelines which recruited a total of twenty-five. It was to these convents that the Catholic gentry sent their daughters to be educated. Thus in 1716 Nicholas Blundell and his wife took their two daughters to the Benedictine convent at Ghent where they stayed for six years. It was from amongst such pupils that the convents recieved their postulants, though most returned home to lead the life of Catholic ladies described by Pope in his *Epistle to Miss Blount on her leaving the town after the coronation* (1715):

> She went, to plain-work, and to purling brooks,
> Old fashioned halls, dull aunts, and croaking rooks;
>
> ...
>
> Up to her godly garret after sev'n,
> There starve and pray, for that's the way to heav'n.[36]

The Lancashire Catholic community was increasingly served by a number of small schools: a free school in Eccleston taught in 1690 by William Harrison who had moved to Childwall by 1701, a Latin school at Sefton taught by James Lunt in 1710, and one in Mawdesley with only four pupils taught the Catholic faith by a teacher called Ball in 1713.[37]

A considerable body of opinion within the secular clergy remained convinced that the English Catholic Church ought to be fully restored by the creation of bishops-in-ordinary, that is by, as far as the penal laws would permit, the establishment of dioceses and parishes. It found expression in Dodd's *Church History*, a fundamental collection of English Catholic documents, and one of the great manifestos of the Anglo-Gallican tradition. Anglo-Gallicanism derived from Gallicanism its respect for the tradition of the local Church and the autonomy of the State. It found reflected in the English Enlightenment its appeal to reason and for toleration, to the values of institutional freedom.[38]

Charles Dodd was the alias of Hugh Tootell, born in Chorley, Lancashire, in 1671. Educated at Douay and Paris, he was ordained in 1698, and came on the English mission, working with his uncle Christopher Tootell at Fernyhalgh, then as chaplain to Molyneux of Mossborough Hall, Rainford, and then to Throckmorton of Harvington, Worcestershire, until his death in 1743. His *Church History of England* was published at Wolverhampton between 1737 and 1742.

He accepted, as all historians must, that 'after all the search I have made the work will be imperfect', but he hoped to give satisfaction 'by providing [him]self with authentic records; being true to them, and so letting every one taste the fruit of his own judgement'. As a child of the Enlightenment he believed that 'Reason' is 'a sufficient criterion in all enquiries whatsoever'. As well as being a work of history, it was a work of apologetics in the French Classical tradition represented by

Bossuet, for the Catholics who 'suffer more by concealement and misrepresentation than by an open and candid declaration'. It was also a work of apologetics for the Anglo-Gallicans, devoted to 'the constant tradition of the British church', quoting with approval the Appellants' declaration 'that the divine institution required hierarchy in every national church', and noting his suspicion that 'a power without appeal is not solicitous about precedents, and those that have power may easily invent reasons to put a gloss upon their actions'.[39]

Despite the defeat of the Jacobite rebellions, the Lancashire Catholic community had survived, ready to share with the county as a whole in the extraordinary economic expansion that was to occur in the second half of the 18th century.

Notes

1. C. Petrie, *The Jacobite Movement* (2 vols, 1948-50)(hereafter Petrie).
2. *HMC Kenyon*, nos.622, 676, 679.
3. *HMC Kenyon*, no.695.
4. Bagley, p.36; W. Beaumont, *The Jacobite Trials at Manchester in 1694* (CS, old series vol.28, 1853).
5. T. C. Porteus, 'New Light on the Lancashire Plot, 1692-4', *Transactions of the Lancashire and Cheshire Antiquarian Society* (henceforth *TLCAS*), vol.50 (1936); G. Scott, 'A Benedictine Conspirator: Henry Joseph Johnston (c.1656-1723)', *RH*, vol.20(1) (1990).
6. Porteus, *TLCAS*, vol.50, p.26; J. Gillow, *Bibliographical Dictionary of the English Catholics* (5 vols, 1885-1902), vol.2, pp.60-62.
7. Bagley, p.36; Petrie, vol.1, p.159.
8. Petrie, vol.1, p.185; S. H. Ware, *The State of Parties in Lancashire before the Rebellion of 1715* (CS, vol.5, 1845), pp.90-91.
9. Petrie, vol.1, p.187; *VCH Lancs*, vol.2, p.245; Blundell, vol.1, p.172.
10. Bagley, p.37; Anstruther, vol.4, p.238.
11. *DNB*, vol.19, p.1026; Bagley, p.37; *VCH Lancs*, vol.2, p.246.
12. T. Burke, *Catholic History of Liverpool* (1910)(hereafter Burke), p.11; C. A. Bolton, *Salford Diocese and its Catholic Past* (1950)(hereafter Bolton), pp.46-47; *Franciscana* (CRS vol.24, 1923), pp.307-308.
13. Lancashire Record Office, DDKe 7/31(1); Pevsner, *Lancashire: the Industrial South* (henceforth *Lancs:South*) (1969), p.212; Bossy, 'Catholic Lancashire in the Eighteenth Century' in Bossy and P. Jupp (eds.), *Essays Presented to Michael Roberts* (1976), p.59; E. E. Estcourt and J. O. Payne (eds.), *The English Catholic Nonjurors of 1715* (1885), pp.89-155; *The Registers of Estates of Lancashire Papists* (RSLC vol.98, 1961, vol.108, 1970, vol.117, 1977).
14. Blundell, vol.2, p.118.
15. Bagley, *Lancashire Diarists* (1975), pp.77-101; J. Gillow and A. Hewitson (eds.), *The Tyldesley Diary* (1973), p.15; M. Blundell (ed.), *Blundell's Diary and Letter Book 1702-1728* (Liverpool, 1952)(hereafter *Blundell's Diary*).
16. O. Rackham, *The History of the Countryside* (1987), p.366; L. Gooch, 'Papists and Profits: The Catholics of Durham and Industrial Development', *Durham County Local History Society Bulletin*, vol.62 (1989).
17. *Blundell's Diary*, pp.25, 80.
18. *Blundell's Diary*, pp.77,126.
19. Foley, vol.7, p.63; *Blundell's Diary*, p.78; Blundell, vol.1, p.46.
20. *Blundell's Diary*, p.19; H. Taylor, 'The Ancient Crosses of Lancashire: The Hundred of West Derby', *TLCAS*, vol.19 (1901), pp.176-80.
21. J. Kirk, *Biographies of English Catholics in the Eighteenth Century* (1909), p.236; *Blundell's Diary*, pp.151, 157.

22. P. Coverdale, 'Ralph Standish Howard's Wooing of Lady Catherine Petre', *Essex Recusant*, vol.22 (1980).

23. P. Bruckmann, 'Pope, Essex, and the Rape of the Lock' in Hilton (ed.), *Catholic Englishmen* (1984); C. S. Foster, *The Catholic Church in Ingatestone* (1982); Foley, vol.7, p.754.

24. Coverdale, *Essex Recusant*, vol.22, p.75.

25. Coverdale, *Essex Recusant*, vol.22, pp.62, 70.

26. Coverdale, *Essex Recusant*, vol.22, p.73; *VCH Lancs*, vol.6, p.422; Forster, *Catholic Church in Ingatestone*, p.41.

27. J. A. Williams, 'Change or Decay? The Provincial Laity 1691-1781' in E. Duffy (ed.), *Challoner and his Church* (1981); Bossy, *Essays*, p.54; J. A. Lancaster (ed.), 'Returns of Papists for the Parishes of Bolton and Deane in the Diocese of Chester, October 1706', *NWCH*, vol.18 (1991).

28. Estcourt and Payne, *English Catholic Nonjurors*, pp.89-155; A. J. Mitchinson (ed.), *The Return of the Papists for the Diocese of Chester, 1705* (1986), p.12; Laslett, *The World we have lost*, pp.36-37.

29. C. M. Haydon, 'Samuel Peploe and Catholicism in Preston, 1714', *RH*, vol.20(1) (1990).

30. Mitchinson, pp.16-18; G. A. Fallon, *The Roman Catholics in Standish* (1976), p.27.

31. Williams, 'The Distribution of Catholic Chaplaincies in the Early Eighteenth Century', *RH*, vol.12 (1),(1973).

32. B. Alger, 'The Priest and Informer Hitchmough', *NWCH*, vol.1(1)(2)(1969); Estcourt and Payne, *English Catholic Nonjurors*, pp.337-364.

33. B. C. Foley, 'Some Papers of a "Riding Priest", Thomas Roydon 1662-1741', *RH*, vol.19(4) (1989); Hemphill, p.131.

34. Hemphill, passim; B.Plumb, *Arundel to Zabi: A Biographical Dictionary of the Catholic Bishops of England and Wales* (1987)(hereafter *Arundel to Zabi*); Anstruther, vol.2, pp.48-49; S. Fairhurst, *St Wilfrid's Church, Standish* (1972), p.18.

35. Bellenger, *Priests*, pp.246-7; *Dominicana* (CRS vol.25, 1925), pp.96, 109.

36. Blundell, vol.3, pp.198-234; M. D. R. Leys, *Catholics in England* (1961)(herafter Leys), p.167.

37. Alger, *NWCH*, vol.1, pp.84-6.

38. G. R. Cragg, *The Church in the Age of Reason* (1970), pp.21-5; Hilton, 'Dodd's Church History', *NWCH*, vol.14 (1987).

39. Tierney, vol.1, pp.xii, xix, xxiii-xxiv, 4, 138, vol.3, p.49.

Chapter V

The Age of Enlightenment, 1746-1789

In the second half of the 18th century Catholic Lancashire benefited from the growing toleration of the age of Enlightenment and from the increasing prosperity of the
Industrial Revolution. It was transformed from a small rural minority largely confined to the west of the county into a vigorous urban community spread throughout
it. Its clergy ceased to be the chaplains of the gentry and became the leaders of
organised congregations. It moved from the centre of the political stage to a much
safer rôle at the centre of the Industrial Revolution.

The Enlightenment was an intellectual movement which sought to apply reason
to nature and to man. Its first significant triumph was the appearance in 1687 of
Newton's *Principia Mathematica* which used reason to reveal the workings of the
entire physical universe. Locke tried explicitly to apply Newton's methods to man
in his *Essay concerning Human Understanding* in 1690, justified the Glorious Revolution of 1688 in his *Two Treatises on Government* (1690), and defended religious
toleration in his *Letters on Toleration* (1689-92). These ideas were taken to the
Continent by Voltaire, and developed there by the *philosophes*. In 1748 Hume published his *Enquiry concerning Human Understanding* including his essay 'Of Miracles' which dealt an apparently fatal blow to Christianity. The Enlightenment succeeded in bringing about the suppression of the Jesuits in 1773. Hume died in 1776,
the year of the publication of the first volume of Gibbon's *Decline and Fall of the
Roman Empire*, which put the lid on the intellectual coffin which Hume had built for
Christianity, and of the publication of Smith's *Wealth of Nations* which expounded
the benefits of the free market economy. 1776 was also the year of the Declaration
of American Independence with its self-evident truths of the rights to life, liberty, and
the pursuit of happiness. The French Revolution of 1789 appeared as the final
culmination of all this promise.[1]

For English Catholics the Enlightenment brought toleration, but not before an
additional burden had been accidentally imposed upon them. Hardwick's Marriage
Act of 1753 aimed to prevent clandestine marriages by insisting that, with the exception of Quakers and Jews, all marriages be performed, after publication of the
banns and the granting of a licence, before an Anglican clergyman. Hitherto the
courts had accepted Catholic marriages, but these now become null under civil law.
Henceforth, until the Registration Act of 1836, Catholics tended to undergo two

ceremonies, though some contented themselves with the Catholic ceremony. In 1771 Lord Chief Justice Mansfield ruled that proof of ordination was required for a Catholic priest to suffer under the penal laws, and henceforth such prosecutions lapsed. The iniquity of the penal laws was increasingly recognised. Thus, when after the death of her husband the estate of the Catholic Ann Fenwick of Hornby was claimed by her Protestant brother-in-law, a special act of parliament was passed to allow her to retain her family estate. The Roman Catholic Relief Act of 1778 permitted Catholics to inherit or to purchase land provided they abjured the Young Pretender, Charles III, and took an oath of allegiance to George III. Henceforth prayers for King George III were said in Catholic chapels. The act aroused Protestant hostility which erupted in the Gordon Riots of 1780, but this was only a temporary aberration. The Catholic Relief Act of 1791 repealed the penal laws, and permitted the public celebration of Catholic worship, though Catholics remained excluded from public office.[2]

The ambivalent Catholic response to the Enlightenment was embodied in Charles Walmesley: he embraced it, and recoiled from it. Born in 1722, the seventh son of John Walmesley esquire of Westwood, Ince, Wigan, he was educated at St Gregory's, Douay, and St Edmund's, Paris, and became a Benedictine monk in 1739, prior of St Edmund's in 1749, procurator general, that is English Benedictine agent in Rome, in 1753, coadjutor bishop of the Western district in 1756, and vicar apostolic of the West in 1763. He was an astronomer who made significant theoretical contributions to the science, including work on the motions of comets and the processions and natations of the moon. These achievements resulted in his being elected a Fellow of the Royal Society, and he belonged to similar societies in Paris, Berlin, and Bologna. He was consulted by the British government on the adoption of the Gregorian calendar or new style in 1752. However, he regarded the advance of atheism as inevitable:

> The times with respect to irreligion though so bad at present, will I apprehend grow gradually worse and worse, till we come to the period intimated by our Saviour: 'When the Son of Man shall come do you think that He will find faith upon earth?' We must strive against the torrent, but nothing will be effectual enough to stop it.

He died in 1797, following an accident to his wheel-chair, but not before he had played a leading rôle in the controversy about the Relief Act of 1791, which brought him into conflict with the gentry. He stares out from his portrait at Lulworth castle, bewigged and with symbols of episcopal authority—rochet, mozetta, pectoral cross, ring, crozier, and mitre—and holding in his hand a scroll bearing the words 'Condemnation of the Oath 1791'.[3]

Catholic Lancashire remained dominated socially by the gentry. Caryll, the sixth Viscount Molyneux, who died in 1745, was succeeded by his brother William, who had joined the Jesuits in 1704, founded the mission at Scholes, Prescot, and became rector of the Lancashire district in 1728. He released the family estates to his brother Thomas, but, when the latter died in 1752, William was ordered by his superior 'to cease parish duty and mount his carriage and servants and appear only in his own rank until his death' (quoted in Foley). When this occurred in 1759, he was succeeded by his nephew Charles William, who was brought up as a Protestant by his Protestant guardians. It was losses such as this which caused contemporary Catholics like Berington to describe the period as one of decline. Nevertheless, the Catholic gentry continued to survive and to flourish.[4]

Their wealth and culture was represented by Charles Towneley of Towneley, the son of William Towneley and Cecilia Standish. He inherited the estate at the age of five in 1742, and was educated at Douay, returning to Towneley in 1758. In 1765 he made the grand tour to Italy, and returned in 1772 a connoiseur to live in London, numbering artists like Reynolds, Nollekens, and Zoffany, as well as scholars like the Abbé Devay, his 'walking library' amongst his friends. He commissioned Turner to do the drawings engraved for Whitaker's *History of the Parish of Whalley* (Turner's *Whalley Abbey* is at the Walker Art Gallery, Liverpool). Gavin Hamilton, painter, excavator, and dealer, acted as Towneley's agent in Italy, sending him antiquities like the Venus he discovered at Ostia which had to be smuggled out of Italy because the papal authorities would not grant export licences. Towneley also acted as financial backer to archaeological excavations in Italy. In the Gordon Riots of 1780 as the mob looted and burned the houses of Catholics, Towneley secured his cabinet of gems and carried his antique bust of the nymph Clytie, which he called his wife, to his carriage to escape to safety with what he valued most. He became a trustee of the British Museum in 1791, and after his death in 1805 the Museum purchased his collection of antique marbles. The collection remains as it was when Towneley, the 'Attic wit', surrounded by his friends and his marbles in his library at Westminster had his portrait, which is now at Towneley Hall, painted by Zoffany.[5]

Meanwhile a Lancashire Catholic contributed to the cult of the picturesque. Thomas West, the Jesuit priest at Dalton-in-Furness from 1756 until his death in 1779, was a Fellow of the Society of Antiquaries and the author of *The Antiquities of Furness*. In 1778 he published his *Guide to the Lakes*, which went through 12 editions in 45 years, aimed to provide connoiseurs of landscape painting and of landscape with examples of 'pastoral and rural landscapes, exhibited in all their styles, the soft, the rude, the romantic, the sublime'.[6]

This civilisation is exemplified in the restrained Palladian elegance of Lytham Hall. Built for the Catholic Thomas Clifton by John Carr in 1757-64 it is now preserved by Guardian Royal Exchange Assurance Ltd. and open to visitors. Its porch and portico, its plaster ceilings, and elaborate chimney pieces, demonstrating the transition from the style of Gibbs to that of Adam, embody the Classical vision of the 18th century.[7]

However, the gentry no longer dominated the organisation of the mission. Reporting in 1773 on the state of his district to Propaganda, the papal department responsible for the English Church, the vicar apostolic of the North, Francis Petre,

5 *Charles Towneley and his friends in the Park Street Gallery, Westminster. By permission of Towneley Hall Art Gallery and Museums, Burnley Borough Council.*

reckoned that out of 137 missions, some 35 only were the chaplaincies of the nobility, but that the rest were independent congregations. The clergy included men like the formidable John Barrow of Claughton. 'The Old Tar' had been pressed into the navy in 1756, deserted, and when re-captured was acquitted by a court-martial as he successfully feigned to be Italian; on hearing the verdict he coolly asked 'Che dice?' (What does he say?). Ordained in 1766, he immediately took residence in Claughton near Garstang. He rebuilt the chapel, which substantially survives, rescued the secular clergy fund from collapse, and served as overseer of the poor and overseer of the highways, seeing off hostile farmers with a brace of pistols.[8]

The great bulk of Lancashire Catholics, therefore, no longer worshipped in the domestic chapels of the gentry but in the new chapels built by the Catholic congregations and their clergy, though the domestic chapels of the gentry continued to be used and built. Thomas Weld built a large chapel at Leagram Hall: it was 60 by 25 feet with five round-headed west windows, and a wooden altar and tabernacle.[9]

The Catholic clergy were quick to realise that the development of industrial towns, as well as the growth of toleration, led to the breakdown of the dependency system of religion and the development of religious pluralism, which provided opportunities for conversion as well as indifference. Religion, including both Catholicism and Protestant Dissent, especially Methodism, was ready to legitimate the social improvement of the bourgeoisie and to ameliorate the anomie of the alienated proletariat. It was not entirely coincidental that the Catholic chapel in Warrington occupied premises in Chapel Yard, Dallam Lane, where Wesley had preached. This free trade in religion was exemplified in Wigan and Warrington, where the clergy referred to the laity as their 'customers'. The religious situation was similar to the industrial North-East.[10]

Permanent clerical missions with public chapels were established throughout the county. Despite difficulties the Jesuit mission in Liverpool flourished. St Mary's chapel, destroyed in 1746, was replaced by another disguised as a warehouse, complete with taking-in doors and block and tackle. However, the comings and goings for Mass could not be hidden, and a Protestant mob destroyed the chapel in 1759, but it was re-built once again. Father John Price took his Catholicism out into the community by preaching annual sermons to raise collections for the Liverpool Royal Infirmary. A permanent mission was established in Manchester in 1776. The Rev. Edward Helme, who had been based in Macclesfield but said Mass once a month in Manchester, left £200 which was used by the Rev. John Orrell to build St Chad's, Rook Street. In Wigan the ex-Jesuit Marmaduke Langdale built a public chapel (St John's) in 1785 (it stood in Standishgate, the site of its altar now marked by the Walmesley cross) with money raised from his congregation and various bequests. In Blackburn in 1770 Mass was celebrated in Wensley Fold in the house of the millowner John Anderton. In 1773 Bishop Petre acquired two cottages in Chapel Street to serve as presbytery and chapel (St Alban's) for the Rev. William Fisher. A public chapel (St Mary's) was built in Friargate, Preston in 1781, partly with a donation from the

Duke of Norfolk. Destroyed by a mob during an election riot in 1768, it was re-built. In 1780 the Benedictine Oswald Eaves built the chapel of St Mary's, Brownedge, Bamber Bridge, near Preston, and in 1789 William Foster, the Jesuit chaplain to the Walmesleys of Showley, built the chapel at Stidd which served the district round Ribchester. In 1789 James Haydock, chaplain to the Traffords of Trafford, Manchester, established an independent mission covering the Trafford estates. The Traffords also provided their house at Strangeways in Hindley near Wigan as a residence for the Benedictines. The ruins of this house remain in this wind-swept moss-land overlooked by the Pennines. In 1789 Dom. George Edward Duckett opened a new public chapel (St Benedict's) in Market Street on land probably provided by Richard Marsh, a local Catholic innkeeper. Money was spent on ale for the builders and clogs for the man who trod the mortar, and on dinner for the 41 members of the Hindley Singers who performed an oratorio at the opening. Similarly, Thurnham Hall near Lancaster, abandoned in 1776 by its owners the Daltons when their neighbour the Duke of Hamilton took to shooting their dogs, was used for monthly Masses. In 1780 Jane Daniel of Euxton, the spinster sister of two priests, Thomas and William Daniel, and the aunt of a third, John Daniel, president of Douay, and of a clockmaker at Kirkham in the Fylde, endowed the Thurnham mission, stipulating that the Daltons should also contribute to the endowment and that her cousin, the Rev. James Foster, should be the first missioner. Accordingly Foster took up residence in the Hall in 1785, and remained there until he built the chapel and house at Woodside in 1802. At Leighton Hall, Yealand Conyers, Warton, the Towneleys and their predecessors had maintained priests. When in 1782 the Towneleys left Leighton they established their chaplain Michael Wharton in an independent mission in a house that contained a chapel alongside it. Since 1677 Woolston Hall, near Warrington, the property of the Standishes of Standish, had been served by Benedictine chaplains. From 1755 Dom. Thomas Benedict Shuttleworth began to enter Warrington, disguised as a packman, to say Mass for the Catholics there. His presence would be advertised by a boy singing 'Sally in our Alley', and the Catholics would gather for Mass in public houses like the *Feathers* in Bridge Street and the *Hole i'th'Wall* in Friars Green. In 1771 he took up permanent residence at Warrington in Bewsey Street, saying Mass at the *Coopers Arms*, though Benedictine chaplains remained at Woolston until 1829. When Shuttleworth died in 1774 he was replaced by his assistant Dom Bernard Anselm Bradshaw, who opened a public chapel (St Alban's) in 1774.[11]

Some of these chapels were controlled by committees of lay trustees. Rook Street chapel in Manchester was built by trustees to whom the land and money had been donated. In Manchester the trustees were co-opted, but in Liverpool they were elected by those members of the congregation whose subscriptions paid the expenses of the Jesuit mission there. This arrangement was overturned by the Jesuit superior William Molyneux, and the priest took charge of the finances. However, in 1778 a dispute arose over the finances between Joseph Gittins alias Williams, the ex-Jesuit missioner, and his assistant Raymond Hormosa alias Harris, a Spanish ex-Jesuit, who won the support of commercial Liverpool by defending the slave trade. In 1779 a meeting of the congregation declared the original arrangement restored and elected trustees who claimed the right to nominate the priests. When Gittins continued to administer the finances, the trustees appealed to the vicar apostolic who suggested that the finances be divided equally between Gittins and his opponents. Gittins refused so the bishop appointed Henry Blundell of Ince and Thomas Clifton of Lytham as arbitrators, but Blundell supported the trustees, and Clifton supported Gittins. When in 1782 the trustees tried to seize the chapel a riot ensued. In 1783 the bishop with the support of most of the ex-Jesuits requested the Benedictines to send a priest, Dom Archibald Benet McDonald, to take over the chapel, but there was further controversy and violence, and a law-suit was settled by the civil courts in favour of McDonald. In 1788 two new chapels were built, one, St Peter's, Seel Street, by the Benedictines, and the other, which eventually was moved to St Nicholas's, Copperas Hill, by the Jesuits and elected trustees.[12]

The trustees defined their essential claim in a statement of 5 April 1783:

> By the aforesaid regulations, no person can serve this congregation as an incumbent without the approbation of the qualified bench-holders. It being therefore unwarrantable for any person to act in that capacity without such an approbation first obtained it is hoped the congregation will never suffer any innovation to take place in a matter of such importance to themselves and posterity as the choice of their own pastors.[13]

The vicar apostolic also identified the issue of principle at stake in a pastoral letter 'To the Catholics of Liverpool' of 8 October 1783 pointing out that the claims of the trustees:

> ... strike at the very being of ecclesiastical authority and subordination ... an irreligious encroachment upon the rights of the sanctuary, a most preposterous attempt to exalt the sheep above the pastor, to direct your teacher, lead your guide, and overawe your prelate, a sacrilegious effort to disturb the order established by our Blessed Redeemer and disturb the system of Infinite Wisdom.[14]

These new congregational chapels were usually attached to the priests' houses and were often under the same roof. It is true that strictly speaking such chapels were until 1791 illegal, and the myth has grown up that they were disguised as houses. There may be a few early examples of such disguised chapels, and they all may have avoided drawing attention to themselves, but their purpose could not be concealed from the local Protestant community. Indeed they shared their restraint with the Protestant, Anglican as well as Nonconformist, churches of the period, later dismissed by the Gothic revivalists as mere 'prattling-boxes', that is preaching-houses. They often had the same two tiers of round-arched windows and their east ends were flat or apsed and expressed in columns or pilasters. They include St Peter's, Seel Street, Liverpool, built in 1788 (its sanctuary enlarged in 1843). It has arched windows, a modest doorway, and recessed, slender, Doric columns. Most of the urban Georgian chapels were replaced by bigger buildings in the 19th century, but they survive, sometimes put to other uses in the rural parishes. Such is the chapel built in 1782 at Yealand Conyers in north Lancashire. There are similar buildings at Brindle, Claughton, and Hornby. They speak the restrained tones of a forgotten Classical architectural and liturgical language.[15]

The Lancashire mission was preserved from the worst consequences of the suppression of the Jesuits by the fact that England was a Protestant country. In 1773 on the eve of the suppression there were in the Northern district 67 chapels staffed by secular priests, 45 by Jesuits, 18 by Benedictines, four by Franciscans, and three by Dominicans. Twenty-eight of these Jesuit mission were in Lancashire, ranging from Liverpool to Dunkenhalgh and from Warrington to Preston. The Jesuit Lancashire district, the college of St Aloysius, had recovered from its earlier decline, growing in numbers from 23 in 1746 to 31 in 1773. The connection between Lancashire and the Maryland mission continued. Robert Molyneux, born near Formby in 1738, entered the Jesuits in 1757, and was sent to Maryland. When the ex-Jesuit John Carroll became the first bishop of the United States of America in 1790 he asked for Molyneux as his coadjutor but was refused. Molyneux became superior of the restored American Jesuit mission in 1805.[16]

An unholy alliance of atheists, deists, Jansenists, Gallicans, and Catholic monarchs suppressed the Jesuits in Portugal, France, Spain, the Sicilies, and Parma, and then secured the election of a pope, Clement XIV, amenable to the suppression of the Jesuits which he decreed in 1773. The Society of Jesus ceased to exist, and throughout Catholic Europe and Latin America its members were banished or imprisoned. In England too it obediently ceased to exist, but its members remained free to function as priests. As a result there were still Lancashire missions served by ex-Jesuits, 15 in 1787. The ecclesiastical autonomy and political independence of the Prince-Bishop of Liège secured the survival of the former Jesuit college at Liège, whither the former English Jesuits moved from St Omers via Bruges. This joint institution was eventually to move to Stonyhurst in Lancashire.[17]

A steady stream of Lancastrians joined the English Continental religious houses during these years. In 1774 the entire community of the English Benedictine priory of St Laurence's at Dieulouard in Lorraine consisted of Lancastrians. At least 70 Lancashire women entered the English Continental convents: the largest concentrations being 12 with the Poor Clares of Gravelines and 17 with the Poor Clares of Rouen. They included Frances Louisa Lancaster who joined the Canonesses Regular of Paris in 1750 and became prioress for 43 years. They also included six with the Blue Nuns at Paris. In 1775 Mrs Thrale, visiting Paris with Samuel Johnson, marvelled at 'a woman of very different rank in the world but the same in a cloister', Elizabeth Simpson, born in Preston who had been maidservant to the Stricklands of Sizergh, Westmorland, and had joined the convent as a lay sister to 'do the office of a servant to these ladies, who finding her devout and docile, I suppose, and happy in a fine voice, admitted her though moneyless to their sisterhood'. Mrs. Thrale observed that Sister Elizabeth 'called the women of quality sister as they did each other, sat down with them at the grate and seemed perfectly at ease. She was however easily distinguishable by her vulgarity and begged some converse with Mrs. Strickland's maid'.[18]

Meanwhile a few Catholic private schools were established in Lancashire of which the most famous was Dame Alice's long established at Fernyhalgh. Alice Harrison, born at Fulwood Row, near Preston, was educated as an Anglican but converted to Catholicism by her reading. As a result she was turned out by her parents, and with the encouragement of the Rev. Christopher Tootell, the priest at Fernyhalgh, decided to make her living by keeping a school there for boys and girls, probably as early as 1710. The school grew so she took on assistants, and she soon had between 100 and 200 pupils, including Protestants, lodging in the village from all over Lancashire and beyond. Her Catholic pupils included Alban Butler, the future president of St Omers and author of *Lives of the Saints*, John Daniel, the future president of Douay, Hugh Kendal, the future president of Sedgley Park, John Gillow, the future president of Ushaw, and Joseph Shepherd, the future president of Valladolid. Every day, pausing to pray at the Ladywell, she took her Catholic pupils to Mass at the chapel there. She eventually retired to Garswood, where she died in 1760, and was buried at Windleshaw, near St Helens.[19]

In 1759 another Catholic school was established by the Rev. Simon Bordley, though he appears not to have taught in it himself, at Ince Blundell, near Liverpool. The school held some forty boys mostly about 11 years old, mainly from Lancashire but also from the rest of England. They were boarded in the village, provided with clothes, pocket-money and books, and they were taught the three Rs (reading, writing, and arithmetic). Some went on to Douay, but many were apprenticed to trades. The school closed in 1764 after the opening of Sedgeley Park.[20]

One of Dame Alice's pupils, Peter Newby, later moved his own school from Great Eccleston in the Fylde to Gerard Hall, Heighton, near Fernyhalgh. Amongst his pupils was Thomas Penswick, the future vicar apostolic of the North. Newby, the 'friend to all mankind', was one of the new Catholic liberal middle-class. Born in 1745 near Kendal in Westmorland, and educated at Fernyhalgh and Douay, he was a schoolmaster for most of his life, though he became a printer at Preston in 1797. He was active in the foundation in 1787 of the Broughton Catholic Charitable Society. Originally founded to relieve the distres caused by an epidemic of smallpox, it still flourishes and now numbers 1,500 members. His early experience aboard an African slaver out of Liverpool turned him into an opponent of the slave trade, an opposition he expressed in the longest of his many published poems:

> The purse-proud Christian, whom no feelings grace,
> May scorn, perhaps, the black, enslaved race.
> But know, that Being, which has plac'd thee here,
> With equal goodness smiles o'er ev'ry sphere,
> And makes no diff'rence in the tints of blood.

He also argued that English Catholics 'Are little less than Slaves', but that:

> Britain is bounded by a lib'ral shore,
> Britons have ask'd what is by birth their due:
> Patient they've waited for that happy hour,
> That places them above a bigot's pow'r.

He was to live to see Catholics tolerated and the slave trade abolished.[21]

Meanwhile the Industrial Revolution was changing Lancashire and transforming the world. In 1733 Kay's flying shuttle had doubled the output of the hand-loom weaver, and in the second half of the 18th century further innovations not only produced a matching increase in spinning with Hargreaves's jenny in 1769 but also created the factory system with Arkwright's water frame in 1769 and Crompton's mule in 1779. By 1776 Watt's steam engine was being used to drain coal mines with a consequent increase in output, and by 1789 it was being applied to both spinning and weaving machines. Powered machinery was increasingly made of iron, and cheaper methods of producing pig and wrought iron became availabe. These rapidly expanding industries were linked to their markets and their raw materials by a network of canals beginning with the Sankey navigation in 1757.[22]

Catholics took an active part in these developments as inventors and entrepreneurs as well as workers, a process paralleled in the industrial North-East. Catholicism had constituted a religious *ancien régime* within the English *ancien régime*, and there were still Catholics who occupied this position, but, in Lancashire, Catholics were engaged in creating the new industrial society. John Sadler, a Liverpool bookseller, invented transfer-printing for pottery, and in 1763 he and his partner, Guy Green, made an exclusive contract with Josiah Wedgwood, whose Etruria factory at Stoke-on-Trent pioneered mass-production. Sir Thomas Gerard, eighth baronet, of Bryn, took advantage of the opening of the Sankey navigation to exploit the coal on his estates at Garswood. He constructed a wagon way to connect Garswood to the canal at Blackbrook. He then undercut the price of coal at Liverpool, where he had a sales-office. The profits enabled him to build Garswood New Hall in 1788 set in a park of 260 acres landscaped by Repton. Thomas Porter gent of Ackhurst Hall, Orrell, near Wigan, left for Oxfordshire but in 1789 leased the coal under his estates to a partnership of Liverpool businessmen and local coal-owners, headed by his brother Charles who remained behind at Ackhurst to manage Chas Porter & Co. The pits, whose abandoned workings lie scattered through Porter's Wood, were linked by wagon ways, which can still be walked past Ackhurst Hall, to the Leeds-Liverpool canal. John Trafford of Trafford, seconded by his steward, John Brettargh, 'the devil's darning needle', developed cobalt and other minerals on his estates between Warrington and Manchester. Robert Gillow, cabinet-maker, opened showrooms in Oxford Street, London, but Lancaster remained the centre of the firm's manufactures, importing timber and other commodities from the Baltic and the West Indies, and exporting furniture and other manufactures. The first cotton mill in Blackburn was opened by the Catholic John Anderton. Increasingly the great bulk of Catholics found employment in these new industries. The development of industry and transport provided an expanding market for agriculture. In response Thomas Eccleston, who held the Eccleston, Scarisbrick, and eventually the Wrightington estates, began the drainage of Martin Mere, the shallow lake that stretched from the River Douglas to the sea.[23]

As a result of the Industrial Revolution the population of the county grew enormously, reaching nearly 70,000 in the first census of 1801, a fourfold increase since 1664. During roughly the same period, 1688-1801, the population of England and Wales almost doubled from an estimated five-and-a-half million to nine million.[24]

There was also an increase in the number of Catholics. The total number of English Catholics increased from an estimated 60,000 in 1680 to 80,000 in 1770, an increase of 33 per cent, whilst the Lancashire Catholic community increased from an estimated 16-18,000 in 1700 to 26,000 in 1770, an increase of 55-60 per cent. It has also been estimated that at about the same time Catholics numbered more than 20 per cent of the population of Lancashire. In 1773 the vicar apostolic reported that Lancashire contained 69 missions each with about two hundred communicants, a total of 13,800, including 1,500 at Liverpool, 1,000 at Preston, 600 at Wigan, 500 at Ormskirk, and 300 at Lancaster. These massively outnumbered the 1,400 Catholics in Yorkshire, 1,200 in Durham, 1,800 in Northumberland, and the few Catholics of Cheshire, Westmorland, and Cumberland, who all put together amounted to little more than 4,400. Similarly the Lancashire Catholics vastly outnumbered the nearly 9,000 Catholics in the Midland district, and the 3,000 Catholics in the Western district. Only the London district with some 22,000 Catholics outnumbered the North.[25]

In response to this obvious growth the House of Lords in 1767 ordered a return to be made of the papists in every parish, giving their sex, age, occupation, and length of residence. Perhaps not all the Anglican clergy were so confident of their diligence and knowledge as the curate of Blackley who could 'speak with the more exactness in this case, as I visited in person every house within the four townships ... allotted to my chapelry' or the vicar of Chipping who 'as I had more than once taken the number of Protestants and papists in this parish, it was not difficult for me to send the exact numbers ... there are few, if any, but I personally know them, as they are all natives of the parish or neighbourhood'. Nevertheless, the return constitutes a remarkably detailed record, invaluable not only to historians of Catholicism but also to social and economic historians. It is, therefore, also a massive document, listing 25,139 papists in the diocese of Chester, printed in one volume, and 42,777 in the rest of the country printed in a second volume. It has received some analysis and would repay further study.[26]

It confirms that Lancastrian Catholicism remained vigorous in its traditional strongholds, the western coastal plain and the Ribble valley, the deaneries of Warrington, Leyland, Amounderness, and Blackburn, but also that it was growing stronger within the developing industrial towns of these districts.

In the far north of the county Catholics remained few and far between. In Lancashire north of the sands, the deanery of Furness, apart from a handful at Ulverston and another at Cartmel, the only sizeable group consisted of the 21 Catholics who formed the immediate congregation of the Rev. John West at Dalton. In Lonsdale deanery there was a handful at Tunstall and a dozen or so at Tatham and at Claughton. There were rather more in Kendal deanery—16 at Halton, 27 at Bolton-le-Sands, and 54 at Warton—an increase attributed by the vicar of Bolton-le-Sands to landowners 'fond of letting their estates to them'. These presumably included such Catholic gentry as George Towneley who resided at Yealand in Warton parish.

This seigneurial Catholicism was in evidence in Amounderness where the parish of Lytham contained 384 Catholics headed by Thomas Clifton esquire and his household. The Catholic clergy in the deanery also included John Barow at Claughton in Garstang, Francis Cliffe at Great Eccleston in St Michael's, and James Tyrer at Lancaster, and the Jesuits Thomas Cuerdon at Kirkham and Joseph Smith at Preston. Farmers and husbandmen predominated amongst the 190 Catholics at Chipping, 537 at Ribchester, 1,459 at Kirkham, 384 at Lytham, 164 at Poulton, 557 at St Michaels, 837 at Garstang, and 119 at Cockerham. They also predominated in the rural townships of the parishes of Lancaster and Preston, which contained 784 and 1,601 Catholics respectively, but these included 237, such as the well-to-do tradesmen the Gillows, in Lancaster town, and 730, mainly weavers, in Preston town.

Weavers predominated amongst the Catholics of Blackburn deanery, who numbered 1,635 in Blackburn and 357 in Whalley. They were served by priests like the Franciscan Robert Painter at Samlesbury, the Benedictine Oswald Eaves at Walton-le-Dale in Blackburn parish, and the Jesuit Andrew Thorpe at Dunkenhalgh, John Harrison at Towneley, and John Moore at Whitewell in Whalley parish.

The western parishes of Leyland deanery were still the settings for agrarian seigneurial congregations but to the east weavers dominated amongst the largely popular congregations. At Croston there were 591 Catholics, mainly husbandmen, headed by Humphrey Trafford esquire and served by the Jesuit Richard Leckonby. At Eccleston there were 283, mainly husbandmen, headed by Edward Dicconson of Wrightington and served by the secular priest William Grimbaldston. However, weavers predominated amongst the 69 Catholics at Penwortham, the 364 served by the Benedictine Joseph Hadley at Brindle, and the 797 served by the Jesuit John Richardson and the secular John White at Leyland. At Standish, which contained 552 Catholics, the rector neglected to record the names but the Standishes still headed the Catholic congregation, and he did remark that the priest, presumably the Benedictine Thomas Patten, was absent for his health at Harrogate or Scarborough. Nevertheless, the 89 Catholics in the township of Coppull were mainly weavers and spinners.

Warrington deanery also displayed this dichotomy between the seigneurial congregations of the agrarian west and the popular clerical congregations of the industrial east. There were a mere three Catholics in North Meols, but Halsall contained 228, Aughton 146, Ormskirk 1,082 (served by the Jesuit Nicholas Founiers at Scarisbrick), Sefton 757, Walton 858, Childwall 409, and Huyton 151, predominantly farmers and husbandmen, though there were numbers of watchmakers in Childwall. Still ensconced amongst them were the Blundells of Ince Blundell and the Blundells of Crosby with their chaplain the Jesuit John Sale. Wigan contained 1,692 Catholics, Prescot 1,294, Winwick 796, Warrington 457, and Leigh 304, predominantly weavers though there were also watchmakers and colliers in Prescot. Wigan was served by three priests: the Jesuit John Worthington in the borough, the Benedictine Evan Anselm Eastham at Hindley, and the secular Thomas Grimbaldston at Billinge. However, the most striking feature of this district was the increase of Catholics in Liverpool from 18 in 1705 to 1,743 in 1767, mainly tradesmen largely associated with shipping.

With the growth of industry Catholicism had begun to make inroads into the deanery of Manchester. There were still none in some parishes and handfuls in others, and just over a dozen at Rochdale, and 18 at Eccles, but there were 21 at Oldham,36 in Blackrod, 41 in Dean, 73 in Bolton, 64 in Salford, predominantly weavers, and 373 in Manchester in a variety of trades. As the parson of Salford put it:

> The number is greater than I could have wished though not more than a sixtieth part of the inhabitants; and perhaps may be in some measure accounted for from the extensive trade of this country which will eventually draw the poor and needy of other countries in order to find employment here.

This conclusion can be illustrated by reference to the township of Atherton in the parish of Leigh on the eastern edge of Warrington deanery. In the 18th century Atherton, apart from Atherton Hall and the hamlet of Atherton, consisted mainly of the village of Chowbent. It can be described in detail from the papers carefully preserved by Richard Hodkinson who arrived there in 1784 to become master of the grammar school. There was an Anglican church and a Unitarian chapel, which divided most of the township between them. John More, fustian merchant, was a Unitarian, a friend of Priestley, and the founder of the local literary society. In 1772 the total population of the village was 1,162 and in 1777 the population of the whole township was 2,200. In 1767 there were 25 Catholics in Atherton, all of them immigrants or the wives and children of immigrants, and most of them engaged in the cotton industry. They included John Hilton, then aged 45 and only arrived in the township three months before. He had a wife five years his senior and six children, five boys and a girl, ranging from the eldest son aged 21 to the youngest aged seven. He was a weaver and so were all his sons except the youngest, whilst his wife and his daughter were spinners. Mary Lee, aged 55, resident for 40 years was another spinner, as was her 22-year-old daughter, and her 14-year-old son was a weaver. There was also a girl aged two in the family, probably Mary's granddaughter. A servant called Arnold Brownlow, aged 30 and resident four years, is next in the list of papists, and may have been employed as a weaver in the Lee household. James Laithwaite, another weaver, aged 50 and resident for eight years had a son, a weaver, and a daughter, a spinner. John Hampson, weaver, aged 64, and Esther Higson, spinner, aged 24, had only been resident three months. Catherine Worthington, spinner, aged 60, had been resident for 17 years. John Stock, aged 30 and resident for seven years, was unusually for this district a collier, but his wife, also aged 30, was a spinner. They had four small children. By the end of the 18th century the Lancashire Catholic community was young and fertile.

These people lived in cottages with flagged floors, horse-hair plastered walls, and brick fireplaces. Large windows lit the largest room, the loom-shop. There the women sat spinning at their wheels, or in some cases their jennies, whilst the men sat at the looms, their hands passing the shuttles and their feet working the treadles in a continual rhythmic din. With wages between five and ten shillings a week they made a good living, for food was cheap with beef at four (old) pence a pound, and potatoes at 20 pence a bushel, as was coal at twopence halfpenny a hundredweight. They presumably attended Mass celebrated by the Jesuits at houses in Bedford Leigh until the chapel was opened there by Father John Shaw in 1789.[27]

The return evinces the migration of Catholics from the countryside to the growing industrial towns. In Manchester the Catholic congregation at Rook Street grew from 300 in 1767 to 600 in 1778 and to 4,000 by 1793, and as many as half of these seem to have been immigrants. In particular they came from such rural areas as Blackburn, the Fylde, Lancaster, Hornby in Lonsdale, and Woolston near Warrington. Moreover, the immigrant was typically fertile which boosted urban Catholic congregations.[28]

Poor Catholics, particularly those with Protestant employers and especially those under the discipline of the factory system, found the number of holydays of obligation burdensome, on which they were expected not only to attend Mass but also to abstain from servile, that is wage-earning, work. Accordingly in 1777 a papal decree confined these holydays to Sundays and to twelve other feast days: Easter Monday, Whit Monday, Christmas, the Circumcision, the Epiphany, the Ascension, Corpus Christi, the Annunciation, the Assumption, Saints Peter and Paul, All Saints, and the patron saint of each individual church. The decree also allowed the vicars apostolic to dispense with the obligation to abstain from servile work on the feasts of Saints Peter and Paul (29 June) and the Assumption (15 August) if they fell in harvest time.[29]

The days of fasting and abstinence, on which Catholics were obliged to restrict themselves to one full meal and to abstain from meat, were also burdensome to working people. However, the papal decree which reduced the feasts transferred the fasts attached to their vigils to the Wednesdays and Fridays of Lent. Nevertheless, in 1781 the Friday fast, but not the abstinence, was abolished, except for the Ember days and those in Lent and Advent. Lent was kept as a time of abstinence, but the vicars apostolic sometimes granted dispensations for three days in the week, except for Passiontide.[30]

Sundays provided the opportunity for Mass and for education. In Blackburn the chapel was guarded by beadles carrying staffs and wearing uniforms of blue with red facings and capes. Young people, carrying their food, came long distances to Mass, and then stayed on for school to learn to read and to write in sand. In the afternoon there was catechism, instruction, and occasionally Benediction of the Blessed Sacrament.[31]

In the rural districts they retained traditional devotions that were dying out elsewhere. At Leagram in the Forest of Bowland they kept the devotion of the teenlay fire: on All Souls Eve, the Catholics led by their priest, the Rev James Lawrenson, assembled on the hillside in the darkness, and prayed for the faithful departed whilst a blazing bundle of straw was held aloft on a pitchfork. The fires could be seen burning throughout north Lancashire.[32]

There was a variety of catechetical and devotional books available to Catholics. At Bordley's school the pupils had the *Catechism*, and some had the *Manual* (a collection of instructions and prayers), whilst others had the new but similar *Garden of the Soul*, and a few had a Bible or New Testament.[33]

At the end of the 18th century the average Lancashire Catholics were recognisably amongst the people described by Engels:

> So the workers vegetated throughout a passably comfortable existence, leading a righteous and peaceful life in all piety and probity ... They regarded their squire, the greatest landholder of the region, as their natural superior ... They had their children the whole day at home, and brought them up in obedience and the fear of God ... [34]

Tolerated, confident, and vigorous, the Lancashire Catholic community was at the centre of the changes that were transforming society.

Notes

1. N. Hampson, *The Enlightenment* (1968).
2. Leys, pp. 126-39; B. C. Foley, *Ann Fenwick of Hornby* (1977); B. C. Foley, *Some People of the Penal Times* (1991), pp.25-38.
3. *DNB*, vol.5, pp.569-70; B. Ward, *The Dawn of the Catholic Revival in England* (hereafter Dawn) (2 vols., 1909), vol.1, pp.4, 16, 150; G. Scott, '"The Times are Fast Approaching": Bishop Charles Walmesley OSB (1722-97) as Prophet', *Journal of Ecclesiastical History*, vol.36 (4) (1985); Blundell, vol.2, pp.83-4.
4. Foley, vol.7, pp.514-5; Ward, *Dawn*, vol.1, pp.8-9.
5. *DNB*, vol.19, pp.1024-5; C. Hibbert, *The Grand Tour* (1987), pp.164, 219; F. Milner, *J. M. W.Turner Paintings in Merseyside Collections* (no date), pp.13-4.
6. T. G. Holt, 'Father Thomas West', *NWCH*, vol.6 (1978); Holt (ed.), *Thomas West: A Guide to the Lakes: A Selection* (1982).
7. Pevsner, *Lancs: North* (1969), p.265; *Lytham Hall* (1981).
8. J. H. Whyte (ed.),'The Vicar Apostolics Returns of 1773', *RH*, vol.9(4) (1968); Anstruther, vol.4, p.22; Lancashire Record Office, 'The Rev John Barrow of Claughton', *NWCH*, vol.3 (1971); Blundell, I, p.118.

9. Bolton, p.75.
10. Bossy, *Community*, pp.298-306; A. D. Gilbert, *Religion and Society in Industrial England* (1976)(hereafter Gilbert), pp.81-93; H. McLeod, *Religion and the People of Western Europe 1789-1870* (1981)(hereafter McLeod), pp.16-7; Blundell, vol.2, p.71; B. Plumb, *The Warrington Mission* (1978), p.6-7; Hilton, 'The Catholic North-East, 1640-1850', *Durham County Local History Society Bulletin*, vol.24 (1980).
11. Burke, pp.11-14; Bolton, pp.87-8; Blundell, vol.2, pp.72-3, 137-8; M. Conlon, *St Alban's, Blackburn* (1973) (hereafter Conlon), pp.12-3; Bolton, pp.79-80; E. O'Gorman, *The History of All Saints Church, Barton-upon-Irwell* (Manchester, 1988), p.11; Hilton, 'A Catholic Congregation in the Age of Revolution: St Benedict's, Hindley', *NWCH*, vol.17 (1990); Hilton, 'The Catholic Revival in Thurnham', *NWCH*, vol.12 (1985); F. J. Singleton, *Mowbreck Hall and The Willows* (1983), p.23; Anstruther, vol.4, pp.80-82; Hilton, *The Catholic Revival in Yealand* (1982); Birt, p.143; Plumb, *Warrington*, pp.4-9.
12. D. Lannon, 'Rook Street Chapel, Manchester', *NWCH*, vol.16 (1989); Burke, pp.14-24; R. J. Stonor, *Liverpool's Hidden Story* (1957), pp.34-5; Bossy, *Essays*, pp.63-4.
13. Burke, pp.20-1.
14. Burke, pp.22-3.
15. B. Little, *Catholic Churches Since 1623* (London, 1966) (hereafter Little), pp.36-50; Pevsner, *Lancs: South*, pp.21-2, 154; Pevsner, *Lancs: North*, p.26; Hilton, *Yealand*, p.6; J. Bamber, 'Yealand Bi-Centenary and Restoration of the Chapel', *NWCH*, vol.10 (1983); Blundell, vol.1, pp.139, 155; Hilton, 'Lingard's Hornby' in Hilton (ed.), *Catholic Englishmen*, p.40.
16. Foley, vol.5, pp.214, 325-6, vol.7, pp.118, 514; Whyte, *RH*, vol.9 (4), p.209.
17. Bellenger, *Priests*, p.18.
18. B. Green, *The English Benedictine Congregation* (1979), p.32; Blundell, vol.3, pp.195-240; M. Tyson and H. Guppy (eds.), *The French Journals of Mrs Thrale and Doctor Johnson* (1932), pp.105-7.
19. Blundell, vol.1, pp.181-86; Foley, *Some People of the Penal Times*, pp.51-58.
20. W. V. Smith, 'The Rev. Simon George Bordley, Schoolmaster', *RH*, vol.13 (4) (1976).
21. M. Whitehead, *Peter Newby* (1980), pp.23, 42.
22. E. J. Hobsbawm, *The Age of Revolution* (1977), pp.42-72; Hobsbawm, *Industry and Empire* (1969), pp.23-108; R. Reid, *The Peterloo Massacre* (1989), pp.11-9; Bagley, pp.51-9; Walton, pp.60-197.
23. L. Gooch, 'Papists and Profits: The Catholics of Durham and Industrial Development', *Durham County Local History Society Bulletin*, vol.42 (1989); L. Hanley, 'John Sadler', *NWCH*, vol.7 (1981); Giblin, 'The Gerard Family', *NWCH*, vol.16 (1990), p.9; D. Anderson, *The Orrell Coalfield* (1975), pp.169-70; G. P. Connolly, 'Shifting Congregations' in Hilton, *Catholic Englishmen*, p.17; Whitehead, 'The Gillows and their Work in Georgian Lancaster' in Hilton, *Catholic Englishmen*; Conlon, p.12; *VCH Lancs*, vol.3, p.269.
24. Walton, p.76.
25. Bossy, *Community*, pp. 185, 189, 408-409; Bossy, *Essays*, pp.54-5; Whyte, *RH*, vol.9 (4), pp.208-14.
26. E. S. Worrall (ed.), *Returns of Papists 1767* (2 vols., 1980-89), vol.1; J. F. Champ, 'St Martin's Parish, Birmingham, in 1767', *RH*, vol.15 (5) (1981).
27. *VCH Lancs*, vol.3, p.435; W. Yates, *A Map of the County of Lancashire, 1786* (1967), p.39; G. Dykes, *Chowbent 1784* (no date); Worall, *Returns of Papists 1767*, vol.1, p.9; V. Foley, p.336.
28. Connoly, *Catholic Englishmen*, pp.13-20.
29. Hemphill, p.184.
30. Hemphill, pp.185-6; Ward, *Dawn*, vol.1, p.32.
31. Conlon, p.13.
32. Bolton, p.75.
33. Smith, *RH*, vol.13I (4), p.281; R. Luckett, 'Bishop Challoner: The Devotionary Writer' in Duffy, *Challoner and his Church* (1981), pp.71-89; J. M. Blom, *The Post-Tridentine English Primer* (London, 1982), pp.112-162.
34. F. Engels, *The Condition of the Working Class in England* (Penguin edition, 1987), pp.51-52.

Chapter VI

The Age of Revolution, 1791-1848

Between the end of the 18th century and the middle of the 19th century Catholic Lancashire underwent continued transformation as the beneficiary of the Industrial and French Revolutions. The progress of the Industrial Revolution, involving urbanisation and immigration not only from the Lancashire but also from the Irish countryside, produced a massive increase in the Lancashire Catholic population. The change from a largely rural seigneurial community into an urban clerical community, and the progress of toleration and emancipation were completed.

The cotton industry continued to lead the Industrial Revolution, and was increasingly concentrated in Lancashire. Cartwright invented the power loom in 1785 and perfected it by 1804, so that weaving followed spinning into steam-powered factories on the coalfields. The long agony of the hand-loom weavers, who made up a large proportion of Catholics, began as their wages and then their numbers fell until by 1850 they vanished. The growth of the cotton industry in the towns round Manchester was matched by the growth of Liverpool as a port. Meanwhile the coal industry expanded as did the iron, copper, chemical, and glass industries in the districts between Liverpool and Manchester. The whole process was accelerated by the introduction of railways, beginning with the Bolton-Leigh line in 1828 and then the Liverpool-Manchester line in 1830, a process that was also complete in outline by 1850. Agriculture remained important to feed the growing population. The population of England and Wales doubled to 18,000,000 in the fifty years after the first census in 1801, but the population of Lancashire increased threefold to two million, and the population of Manchester fourfold to three hundred thousand.[1]

Shrewd Catholics with resources to invest profited from the Industrial Revolution. In 1798 Edward Standish of Standish, on the advice of his friend Thomas Eccleston, leased the coal on his estate to a group of Yorkshire Quakers, whose agent developed the mines. In 1814 Richard Ainscough with the help of his father, a yeoman farmer in Mawdesley, set up as a grocer in Parbold, and then took over the village windmill. His son Hugh, having studied for the priesthood and for a career in medicine, joined his brother Richard Ainscough junior in the family business. They built steam-powered flour-mills, and went into farming. Hugh Ainscough also built an hotel in Southport, and went into banking. Bartholomew Bretherton, the owner of the largest stage-coach company operating out of Liverpool, raced one of his coaches against one of the new trains, beat it, sold his firm, and invested the proceeds in the railways.[2]

The French Revolution of 1789 had immediate and profound effects on the Catholic Church. The fall of the *ancien régime* in 1789 was followed by the civil constitution of the clergy which reduced the French clergy to servants of the state, and was condemned by the pope in 1791. Many of the clerical opponents of the constitution fled to England, not least to Lancashire. In 1792 Revolutionary France went to war with the German states, and by 1793 was at war with most of Europe including England. The Revolution closed the English colleges and convents in the territory it controlled, and they returned to England. The execution of the king in 1793 and the foundation of the French Republic heralded the Reign of Terror, and coupled atheism with republicanism as the enemies of England. In 1798 Ireland revolted, was defeated, and was united with Britain in 1800. In 1799 Bonaparte made himself dictator and came to a compromise with the Church in the concordat of 1802. The fall of Bonaparte in 1814-15 resulted in the restoration of European monarchies, and was followed by the restoration of the Jesuits.[3]

In Britain increasing tolerance and the continual threat of Irish rebellion led to toleration and emancipation for Catholics. The Relief Act of 1791 abolished the double land tax on Catholics and permitted the celebration of Catholic worship in public chapels. The Emancipation Act of 1829 allowed Catholics to hold government office, except for Lord Chancellor, Lord Keeper, or Lord Lieutenant of Ireland. Turner commemorated the event with an allegorical painting of the Jesuit college at Stonyhurst in Lancashire. He placed shining crosses on the twin towers of the college, overlooking the pond where Catholic boys seize the boat of emancipation under the protection of a horseman who represents the king. At last in 1831 Peregrine Edward Towneley of Towneley became a justice of the peace, a deputy lieutenant, and high sheriff of Lancashire. Bewhiskered, high-collared, and black-coated, he sat for his portrait beside a table of books and a window which apparently looked out on Towneley Hall. A last disability was removed by the Marriage Act of 1836 which allowed for the presence of a civil registrar at a Catholic wedding, thus making such marriages valid in law.[4]

The Enlightenment continued to have destructive consequences for Christianity. Hegel's dialectic, the reconciliation of intellectual conflict in synthesis, was used to attack Christianity from without and to modernise it from within. Strauss applied Hegelianism to Christianity in his *Life of Jesus* (1835), which argued that the Gospels were not history but myth. According to Engels, this work and the works of deists and atheists circulated amongst the Lancashire working class who were generally indifferent and even hostile to religion. Marx and Engels applied Hegelianism, deprived of its idealism, as dialectical materialism to history, and in *The Communist Manifesto* of 1848 described the pope as one of the 'Powers of old Europe' haunted by 'the spectre of Communism'. Darwin's *Origin of the Species* (1859) undermined the concept of a benevolent creator.[5]

The Catholic gentry remained patrons of the Classical arts. Henry Blundell of Ince Blundell emulated Charles Towneley in the collection of antique statuary. In about 1780 he built a Tuscan temple at Ince Blundell to house the collection. Then in 1804 he moved it to his Ionic Pantheon based on the Roman Pantheon. He was also an admirer of the Greek Revivial architecture being built in Liverpool at the time. His collection is now housed in the Walker Art Gallery at Liverpool.[6]

The attempts to secure toleration for Catholics involved the Catholic nobility and gentry, who remained the leaders of the Catholic community, in the expression of Cisalpine views. Cisalpinism was a development of the Anglo-Gallicanism of the 17th century. It asserted the autonomy of the English Catholic Church while seeking an accommodation with the English Protestant State. In 1782 a meeting of 30 leading Catholic laymen elected a committee to try to secure a further measure of toleration. The committee consisted of five members, one for each of the four vicarates and a fifth for Lancashire, John Towneley of Towneley. In 1783 the committee wrote to the vicars apostolic pointing out that the government viewed with suspicion 'the absolute and unlimited dependence of their superior clergy upon the court of Rome' and urged that the vicars apostolic should be created ordinaries, that is diocesan bishops. However, Bishop Walmesley feared that that was not all they wanted, but that as well as proposing a new oath of allegiance 'to exclude the pope's spiritual jurisdiction' they wanted 'to diminish our dependence in spirituals on the see of Rome, and by degrees to shake it off entirely; likewise to take off the abstinence of Saturday, to reduce Lent to a fortnight before Easter, and to have the liturgy in English'. In other words there was a hidden Cisalpine agenda which, behind the attempt to secure toleration, sought to make the English Church autonomous and to come to terms with the exigencies of the Industrial Revolution and the demands of the Enlightenment.[7]

The committee elaborated their views in an address of 1787. They declared that the vicars apostolic were:

> ... appointed by the court of Rome, without any election either by the clergy or laity ... But ... ecclesiastical government by vicars apostolic ... is ... contrary to the primitive practices of the Church and ... it is incumbent upon us to use our endeavours to procure the nomination of bishops in ordinary ... pastors thus chosen by the flock which they are to teach and direct, and in conjunction with which they would be competent to regulate every part of the national Church discipline ...

In effect they wanted an elected episcopate ready to adapt ecclesiastical discipline to industrial society.[8]

At the same time, mindful of the needs of the rising Catholic middle class they called for the establishment of a Catholic school in England 'which shall afford a system of education proper for those who are destined for civil or commercial life'.[9]

The committee was opposed not only by the bishops but also by a group of laymen which included such Lancastrians as Trafford and Blundell who objected to any proposal not supported by the bishops and who maintained that the continental English schools were perfectly adequate.[10]

Nevertheless the committee negotiated with the government to bring in another Catholic Relief Bill which contained an oath of allegiance accepting the Hanoverian succession and denying papal temporal supremacy and infallibility. The proposed oath met with opposition from the Lancashire clergy who met to condemn it, and in 1789 it was solemnly condemned by the vicars apostolic.[11]

The Rev. John Barrow of Claughton expressed himself thus to the Cisalpine Bishop Berington in 1790:

> I have seen your long, elaborate unmeaning letter addressed to the Lancashire brethren, who so laudably condemned the execrable oath of which you seem to own yourself the invincible champion. But you must permit me to tell you that neither the undeserving ornament of a mitre nor the flimsy badge of a Parisian double DD tacked to your now unimportant name will ever make me or my brethren, who had the honour to oppose your unwarrantable measures, advocates of your dangerous doctrines ...[12]

An open meeting of the committee including Towneley adopted an amended oath but it was condemned by the four vicars apostolic. In response to these pressures the oath was eventually amended into an acceptable form, and in 1791 the Second Catholic Relief Act was passed abolishing all the penal laws and permitting the public celebration of Catholic worship.[13]

Meanwhile Bishop Walmesley suspended a leading Cisalpine, the Benedictine Joseph Wilkes. The Staffordshire clergy, who contained a hard core of native Lancastrians, came to Wilkes's defence with an 'Appeal to the Catholics of England'. It contained the 'Staffordshire Creed', a conservative statement of Gallican and indeed Richerist principles, that is a defence not only of the rights of the episcopate with regard to the papacy but also of the priesthood with regard to the episcopate, all based on the appeal to antiquity:

> We know as others do what our faith is and we have learnt to distinguish what is human from what is divine. We believe our Church to be an infallible guide in all that appertains to salvation. Of this Church we believe the bishop of Rome to be the head, supreme in spirituals by divine appointment, supreme in discipline by ecclesiastical institution; but in the concerns of state or civil life we believe him to be no governor, no master, no guide. We believe that the jurisdiction of bishops is of divine origin; but that that jurisdiction is distinctly defined, that its limits are all known, that is, that its exercise must be circumscribed within the sphere and be conformable to the rules of established order. We believe that the priesthood is from Christ, the rights of which are as sacred as those of the pontifical and of the episcopal order, and that the forms of ancient practice, which must ever be revered, have sanctioned the exercise of those rights and marked their limits.[14]

To maintain their influence, some members of the committee formed themselves into the Cisalpine Club in 1792, and were joined by John Towneley. The

French threat to the English Continental schools revived the scheme to establish a Catholic school in England, and the club set up a committee including Towneley to examine the matter. It was proposed to establish the school in Staffordshire, and John Towneley's son Peregrine was to be one of the governors. The Rev. John Bew, former president of the English seminary at Paris, was asked to be its principal but Bishop Walmesley refused him permission to accept the post.[15]

In 1797 Walmesley publicly excommunicated the signatories of the Staffordshire creed. He died a few months later, as did their defender, Bishop Berington. In 1801, the newly appointed vicar apostolic of the Midlands, Bishop Stapleton, attempted to persuade the surviving signatories of the Staffordshire creed to accept a compromise. Four of the remaining five, including Thomas Southworth, born at Fernyhalgh and president of Sedgeley Park School, accepted the compromise, but another Lancastrian, John Carter, the priest at Wolverhampton, held out until his death in 1803. His will is the perfect expression of the devotion of a conservative Anglo-Gallican pastor to his faith and to his flock:

> Self love prompts us to speak of ourselves to the last, and self defence is an inalienable right of our nature when we are attacked by calumny. I loved my people, and taught them with undeviating fidelity the saving and orthodox doctrines of the one holy Catholic and apostolic Church, and I hope they will in return pray God to forgive my offences against Him. In His boundless mercy and the merits of His crucified and sinless Son, Jesus Christ, is my humble reliance, my only hope. Various motives have been assigned for my declining to subscribe certain formulas. Truth will be alive when I am dead. It is, was and ever will be simply this: I conscientiously—Domine tu scisti [Lord, thou knowest]—refused to sign away the canonical liberties of the Christian clergy, and obliquely to wound the reputation of two beloved superiors. My enemies themselves (whom I cordially forgive) cannot blame such disinterested, even were they to prove mistaken, principles. Odio oderunt me gratis [They hate me with a free hatred]. Peace was my dear delight; but no frowns, no terrors, neither poverty nor fear of temporary disgrace could ever shake my attachment to truth.[16]

Despite the apparent defeat of Cisalpinism and the collapse of its organisation, it remained a powerful intellectual force, and its leader throughout the later part of this period was John Lingard. Born in Winchester in 1771, educated at Douay, ordained in 1795, and first vice-president of Ushaw, he was appointed to the mission at Hornby in Lancashire in 1811. From the appearance of the first volume of his *History of England* in 1819 until his death in 1851 the intellectual centre of gravity of English Catholicism rested in Hornby.

In this rural retreat, painted by Turner in 1818, Lingard lived in the presbytery built in 1762 by the generosity of Ann Fenwick. Lingard, with his poodle Ettie, would walk in the walled garden with its sundial, pear trees, and the oak from Lake Trasimene which he planted. There he kept his tortoise, Moses, which survived him by 50 years and is still preserved. In 1820 he built the chapel with its Venetian

6 *John Lingard. From a print in the possession of the author.*

doorway, its busts of Constantine and Oswy (rulers who summoned Church councils and therefore symbolic of the Gallican respect for the rights of the state), and his Roman altar piece. The friend of the parson, the squire, and the poor who were never turned empty from his door, he is commemorated by tablets in his own chapel and in the Anglican church.[17]

Lingard was a prolific writer and controversialist, always ready in the defence of the Catholic Faith and the Cisalpine position. The friend of Butler, the active lay leader of the Cisalpines, and the correspondent of Dollinger, the leader of the German Liberal Catholics, he helped Tierney to prepare his edition of Dodd's Gallican *Church History*. His ten-volume *History of England* was his magnum opus, a pioneering work of history in its use of the sources and the monumental manifesto of the Catholic Enlightenment, though his best known work is the still popular hymn 'Hail Queen of Heaven'. Although a pioneer of the vernacular liturgy, he disliked 'new-fangled devotion', and urged the clergy 'to make our religion appear venerable and heavenly to those around us' (quoted by Haile and Bonney). His theology was accordingly conservative: 'In matters of faith and essential discipline, no change whatsoever can be admitted' (quoted by Chinnici) because 'Christianity is not an art or science in which new discoveries may be made. It must come in perfect shape from the hands of its divine author, and have been delivered in that shape by the apostles to their disciples' (quoted by Chinnici).[18]

The Cisalpine tradition was continued by Daniel Rock. Born in Liverpool in 1799, he was ordained in 1824, and from 1827 to 1840 he was the chaplain of Lord Shrewsbury at Alton Towers in Staffordshire. There he wrote for the benefit of Protestants *Hieurgia, or the Holy Sacrifice of the Mass*, published in 1833, an account of the liturgy in which he insisted on 'the venerable and apostolic antiquity of this service'. He then became chaplain to Sir Robert Throckmorton at Buckland, Berkshire, where he wrote *The Church of Our Fathers*, published between 1849 and 1854, on the Sarum rite. He was the leading figure in the Adelphi, a national society of priests, dominated by Lancastrians and Londoners, who began in 1845 to agitate for the restoration of the hierarchy.[19]

Meanwhile the French Revolutionary government closed the convents and expelled the English communities, some of whom found a temporary asylum in Lancashire. The English Benedictine nuns of Cambray (Cambrai) were arrested in 1793, and during their imprisonment the chaplain and five of the 25 nuns died of their privations, so that Dame Agnes trembled from head to foot for the rest of her life. They were expelled to England, and on the invitation of the Benedictine priest at Woolton, Liverpool, they made their way there and kept a school until they left for Stanbrook, near Worcester, in 1808. The Benedictine nuns of Montargis, near Orleans, left for England in 1792, and in 1821 they opened a school at Orrell Mount, near Wigan, but threatened with mining subsidence in 1835 they left for Princethorpe, near Rugby, leaving their house, the Nunnery, which still survives. The Benedictine nuns of Ghent fled in 1794 via Antwerp, whither William Dicconson of Wrightington went to fetch them. Some went temporarily to Fernyhalgh, some to Little Singleton, and some to Wrightington. Since the Reformation nuns had apparently become such unknown quantities that when the improving squire Dicconson ordered his coach-man to Wigan to collect the nuns, the coachman asked a fellow-servant, 'What are nuns?', and was told, 'I don't know. Some new sort of potato perhaps'. A year later the nuns were re-united at Winckley Square, Preston, to open a school, but they left and finally settled at Oulton in Staffordshire.[20]

The expulsion of the English ex-Jesuits brought their college permanently to Lancashire. On the dissolution by the French monarchy of the English Jesuit college at St Omers in 1762, it had been re-established at Bruges in the Austrian Netherlands. When the Austrian government dissolved it in 1773, it took refuge in the territory of the Prince-Bishop of Liège. Invasion by the French Republican forces in 1794 forced it to seek refuge in England. Thomas Weld of Lulworth, an alumnus of the college at Bruges, gave it Stonyhurst Hall and its 44 acres in the Ribble valley, which he had acquired as the heir of the Shireburns. Although technically secular priests the ex-Jesuits wished to elect their own rector, as they had done at Liège, but Bishop Gibson objected until a papal brief of 1796 overruled him. The school flourished, and in 1808 the buildings were extended. Weld attended the inauguration and in the festivities proceeded to sing one of his favourite songs, 'I am mad Tom, behold me'. However, he began it at too high a pitch but persisted in it, bringing on a fit of apoplexy, which resulted in his death, a melancholy example of the danger of persisting in error.[21]

The English secular college at Douay closed in 1792 was re-founded at Ushaw with the help of the Rev. John Barrow. He opposed any suggestion that the college return to the Continent, urging that it should be re-established at Claughton. When Ushaw in County Durham was finally decided on for its site, Barrow cut through the legal difficulties, and conveyed the land to the bishop. When the new college finally opened in 1809 he rode across the Pennines to Ushaw to say Mass. The big-boned septuagenarian hobbled up to the altar where he placed his red wig while he vested.[22]

The French Revolutionary programme of dechristianisation, begun in 1793, brought many French priests as refugees to Lancashire. They came mainly from the royalist west of France, the Vendée, Anjou, Poitou, and Guyenne. Here most of the émigrés lived the life of refugees, dependent on the relief fund administered by the British government or trying to earn a living teaching French. Many of them returned to France after the concordat of 1801, and the bulk of the remainder after the restoration of the French monarchy in 1814-15.[23]

At least one of these émigrés, Jean Begué who arrived in Liverpool in 1799 was an active supporter of the Blanchardist schism which asserted Gallican principles against Ultramontanism. The concordat called for all the bishops of the *ancien régime* to resign their sees, but there were those like Blanchard who argued that the episcopate was of divine foundation, and that bishops were married to their sees which they ought not to resign. This view was condemned by the English vicars apostolic in 1808, and it seems to have had little influence on the English Catholic Church.[24]

A minority of the émigré clergy served as pastors in Catholic Lancashire. They included Joseph-Louis Dorrival who was chaplain to the Ecclestons of Scarisbrick from 1801 until his death in 1824; Louis Merlin, chaplain to the Towneleys of Towneley from 1811 until his death in 1819, according to his epitaph (quoted by Blundell) 'dear to God and the poor'; Félix de Lalond who was chaplain to the Dicconsons of Wrightington from at least 1804 until his death in 1806; and Louis Richebeque who served the Catholic congregation at Croft, near Warrington (where he built the church in 1827) from 1798 until his death in 1845. The most outstanding was Jean-Baptiste Géradot. He arrived in Liverpool in 1795, taught in the Catholic school at Vernon Hall and in the Catholic Charity School, and in 1804 with the financial support of the local Protestants opened the chapel of St Anthony's, Scotland Road, which he served until his death in 1825.[25]

Midnight Mass of Christmas at St Anthony's in 1813 provides a description of the liturgy of the period in this tiny chapel 55 feet long by 32 feet wide. The front was illuminated with candles in the shape of a star and the letters 'J.S.' (the initials of Jesus Salvator, that is Jesus the Saviour). The music was by Webbe and Cassuli, together with Novello's version of the *Adeste Fideles*, Handel's Pastoral Symphony from *Messiah* and the sung *Te Deum*.[26]

These Lancashire Catholics living in the last heyday of classical music had a passion for choral performance. In his old age, the Rev. John Barrow turned from the cry of the pack of hounds he kept in his youth to learn music and to teach his own choir which he boasted 'bore the bell of all our Lancashire choirs'. The opening of St Wilfrid's, Preston, in 1793 was followed by a performance of Handel's *Messiah* and a concert of sacred music, which according to the *Blackburn Mail* (quoted by Warren) was sung 'with so much true taste, animation and feeling as went to the heart of every lover of sacred harmony'.[27]

The growing strength of the Catholic community and of its clergy was marked by the division in 1840 of the Northern vicariate into a Northern, a Yorkshire, and a Lancashire district (which also included Cheshire), each with its own vicar apostolic. The new vicar apostolic of Lancashire was George Hilary Brown, born at Clifton, Lytham, educated at Ushaw under Lingard, a vice-rector of Ushaw and priest at St Peter's, Lancaster. He was consecrated bishop in St Anthony's, Liverpool.[28]

The vicars apostolic presided over a Church in which the rights of the laity were deeply rooted. The oldest and strongest of these roots was the seigneurial authority of the Catholic gentry who provided the chapels and regarded the clergy as their chaplains. Thus although the mission at Wrightington was financed out of the Finch Mill estate of Bishop Edward Dicconson, in 1806 the squire of Wrightington, Captain Edward Dicconson insisted, despite the wish of the vicar general, on the appointment as priest at Wrightington of the Benedictine Louis Francis Cooper, who had been supplying Wrightington from Parbold. The squire maintained that the Finch Mill estate belonged to him, and challenged the ecclesiastical authorities to take him to court. To avoid this open dispute, the bishop, with the mediation of the Benedictine

Father Richard Marsh of Hindley, approved the apointment of Cooper whilst reserving his rights to Finch Mill.[29]

Some of the urban congregations were just as committed to the rights of the laity embodied in lay trustees who built chapels and controlled clerical appointments, a movement which swept through English-speaking Catholicism. In New York the trustees forced the retirement of their priests, and in Albany and Philadelphia they went into schism.

In Wigan the movement resulted in the simultaneous erection of two rival chapels almost side by side. By the early 19th century the existing chapel built in 1785 to house the 900 Catholics was no longer big enough to hold the congregation which had grown to 3,000, especially as the nearby chapel at Ince Hall had been closed by the removal of the Ince-Andertons. In 1817 a committee led by Peter Greenough, a cotton manufacturer, was formed to build a new chapel by subscription amongst the congregation including the poor, and applied to the vicar apostolic for the appointment of a priest. Charles Walmesley esq of Westwood House, Ince, one of the local gentry, called for the re-building of the old chapel to be staffed by its ex-Jesuit priests. Richard Thompson, the vicar general of Lancashire, declared that the vicar apostolic withheld his approval from the ex-Jesuits and that support for their chapel amounted to opposition to episcopal authority. Thomas Plowden, the rector of Stonyhurst, weighed in on behalf of his colleagues. He argued that chapels remained the private property of their founders who had a right of patronage. Thompson, with the help of Lingard, denied that there was any right of patronage, and insisted that clergy and laity were subject to their bishop. Both sides appealed to Rome which ordered Bishop Gibson, the vicar apostolic of the North, to enforce a compromise, suggested by John Milner, the vicar apostolic of the Midlands. Gibson therefore allowed both chapels to proceed, and neo-Gothic St Mary's for the secular clergy went up a couple of hundred yards away from neo-Classical St John's for the Jesuits. Wigan, therefore, remains in Little's words, 'England's vintage town for Regency Catholic churches'.[30]

In Preston St Wilfrid's was built in 1792 and placed in the care of three lay trustees. In 1815 the surviving trustee released the trust to its ex-Jesuit priests. However, some members of the congregation insisted on the property's being surrendered to lay trustees.[31]

This three-cornered struggle for control between the bishops, the clergy, and the laity was at its most intense in the little mission of Lee House near Chipping in the fells above the River Hodder. The mission had been founded in 1738 for the Franciscans and placed under the control of lay trustees. Eventually the Franciscans abandoned the mission and in 1827 the Rev. Francis Trappes was appointed to the mission. He built a chapel, school, and presbytery, and the size of the congregation increased from eighty or ninety to three hundred. However, in 1841 the vicar apostolic, Bishop Brown, suspended Trappes on suspicion of his being the author of a pamphlet on abuses which had slandered the bishop. The real author acknowledged his pamphlet, and the bishop removed the suspension in 1843. Meanwhile in 1841 the papacy ruled that lay trustees were entirely dependent on episcopal authority, and in 1844 Bishop Brown declared them abolished. In order to rid himself of both Trappes and the trustees, he followed up the suspension with an interdict forbidding the administration of the sacraments in the Lee House mission, and it was only withdrawn in 1859 when Trappes surrendered the mission to the Benedictines.[32]

Although the growth of urban Catholicism was dramatic, rural Catholicism continued to flourish. Agriculture prospered in response to the expanding urban market, and remained especially strong north of the Ribble. There was some decline in rural population, especially after the Poor Law Amendment Act of 1834 faced the poor with the choice of entering the workhouse or receiving no relief so that the rural poor migrated to the towns and employment. Thus the Catholic population of Hornby in Lonsdale fell from 200 in the 1810s to about 170 in the 1840s, most of the emigrants moving to the industrial towns of Lancashire. However, on the coast at Yealand north of Lancaster and at Thurnham to the south, the Catholic congregations increased from less than 80 in 1801 to 180 in 1839 at Yealand and from 186 in 1800 to 420 in the 1830s at Thurnham.[33]

These flourishing rural congregations were apparently headed by seigneurial households which maintained their priests and provided their chapels, but their finances were rather more complex. At Thurnham the priest was maintained partly by the Daltons of Thurnham Hall and partly by an endowment left by Jane Daniel, a member of a family of clockmakers and clerics from Kirkham in the Fylde. The chapel was built in 1817 with money provided by the Daltons, the Gillows, the Lancaster cabinet-makers, and the Worswicks, the Lancaster bankers. This chapel was replaced in 1847-8 by Charles Hansom's Gothic church, partly paid for by Elizabeth Dalton and partly by the Rev. Thomas Crowe out of profitable speculation in the railways. (The churchyard contains the Gillows' Egyptian mausoleum.) However, Elizabeth Dalton's claim to be the sole founder of the church led to Crowe's resignation. At Yealand, where the Towneleys had established the mission in 1782, Leighton Hall was purchased by the Worswicks who sold it in 1827 to the Gillows. There too the Georgian chapel was replaced in 1852 by Paley's Gothic St Mary's, paid for by the Gillows.[34]

These Gothic churches completed an architectural progress that had begun in the halls. At Leighton Hall the Worswicks began the transformation of a Classical into a Gothic house, probably employing as architect Thomas Harrison who had introduced this decorative Georgian Gothic to the district with his additions to Lancaster Castle in 1788. The alterations at Leighton were taken a stage further by the addition of a new Gothic wing by Paley and Austin in 1870. The Daltons, who might have imbibed the Gothic sensibility in the Bath of Jane Austen's *Northanger Abbey*, added Gothic decoration to Thurnham Hall in 1823 and a Gothic chapel in 1854-55. The apogee of these Gothic Catholic houses is Scarisbrick Hall, near Ormskirk. In 1836 Charles Scarisbrick, growing rich on his Southport properties, gave Augustus Welby Pugin, the high priest of the Gothic, his first major commission, to re-build his house, a task which was finally completed by E. W. Pugin. These Gothic houses challenged the secularisation of the 19th century with a vision of reactionary romanticism that Disraeli described with relish in *Coningsby*.[35]

Although the old gentry and the nouveaux riches continued to dream their rural idyll, the fundamental trend was the growth of urban Catholicism. This development was part of a general process of urbanisation, which involved not only local immigration but also, especially for the Catholics, immigration from Ireland.

Simon Bordley, the priest at Aughton near Ormskirk, lamented the changes as early as 1789:

> I am now an old man within half a year of fourscore and I love the old ways and old customs better than new ones, and I think myself authorised to do so both by the Old and New Testament ... Our Saviour says 'No man drinking old wine calls for new, for the old is better'. And so think I; for the Catholics I found in Lancashire fifty years ago were incomparably better than what we have at present.[36]

The older urban Catholic centres, Preston and Wigan, continued to grow, as did the newer one, Liverpool, and they were joined by a fourth, Manchester. By 1810 their estimated Catholic populations were: Preston, 4,000; Wigan, 2,100; Liverpool, 9,300; Manchester, 6,300; a total of twenty-one thousand six hundred. By 1834 they were: Preston, 8,892; Wigan, 7,000; Liverpool, 20,000; Manchester, 18,000; a total of fifty-four thousand. By 1851 they were: Preston, 19,420; Wigan, 12,767; Liverpool, 69,125; Manchester, 44,105; a total of a hundred and twenty thousand.[37]

This growth was due partly to natural increase and continued immigration from the Lancashire countryside but it was mainly the result of Irish immigration. The Irish came to escape their native poverty in response to the increased demand for labour created by the Industrial Revolution. They came in successively larger waves: the first about 1790, the second after 1820, and the third in the famine years of the late 1840s. By 1834 they totalled 31,800 (58 per cent) of the 54,000 Catholics in Preston, Wigan, Liverpool, and Manchester.[38]

The strength of the Irish varied from place to place. Preston was the least Irish of these congregations. The Irish numbered less than 1,000 out of a Catholic congregation of 8-9,000. In Wigan 3,000 Irish made up a large minority (over 40 per cent) of the 7,000 Catholics. However, in Liverpool the 9,000 Irish constituted nearly 70 per cent of the 13,000 Catholics, though they were less than 10 per cent of the city's population, and in Manchester over 15,000 Irish made up 83 per cent of the 18,000 Catholics. The Irish also found their way to St Helens and to some of the cotton towns that ringed Manchester.[39]

The Irish Catholics were alienated not only by their religion but also by their language or, at least, their accent, by their socio-economic status—they took the most lowly paid and the most unpleasant jobs—and by their way of life. All but their religion tended to alienate them from the native Lancashire Catholics. In addition to the hostility betweeen Irish Catholics and Irish Protestants there were also divisions between Irish Catholics from different provinces and counties.[40]

In Manchester they lived in their own ghettos: New Town or Irish Town with 20,000 Irish and the much smaller Little Ireland with a mere two thousand. They inhabited back-to-back houses or cellars, and were employed as hand-loom weavers and brick-layers' labourers. Poor, ignorant, diseased, prone to drink and violence, they were the victims of ethnic, social, and religious prejudices. Engels described them thus:

> A horde of ragged women and children swarm about here, as filthy as the swine that thrive upon the garbage heaps and in the puddles... The race that lives in these ruinous cottages ... in dark, wet cellars, in measureless filth and stench, in this atmosphere penned in as if with a purpose, this race must really have reached the lowest stage of humanity.[41]

However, the Irish and Lancastrian Catholics were integrated by their religion, by marriage, and by their schools, despite the 'dropping off' or 'leakage' of large numbers, amounting to fifty per cent, of Irish from the practice of their religion. This was caused partly by the failure of the English clergy to cope, partly by the inadequacy of the instruction given in Ireland, partly by the folk religion of the Irish which did not necessarily include the Counter-Reformation discipline of weekly Mass attendance, and partly by the general secularising pressures of an urban industrial environment.[42]

Whilst some of the rural clergy, like 'Lazybones' Lingard, continued to manage decline, the urban clergy did their best to manage growth, despite the rise in the ratio of Catholics per priest from 300 in the 1780s to 1,000 in the 1830s.[43]

The lead was taken by 'Daddy' Dunn in Preston. Born in Yorkshire in 1764, he was ordained as a Jesuit in 1771, and came to Preston in 1776. After the suppression and restoration of the Jesuits, he did not rejoin the Society but remained in charge of the Preston mission until his death in 1827. He built St Wilfrid's in 1793, re-opened St Mary's in 1793, opened a Sunday school in 1787, and a day school in 1814. He also took an active part in Preston's public life, helping to found the House of Recovery, the Literary and Philosophical Society, the Savings Bank, the Clothing Society, and the Gas Company.[44]

Overwhelmed by the growth of his congregation from 1,000 to 40,000, Roland Broomhead in Manchester had to ignore secular matters and to concentrate on administering the sacraments and giving public instructions to get his flock to the sacraments. Another Yorkshireman, he was born in 1751. He took over St Chad's in 1778, built St Mary's in 1794, and St Augustine's in 1820. After ten hours in the confessional he would emerge to soak his feet in hot water and to complain, 'At my time of life, I cannot stand it much longer' (quoted by Connolly). He died worn out in 1820.[45]

With successive vicars apostolic resident in the North-East, the burden of organising the Lancashire mission fell after 1824 on Thomas Penswick as coadjutor. Born in 1772 in Ashton-in-Makerfield, the son of Lord Gerard's steward, he was a pupil of Newby at Fernyhalgh and a student at Douay, whence he escaped imprisonment during the Terror, burying the college treasure. He went to Ware, Hertford-shire, but left for Crook Hall, Durham, walking all the way, and was ordained in 1797. He was appointed to St Nicholas's, Liverpool, in 1814. A campaigner for Catholic emancipation and against the Anglican tithes, he toured the Lancashire missions, preaching, hearing confessions, and taking sick calls. He succeeded as vicar apostolic in 1831, and died at Ashton in 1836, and was buried at Windleshaw.[46]

The labours of the English clergy were heroic; they also risked martyrdom from disease. Cholera, dysentry, typhoid, and typhus swept through the insanitary streets of the industrial towns in the second quarter of the 19th century killing thousands, especially in the aftermath of the Irish famine of 1846. The priests were called out to administer the sacraments to the sick and dying, and fell victims to contagion. In 1838 Bishop Briggs recorded the death from disease of 26 priests in the Northern district in 18 months. Between April and September 1847 ten Liverpool priests died from the typhus, and throughout the county there were other 'martyrs of charity'.[47]

The living and working conditions of Lancashire in the Industrial Revolution were the breeding grounds of radicalism and trade unionism in which Catholics played their part. The Irish immigrants, in their eagerness to work, no matter how low the wage, stood aside from working-class organisations and were notorious as blacklegs, strike-breakers, and violent opponents of Chartism and other Radical move-ments. However, they were also the heirs of their own revolutionary nationalist tradition, though this also tended to put them at odds with English Radicalism.[48]

Nevertheless, it was from the ranks of the immigrant Irish that John Doherty stepped forward as the champion of the working class. Born in Ireland in 1797 and a devout Catholic he came in 1816 to work as a spinner in Manchester. He built up a Manchester cotton spinners' union, but found that new machinery weakened their position and led to the failure of their strike in 1829. He therefore set up a national cotton spinners' union, and then went on to form a general union of all trades, the National Association for the Protection of Labour. In 1830 the cotton manufacturers of Ashton-under-Lyne imposed a wage cut, and Doherty led his union into a strike. However, the strike was far from solid and ended not only in failure but also in the collapse of both the cotton spinners union and of the general union. Doherty's was the precursor of the equally unsuccessful Grand National Consolidated Trade Union associated with the co-operative Socialism of Robert Owen. The future, however, lay with the single-craft trade unions.[49]

The attitude of the clergy to the trade union movement was ambivalent. They tended to lump it together with all the secret societies of which they disapproved on principle and to which they applied an interdict. However, they did realise that conditions required workers to unite to protect their wages and conditions of work. As the Rev. Henry Gillow of St Mary's, Manchester (quoted by Connolly) put it in 1836, 'These men must combine'. Bishop Penswick summed up the ecclesiastical attitude in a pastoral of 1834 which, whilst condemning violence, accepted the rights of the workers to defend their standard of living.[50]

Catholicism, like Methodism and Dissent, performed the functions of legiti-
mating protest and social improvement and of ameliorating anomie or alienation.
Indeed in its commitment to conversion, its itinerant mission, and its reliance on lay
support, Catholicism shared many of the features of Protestant Evangelicalism.
Moreover, whilst Catholicism claimed to be a universal church, that is an inclusive
organisation comprehending the total population, it had ceased to be so in England
at the Reformation. By the early 18th century it had become, like Protestant Dissent,
a sect, an exclusive body demanding and receiving total adherence. By the middle
of the 19th century, like Protestant Dissent, it was turning into a denomination in so
far as it was failing to maintain the total adherence of its membership. As the
dependency system, in which people followed the lead of their social superiors, gave
way to religious pluralism, Catholicism, like Methodism and Dissent, was a beneficiary of the Industrial Revolution.[51]

In early August 1848 the English bishops assembled together in Manchester
to open St John's church in Salford, soon to be the cathedral, and to plan the
restoration of the diocesan hierarchy. Built by Matthew Hadfield and praised by
A. W. Pugin, its Gothic style and its steeple, at the time the highest in Lancashire,
asserted the claim of Victorian Lancastrian Catholicism to continuity with the universal church of the middle ages, but it stood in a city dedicated to economic and
religious *laissez-faire*.[52]

Notes

1.   Hobsbawm, *Age of Revolution*, pp.42-72; 207-23; Hobsbawm, *Industry and Empire*, pp.56-133;
      Reid, *Peterloo Massacre*, pp.6-19; Engels, *Condition of Working Class*, pp.50-64; Walton,
      pp.102-24.

2.   D. Anderson, J. Lane and A. A. France, *The Standish Collieries, Wigan, Lancashire, 1635-1953*
      (1984), pp.11-8; Plumb, *Our Lady and All Saints, Parbold, Lancashire* (1984), pp.11-12;
      Giblin, 'The Stapleton-Bretherton Family and the Mission of St Bartholomew's, Rainhill',
      NWCH, vol.9 (1982), pp.12-13.

3.   E. E. Y. Hales, *Revolution and Papacy* (1960); A. Vidler, *The Church in an Age of Revolution*
      (1971) (hereafter Vidler), pp.11-22, 33-43; Bellenger, 'A Tale of Two Churches' in Hilton, *The
      Loveable West* (1990); Bellenger, *The French Exiled Clergy* (1986).

4.   Leys, pp.140-53; E. Shanes, *Turner's England* (London, 1990), pp.198-99; *Burke's Landed
      Gentry* (2 vols., 1875), vol.2, pp.1396-7; Blundell, vol.2, p.25; Ward, *The Sequel to Catholic
      Emancipation* (hereafter *Sequel*) (2 vols., 1915), I, pp.191-4.

5.   Vidler, pp.27-31, 101-4, 210; O. Chadwick, *The Secularization of the European Mind in the
      Nineteenth Century* (1990), pp.48-87, 161-88, 223-6; K. Marx and F. Engels, *Manifesto of the
      Communist Party* (Foreign Languages Publishing House edition, Moscow, no date), p.44.

6.   Pevsner, *Lancs: South*, pp. 26, 128; J. M. Crook, *The Greek Revival* (1972), p.118.

7.   Ward, *Dawn*, vol.1, pp.93-4, 97, 100.

8.   Ward, *Dawn*, vol.1, p.109, vol.2, pp.260-5.

9.   Ward, *Dawn*, vol.1, p.110, vol.2, pp.260-5.

10.   Ward, *Dawn*, vol.1, pp.109-25.

11.   Ward, *Dawn*, vol.1, pp.12-86.

12.   Lancashire Record Office, 'The Rev. John Barrow of Claughton', *NWCH*, vol.3 (1971), p.36.

13.   Ward, *Dawn*, vol.1, pp.226-97.

14.   Ward, *Dawn*, vol.1, pp.316-38; Hales, *Revolution and Papacy*, pp.16-17, 296-7.

15.   Ward, *Dawn*, vol.2, pp.51-57.

16.   Ward, *Dawn*, vol.2, pp.145-62, 235-56; Anstruther, vol.4, pp.56-7, 255.

17.   Hilton, 'Lingard's Hornby' in Hilton, *Catholic Englishmen*; Shanes, *Turner's England*, p.94.

18.   M. Haile and E. Bonney, *Life and Letters of John Lingard* (1912) (hereafter Haile and Bonney), pp. 307-8; J. P. Chinnici, *The English Catholic Enlightenment* (1980), pp.32, 140.

19.   *CE*, p.105; 25. D. Rock, *Hierurgia* (2 vols., 1833), vol.2, p.769; Ward, *Sequel*, vol.2, pp.159-60.

20.   Ward, *Dawn*, vol.2, pp.83, 92-3, 128; Bellenger, *Loveable West*, p.21; Stonor, *Liverpool's Hidden Story*, p.105; A. Bentley,'Lancashire Missions: Crossbrook', *NWCH*, vol.1 (2) (1969); V. Marsh, *St Joseph's, Wrightington* (1969), pp.39-40.

21.   Blundell, vol.2, pp.121-27; Ward, *Dawn*, vol.2, pp.103-4; Ward, *Eve*, vol.1, p.211; D. Mathew, Catholicism in England (1948) (hereafter Mathew), p.179; J. Gerard, *Stonyhurst Centenary Record* (1894), p.136.

22.   Lancs. R. O., *NWCH*, vol.3, pp.37-9.

23.   Bellenger, *Loveable West*, pp.15-26.

24.   Bellenger, *Loveable West*, p.23.

25.   Bellenger, *Loveable West*, p.25; Bellenger, *The French Exiled Clergy* (1986), pp.208, 272; Blundell, vol.1, p.29; Marsh, *St Joseph's, Wrightington*, p.40; B. Kelly, *Historical Dictionary of English Catholic Missions* (1907), p.147; Burke, pp.31-2.

26.   Burke, p.32.

27.   Lancs. R. O., *NWCH*, vol.3, pp.3-34; L. Warren, *A Short History of St Wilfrid's Church, Preston* (1972), p.10.

28.   *English and Welsh Hierarchical Structure* (1990), p.4; Plumb, *Arundel to Zabi*.

29.   Marsh, *St Joseph's, Wrightington*, pp.38-41.

30.   Hilton, 'The Case of Wigan', *NWCH*, vol.10 (1983); Little, p.56.

31.   Warren, *St Wilfrid's, Preston*, pp.8, 14-15.

32.   R. Trappes-Lomax (ed.), *Lancashire Register VI* (*CRS* vol.36, 1936), pp.74-6; Plumb, *Arundel to Zabi*.

33.   Walton, pp.121-3; Hilton, *Catholic Englishmen*, p.42; Hilton, *Yealand*, p.6; Hilton, *NWCH*, vol.12, p.3.

34.   Hilton, *NWCH*, vol.12, p.3; Anstruther, vol.4, pp.80-3; Singleton, *Mowbreck Hall and The Willows*, p.31; Hilton, *Yealand*.

35.   Little, pp.51-78; Pevsner, *Lancs: North*, pp.218-23.

36.   Hemphill, p.94.

37.   Bossy, *Community*, pp.303-7, 424.

38.   J. Hickey, *Urban Catholics* (1967), p.39; Bossy, *Community*, pp.306-8.

39.   Walton, p.183.

40.   Walton, p.183; Hickey, *Urban Catholics*, pp.46-55.

41.   J. W. Werly, 'The Irish in Manchester, 1832-49', *Irish Historical Studies*, vol.18 (71) (1973); Engels, *Condition of Working Class*, p.98.

42.   Bossy, *Community*, pp.309, 313-6; T. G. McGrath, 'The Tridentine Evolution of Modern Irish Catholicism, 1563-1962', *RH*, vol.20 (4) (1991).

43.   G. P. Connolly, '"With more than ordinary devotion to God": The Secular Missioner of the North in the Evangelical Age of the English Mission', *NWCH*, vol.10 (1983).

44.   T. G. Holt, 'Joseph Dunn of Preston from his Correspondence' in Hilton, *Catholic Englishmen*.

45.   Anstruther, vol.4, p.48; Connolly, *NWCH*, vol.10, p.16.

46.   Anstruther, vol.4, pp.208-9; Plumb, *Arundel to Zabi*.

47.   Connolly, *NWCH*, vol.10, pp.8-9; Burke, pp.86-7; Bolton, pp.123-9.

48.   Walton, pp.141-97; Hickey, *Urban Catholics*, pp.32-55, 135-44.

49.   R. G. Kirby and A. E. Mason, *The Voice of the People: John Doherty* (1975); H. Pelling, *A History of British Trade Unionism* (1963), pp.36-8.

50.   Connolly, 'The Catholic Church and the First Manchester and Salford Trade Unions in the Age of the Industrial Revolution', *TLCAS*, vol.83 (1985).

51.   Gilbert, pp.53-9, 81-93, 97, 139-41.

52.   Bolton, pp.115-7.

Chapter VII

Celtic Ultramontanism, 1848-1918

In the second half of the 19th century and the early years of the 20th century Catholic Lancashire continued to grow with the increasing prosperity of the county and as a consequence of Irish immigration. As it grew in size it developed more complex structures inspired by the rise of Ultramontanism, a movement which sought to subject the Church to the papacy and society to the Church. The hierarchy was restored, religious orders proliferated, and a Catholic system of formal education was established. The whole process was paralleled on the other side of the Pennines. It was a period when in some eyes Catholic Lancashire appeared as the Italian mission to the Irish.[1]

Catholic Lancashire benefited from the economic, social, and political progress of the period. Cotton, engineering, coal, chemicals, and agriculture increased their output. Central and local government became increasingly democratic, and both politics and society became increasingly stable. The working class, especially in the cotton towns (but less so in Liverpool), achieved an improved standard of living. Wages increased, food prices fell, and housing and sanitation improved. Increasingly, workers had money and time that gave them leisure to enjoy seaside holidays, football, cricket, rambling, music hall, pubs, music, literature, and religion. For Catholicism and the other denominations this was in Walton's words a 'golden age of church and school building'.[2]

In 1851, when the decennial census was accompanied for the first and only time by a religious census, Lancashire was still the most Catholic county in England. The number of Catholics counted at Mass in Lancashire on Sunday 31 March 1851 was 102,812, 42.5 per cent of 241,482 Catholics in England. However, it was still only a small minority (4.9 per cent) of the total Lancashire population of two million sixty-seven thousand four hundred and one. It was also only a slight majority (53.4 per cent) of the total Irish-born population of Lancashire which numbered a hundred and ninety-two thousand five hundred and ten. It consisted of 69,783 Catholics in the diocese of Liverpool, which had 84 churches and chapels served by 113 priests, and 33,092 Catholics in the diocese of Salford, which had 32 churches and chapels served by 37 priests.[3]

By 1910 the Catholic population of Lancashire had increased sixfold to 666,600, consisting of 366,000 in the diocese of Liverpool and 300,000 in the diocese of Salford. The former had 332 secular and 122 regular priests serving 184 churches and chapels, and the latter had 235 seculars and 86 regulars serving 138 churches and chapels.[4]

Native Lancastrian Catholics were reinforced massively by Irish immigrants, and the Irish were grafted onto the Lancastrian stock. Between 1841 and 1851 the Irish immigrant population of Lancashire almost doubled to over 191,000, 10 per cent of the county's total population. They continued to be strongest in both Liverpool and Manchester, but growth was more rapid in the smaller cotton towns. Thus in 1851 Irish immigrants made up 17 per cent of the population of Manchester, 7 per cent of Ashton-under-Lyne, and 10 per cent of Stockport, and in 1881 they were 13 per cent of the population of Liverpool, 7.5 per cent of Manchester, and 9 per cent of St Helens.[5]

Typical immigrants, poor and alien, the Irish aroused the hostility of the English. They were seen as a burden on the poor rates, as undercutting English labour, as black-legs and strike-breakers, as dirty, drunken, promiscuous, and violent. These views were strengthened by anti-Popery, fomented by Evangelical Protestantism, by the Orange Order which came from Ulster, and by local Tories, especially in Liverpool, who sought to make party political gains from these fears. As a result there were anti-Irish riots, beginning in Stockport in 1852, and continuing throughout the cotton towns into the 1860s, involving the defence of the Catholic church at Haslingden by the young Michael Davitt.[6]

The Irish were even despised by some of the native Lancashire Catholics. As Redmond (quoted by Steele) declared in Manchester in 1910:

> The English Catholics ... have always been the most bitter enemies of Ireland. Why, I do not know ... We have fought their battles, we emancipated them ... But ... not even the Orangemen in Belfast today are more bitter opponents of the cause of Irish freedom than are the average English Catholics ...[7]

Nevertheless, the Lancashire Irish were virtually unique in the whole Irish diaspora in so far as only in Lancashire, and perhaps to a certain extent in some other parts of England, did the Irish immigrants find a strong local Catholic Church already in existence. In Canada they found a strong Catholic Church, but it was French-speaking. In Wales, Scotland, Australia, and America, the Irish in effect created their own extension of the Irish Catholic Church. After 1850 the great majority of the Lancashire Catholic laity may have been Irish or of Irish descent, but the great majority of the clergy were English. The clergy were increasingly reinforced by native Irishmen or Lancastrians of Irish descent. From the foundation of the diocese of Liverpool in 1850 until 1986 over a quarter (248 out of 857) of the diocesan clergy were Irish-born.[8]

The Catholic Church in Lancashire was the primary social institution for the immigrant Irish. As the *Northern Press* (quoted by Lowe) put it in 1860, 'Irish and Catholic are to us the same'. The generation that arrived after the famine of 1845-7 came from an Ireland where the Church's rôle was even more central, but where less than 40 per cent regularly attended Mass. They found in Lancashire a

Catholic Church which provided them with continuity and security. Nevertheless, despite reinforcements by later generations which experienced a devotional revolution in Ireland, they remained only partly attached to the practice of their religion. In Liverpool, where the Irish formed the overwhelming majority of Catholics, much less than 50 per cent of Catholics attended Mass or performed their Easter duties by making their confession and communion. In Preston, where the Irish were less than a third of the local Catholics, 50 per cent or more of Catholics attended Mass or made their Easter duties. In St Helens and Widnes Catholics were more fervent than in Liverpool but less fervent than in Preston. Succeeding generations were integrated into the Lancashire Catholic community by Catholic schools, and by guilds and confraternities.[9]

The Irish middle class was eminently successful in integrating itself into the host community. Charles Barry, a lawyer, came over to Liverpool where he built up a successful practice. He was elected as a Liverpool M.P., and was appointed attorney general and then lord chief justice.[10]

In remaining Catholics the immigrants stayed Irish and were supporters of Irish political nationalism. In 1847 the corpse of Daniel O'Connell, 'the Liberator', the leader of the campaign for Catholic emancipation, had lain in state on a steamer in the Mersey, while relays of Irish immigrants knelt before it. In the 1860s the Fenians, dedicated to winning Irish independence by armed force, had their supporters among the Lancashire Irish. John Denvir was a leading Liverpool Irishmen who joined the Fenians in 1866. Some of the Fenians who attempted to seize Chester Castle in 1867 called at Wigan to make their confessions to Fr. Hugh Nugent McCormick, a native of Ireland and the rector of St Patrick's. The Fenians reorganised at a secret convention in Manchester in 1867. The Fenian leaders were arrested in Mancester, but rescued. Three of the rescuers—Allen, Larkin, and O'Brien—were captured, and executed for killing a policeman. For Irish Catholics they became 'the Manchester Martyrs'.[11]

Nevertheless, Fenianism failed, and Irish support switched to the Home Rule League, founded in 1873. In Liverpool its spokesman was the former Fenian John Denvir, first governor of the Catholic Boys' Refuge, first editor of the *Catholic Times*, editor of the *United Irishman* and the *Nationalist*. In 1885 he moved to London as British organiser of the Home Rule Association.[12]

The outstanding Irish Lancastrian in the nationalist movement was Michael Davitt. He came as a child with his family from Mayo to Haslingden in 1850. At the age of 10 he lost an arm in an accident in a cotton mill. As a young man he joined the Fenians, and was imprisoned. In 1879 he formed the Irish National Land League to work for tenant right. He became an M.P. but resigned in protest at the Boer War. He founded *The Labour World* in which he urged the trade unions to sponsor their own parliamentary candidates, and therefore ranks among the founding fathers of the British Labour Party. He died in Dublin in 1906, and was commemorated in St Mary's, Haslingden, by the organ and by a tablet unveiled at a High Mass.[13]

The great triumph of Irish nationalism in England was the election of T. P. O'Connor as Nationalist MP for Liverpool Scotland in 1885, a seat he held until 1929. Short of seceding from England and joining the Irish Free State, Catholic Lancashire could go no further in its assertion of its Irish nationalism.[14]

Italian nationalism was the catalyst of the Ultramontanism imposed on the Church during the pontificate of Pius IX (1846-1878). After an initial flirtation with Italian liberalism, the Pope was convinced by the revolution of 1848 that Christendom was in apostasy, and that the appropriate response for Catholics was loyalty to the papacy, unity amongst themselves, and separation from the rest of the world. In 1854 the papal definition of the dogma of the Immaculate Conception of the Blessed Virgin Mary marked the first major expression of papal claims. In 1864 in the encyclical *Quanta Cura* and the Syllabus of Errors he condemned 'progress, liberalism, and modern civilization' (quoted in Vidler). Non-Catholic Liberals like Cavour and Gladstone could ignore such sanctions but Liberal Catholics like Montalembert, who wanted 'a free Church in a free State' (quoted in Vidler), and Acton could not. The First Vatican Council ended in 1870 with the definition of papal infallibility.[15]

The less reactionary attitude of Pope Leo XIII (1878-1903) encouraged some Catholic scholars such as Loisy to attempt to reconcile modern Biblical criticism with Catholicism, but this modernism was condemned in 1907 by the encyclical *Pascendi Dominici Gregis* and the syllabus *Lamentabili Sane* issued by Pope Pius X (1903-1914).[16]

The immediate effect on Lancashire of this new temper was the restoration of the English hierarchy in 1850. The Lancashire district was divided into the new dioceses of Liverpool and Salford. Cheshire, which had been part of the old Lancashire district, was included in the new diocese of Shrewsbury. The diocese of Liverpool was to have included the Isle of Man, and the hundreds of West Derby, Amounderness, and Lonsdale, whilst Salford was to have included the hundreds of Salford, Blackburn, and Leyland. However, this arrangement would have cut the diocese of Liverpool in two, so in 1851 Leyland was transferred from Salford to Liverpool. Unfortunately this division, giving Liverpool roughly twice as many churches, priests, and people as Salford created a serious imbalance between what were originally intended to be two roughly equal dioceses. As a result when in 1911 England was divided into three provinces, it was Liverpool that was elevated into an archdiocese at the head of the northern province including Salford, Leeds, Middlesbrough, and Hexham and Newcastle.[17]

To the Anglo-Gallican Cisalpines who had campaigned so long for the restoration of the hierarchy it was disappointing. As far as Rome was concerned the English Church was still a missionary Church. The English bishops continued to be subject to the Congregation of Propaganda until 1908. Canons were appointed, but they did not form clerical cathedral communities, and they had no right even to elect their own dean, still less their bishop. Parishes were not established until 1918: the local congregations and their churches remained missions, and their priests could be appointed and removed at the will of the bishop. Rock and his friend Tierney petitioned Rome for the complete restoration of the hierarchy, but without success. Instead of a proper hierarchy in which bishops, priests, and laity exercised their rights, the bishops remained subject to the pope, and the priests to the bishops. The next step was to subject the laity to the priests.[18]

The first bishop of Liverpool, George Hilary Brown (1850-56) had already in 1844 as vicar apostolic of Lancashire abolished the lay patronage of missions. His coadjutor and successor, Alexander Goss (1856-72), set about restricting the gentry's right to appoint their chaplains where these chaplains were also the local missioners. Thus in 1860 he vetoed the appointment by Major Blundell of a Capuchin or Vincentian to the chaplaincy-mission at Little Crosby. He also refused to allow the gentry to have the Blessed Sacrament reserved in their private chapels. When he refused this privilege to Sir Robert Gerard he was accused of an inclination 'to sacrifice the liberties of the English Church to Italian notions acquired by a Roman education' (quoted by Doyle). Goss replied that he could not grant permission because 'the government of the bishops was reduced to a more constitutional form, and hence the bishops do not now possess the extensive authority enjoyed by their predecessors. During the persecution also the laws of the Church were in abeyance, and hence many things were allowed which are now prohibited' (quoted by Doyle), a classic expression of the propensity of clerics to invoke canon law to allow them to do what they intend to do anyway.[19]

Goss was hostile to Roman interference with his own authority. 'The dealings of Rome, at any time, with the bishops,' he wrote, 'have been of the ferula and bonbons type; they are not dealt with as grown-up men but as difficult children' (quoted by Doyle). He insisted that 'we are not Italians but Englishmen'(quoted by Doyle). As the Ultramontane Cardinal Wiseman told Propaganda, Goss was always telling his people, 'I am English, I am a real John Bull, indeed I am a Lancashire man' (quoted by Doyle). When Acton and Simpson's Liberal Catholic magazine the *Rambler* was censured by Propaganda in 1862 for attacking the temporal sovereignty of the papacy, Goss complained that 'Rome is only Manning in Italian. It learns all from him and acts by his suggestion. ... Rome lives in an ideal world in a cloud of incense offered by the nauseous *Tablet, Universe* [*L'Univers*], *Civilta* and *Osservatore.* Who is Herbert Vaughan or Veuillot to dictate a Catholic policy to the world?' (quoted by Doyle). Accordingly he was the only English bishop not to issue a pastoral condemning the *Rambler*. Ill-health prevented his attending the Vatican Council, but he denounced the infallibilists led by Manning: 'Truth, staple English truth, seems to have departed from the whole faction. I generally believe any assertion which they are unanimous in contradicting' (quoted by Doyle). He feared that infallibility would change 'the patriarchal sceptre' into 'the dictator's truncheon' (quoted by Doyle).[20]

From the Italian State's annexation of the Papal States in 1860 until its annexation of Rome in 1870, the litmus test for Liberalism and Ultramontanism was the question of the temporal sovereignty of the papacy. Michael James Whitty, an Irish immigrant, the editor of the *Liverpool Daily Post* (quoted by Burke), proclaimed in 1860 that 'frankly accepted and boldy turned to acount, the loss of the Temporal Power might have secured to the Catholic Church a new lease of life, more vigorous and beneficent that it had ever yet enjoyed', and he asserted that 'the Ultramontanes did not represent the Roman Catholics of England and Ireland'. His rival, the convert S. B. Harper, the editor of the *Liverpool Northern Press* (quoted by Burke), complained that 'the Pope may fall to the ground for all these liberal minded Catholics care. Catholics are to blame for the shame and obloquy that has of late been thrown on their religion. We truckle to the spirit of the world; we sneak along, and hide our honest feelings, because we are too cowardly to stand up for them and bear the battle with the world'. In 1870 a detachment of Papal Zouaves, volunteers in the Papal army, arrived in Liverpool to be feted in a public lunch. One of them, Francis Woodwark, fell fatally ill, and was buried at Anfield in the presence of his comrades.[21]

Threatened by the hostile forces of the modern world, of which Italian Liberalism was only the most manifest to the papacy, Catholics responded by trying to separate themselves from that world, rather like the early Christians in the midst of the pagan Roman empire. Indeed, as the old order collapsed, Protestants, Liberals, and Socialists, as well as Catholics, retreated (in McLeod's words) into 'self-built ideological ghettos', and sectarianism came to provide for many, like the immigrant Irish, 'the strongest basis for social identity'. Nowhere was this process more obvious than in education.[22]

From the late 18th century, if not before, Anglicans, Nonconformists, and Catholics had attempted to provide some formal education for the poor. It consisted of the three Rs, reading, writing, and arithmetic, together with the fourth R, religion. Short of funds and teachers, schools adopted the monitorial system whereby the abler older pupils passed on instruction to the younger. Eventually some monitors would go as pupil teachers to train to become qualified teachers. Nevertheless, these voluntary schools were unable to keep up with the expanding population.[23]

Accordingly they turned increasingly to the government for help. Government was aware of the benefit of education in creating a law-abiding population. It was also responsive to the demands of an industrial economy for literate, numerate workers. Advancing democracy also created a demand for an educated mass electorate.

The result was increasing financial assistance from government accompanied by increasing government intervention. The first government grant was made to the Protestant schools in 1833. Meanwhile the Factory Act of 1802 had made provision for the teaching of children employed in factories, and this provision was included in the Factory Act of 1833 which fixed the minimum age for factory workers at nine, and the Factory Act of 1844 which reduced working hours but reduced the minimum age to eight. The revised education code of 1862, which remained in effect until 1890, introduced payment by results, that is, it made the government grants proportionate to the pupils' attendance and performance in examinations in the three Rs.

Forster's Education Act of 1870 made universal elementary education available by providing for the establishment of local board schools financed out of the rates where there were insufficient church school places. The school leaving age was fixed at ten in 1876, and increased to eleven in 1893, and to twelve in 1899, and Mundela's Education Act of 1880 made elementary education compulsory. Meanwhile elementary education became free in practice in 1891 though it was not until 1918 that it became free in law. Balfour's Education Act of 1902 made local government responsible for the finance and administration of elementary education, and allowed it to aid secondary and technical education. By the beginning of the 20th century, therefore, a system of universal, compulsory, free, elementary education had been established, within which Catholic schools functioned along with Anglican and council (formerly board) schools, the Nonconformists having dropped out.

The first Catholic approach for government funds towards education was made by the Catholic Institute, set up in 1838 as a representative body for the Catholic laity, with branches in Liverpool and Manchester. It found that some 30,000 Catholic children were receiving formal education but that 35,000 were not. In 1845 therefore it made a public appeal for donations, and in 1847 its chairman, Charles Langdale, opened negotiations with the government. In 1847 the bishops appointed the Catholic Poor Schools Committee, with Langdale as chairman, to act as the Church's representatives, and in that year it received a government grant.[24]

The test case in these negotiations was a formal application for a grant towards the Catholic school at Blackburn. By 1818 there was a Catholic Sunday school in Blackburn, and by 1820 there existed a free school with a full-time lay teacher. Teacher and pupils walked in the procession for the coronation of William IV, and they did so again, placed between the Presbyterians and the Methodists, in 1838 for the coronation of Victoria. The school was partly financed by annual sermons, which in 1834 were supported by Blackburn Choral Society and by a part of a regimental band playing Mozart. In 1848 a local Poor Schools Committee was formed to receive its share of the national grant. Moreover, in 1850 the Catholic mill-owners John and Thomas Sparrow established a factory school where the Catholic children were given religious instruction. In the same year the Notre Dame nuns arrived to take over the parochial schools. In their struggles to secure good attendance and examination results (offering to pupils the bribe of a post-examination tea-party), in their failings (the monitor caught playing with his class instead of teaching), and in their humanity (a half-timer having fallen asleep in class was sent into a little room to get some sleep so that he could get up at a quarter past five in the morning to go to work in the factory), the Blackburn schools were typical of these Catholic parish schools. They remained, like the Church as a whole, excessively dependent on women. In Blackburn in 1866, 24 girls presented themselves for examination as pupil teachers compared to only two boys.[25]

By 1910 the diocese of Liverpool had 175 elementary schools with 74,100 pupils and 1,720 teachers, and Salford had 140 elementary schools with 55,000 pupils and 1,591 teachers.[26]

Catholic education was assisted by the proliferation of active religious congregations, especially of women. They provided teams of specialists to meet the new social circumstances. As international bodies under pontifical jurisdiction they fitted Ultramontane ideals. They also provided women with the opportunity of a professional career.[27]

The Sisters of Notre Dame de Namur came to England in 1845 at the invitation of the Redemptorists. By the end of the 1850s they were running schools in Blackburn, Liverpool, Manchester, Wigan, and St Helens, and in 1868 in Southport. In each they ran a variety of parochial schools for the poor—elementary, evening, and Sunday schools—together with secondary schools for the fee-paying middle class, which helped to finance their work. They also ran the Catholic women's teacher training college at Mount Pleasant in Liverpool, established in 1855.[28]

Native congregations included the Sisters of the Cross and Passion, founded in Manchester in 1851 by Elizabeth Prout (Mother Mary Joseph) under the influence of the Passionist Father Rossi. Originally intended as a means of sanctification for working-class women who would continue to earn their living in the factories, the congregation soon adopted teaching as its active vocation and means of finance.[29]

As the women religious pioneered Catholic secondary education for girls, the men religious did so for boys. In 1842 at the suggestion of Cardinal Acton, the Jesuits opened a day school in Liverpool to provide secondary education for boys. In 1851 it was formally re-constituted as St Francis Xavier's College, and by 1883 with 400 pupils it was the largest Catholic secondary day school in England. The Jesuits also set up Preston Catholic College in 1860. The Xaverian Brothers established the Xaverian College at Manchester in 1860 (St Bede's, Manchester, established in 1875 under the Salford diocesan clergy was an exception), the Irish Christian Brothers St Edward's, Liverpool, in 1900, and the De La Salle Brothers, De La Salle Grammar School at St Helens in 1911.[30]

Additional provision was also made for the training of priests. Salford diocese in particular recruited priests from the seminary at Bruges, which between 1859 and 1873 trained English, Belgian, and Dutch priests to work in England. Bishop Vaughan set up a seminary of pastoral theology attached to Salford cathedral to complete this training. The Bruges college helped to produce such men as John Lathouwers, ordained at Ushaw in 1875, who served in Salford, Darwen, Blackley, Oldham, Blackburn, Nottinghamshire, and Manchester, before his death in 1906. Liverpool diocese established a junior seminary at St Edward's, Liverpool, and then in 1883 opened a senior seminary at St Joseph's, Upholland. As a result of these measures, the number of secular priests in the diocese of Liverpool increased from 58 in 1850 to 246 in 1890, though in 1894 the Rev. George Teebay argued that the expenditure of £240,000 in twenty years had not produced value for money, and by 1910 it had increased to 333.[31]

The parochial work of the secular clergy was supplemented by the new religious congregations dedicated to providing popular missions aimed at strengthening the converted and converting the lost. The mission consisted of a series of services, including sermons, over a number of days, culminating in a renewal of baptismal vows. In 1845 the Passionists, led by Dominic Barberi, were established at Sutton in St Helens, and in 1851 the Redemptorists were established at Bishop Eton in Liverpool.[32]

The Ultramontane Church responded to a whole range of social needs, a concern personified by Monsignor James Nugent in Liverpool, and commemorated by his statue in St John's Gardens. Born in the city in 1822, educated at Ushaw and Rome, and ordained in 1846, Nugent worked in Blackburn and Wigan before returning to Liverpool in 1853. He founded schools, invited the Notre Dame nuns to Liverpool, preached temperance, served as chaplain to Walton gaol, and above all, sought to 'Save the Boy'. He set up the Boys' Refuge where he housed 500 saved from the streets, and in 1870 he began the programme of settling the orphanage boys in Canada and the United States. Inspired by Nugent, agencies were founded to care for the orphaned and the blind.[33]

Similar provision was made in the diocese of Salford, especially under Bishop Vaughan. Born in Gloucester in 1832, and educated at Stonyhurst, Brugelette, Downside, and Rome, Herbert Vaughan was ordained in 1854 for the Westminster diocese. In 1866 he began the Mill Hill College to train priests for the foreign missions, but in 1872 he was appointed bishop of Salford, a see he held until he was promoted to Westminster in 1892. He was Ultramontane in his respect for the papacy, insisting on Peter's Pence being collected in his diocese, and in his Marian devotion, distributing de Montfort's book to the clergy. He was an efficient administrator who placed the finances of the diocese on a firm foundation by his insistence on paying off the capital as well as the interest of any debts incurred to build churches. He was jealous of his episcopal authority, forbidding the Jesuits to open a school in Manchester, and securing the papal bull which regulated the relations of the religious orders with the bishop in favour of the latter. He was responsible for establishing the Catholic Protection and Rescue Society to care for orphans and to run houses which would take Catholic children from the workhouses.[34]

 The clergy and the religious were seconded in their charitable concern by lay activists. Organised in such bodies as the Society of St Vincent de Paul, the active laity endeavoured to extend practical charity towards the poor, collecting and distributing money to the old, the sick, and the unemployed. Moreover, Catholic societies and guilds provided leisure and recreational facilities within a framework of Catholic observance and spirituality.[35]

The laity produced their own leaders, such as the convert John Yates (1807-1878). He was a Liverpool solicitor who helped to form the Catholic Defence Association and the committees which raised the funds to build St Francis Xavier's and St Mary's. A Liberal politician, he was elected a town councillor, a member of the school board, and a poor law guardian. Yates was typical of the new middle-class lay leadership of the Victorian Church.[36]

7 *The Nugent Memorial, St John's Gardens, Liverpool. By permission of Mr. Brian Plumb.*

An attempt to concert these activities was made by Louis Charles Casartelli, a Mancunian of Italian descent who was bishop of Salford from 1903 until 1925. In 1906 he set up the Catholic Federation to co-ordinate the work of existing Catholic societies within the diocese and to mobilise Catholic opinion to defend Catholic interests. However, the Federation was condemned by the United Irish League for its intervention over education in the Manchester North West by-election of 1908, and its popular support collapsed.[37]

The Ultramontane clergy led by Wiseman, including some of the Oxford converts led by Faber, introduced Italian practices and devotions. These included the wearing by the clergy of cassock and biretta outside services, the everyday wearing of black suits and Roman collars, the replacement of the old English pronunciation of Latin—'continental vowels with English consonants'—by the Italian pronunciation, nicknamed 'cheese and chaws' by the old English Catholics (according to Haile and Bonney), the lighting of candles before images of the Blessed Virgin Mary and saints, and the increased celebration of benediction and exposition of the Blessed Sacrament (often sung throughout the English-speaking world to settings by the Preston-born Benedictine Joseph Egbert Turner), including the *quarante ore* or forty-hours exposition.[38]

The public manifestations of this piety were the Whit walks which processed through the Lancashire towns from the mid-19th century onwards. The first Catholic walk in Manchester was in 1844. Beginning with the singing of the Catholic anthem 'Faith of our Fathers', Catholics paraded through the crowded streets with their vestments, banners, uniforms, and brass bands in a colourful demonstration of religious allegiance.[39]

The Ultramontanes turned to contemporary Rome for inspiration but Pugin and his supporters looked to medieval England, and were denounced as Gallicans by Faber. Pugin sought the conversion of England by the revival of plainchant and the restoration of Gothic architecture, and the means, if not the end, of his programme were realised.[40]

In 1903 the *motu proprio* of Pope Pius X reasserted plainsong as the liturgical music of the Latin rite, permitted the use of polyphonic choral music, and restricted the use of musical instruments other than the organ, in effect banning the use of orchestral music in church.[41]

Although Pugin was unsuccessful in his attempt to revive the use of Gothic vestments and of rood screens, he was overwhelmingly successful in the revival of Gothic architecture, and Catholic Lancashire was endowed with a wealth of neo-Gothic churches, often accompanied by Gothic schools. Restricted by financial considerations, Pugin and his disciples frequently built in the lancet or Early English style but occasionally they could let themselves go with the Decorated style. Pugin built his archetypal Early English St Wilfrid's, Hulme, Manchester, in 1842, and the Decorated St Oswald's, Old Swan, Liverpool, of which only his steeple survives, in 1842, and the Decorated St John the Evangelist's, The Willows, Kirkham, paid for by the Gillows, in 1845. His son, E. W. Pugin, built St Vincent de Paul's, Liverpool, in 1856, St Mary's, Barrow-in-Furness, in 1866, St Anne's, Stretford, in 1867, (what Pevsner calls) his 'showpiece' St Francis's, Gorton, Manchester, in 1867, and (what Pevsner calls) his 'masterwork' All Saints, Barton-upon-Irwell in 1867. Scoles built St Francis Xavier's, Liverpool, in 1849. J. A. Hansom built his towering St Walburge's, Preston, in 1854, and possibly his finest, Holy Name, Chorlton-on-Medlock, Manchester, in 1871. Clutton built Our Lady's, Formby, in 1864, and St Michael's, Ditton, in 1879. Paley built St Peter's, Lancaster, in 1859. These are only a few of the more outstanding churches listed and described by Pevsner, and elucidated by Little. They were enriched with stained glass, frescoes, mosaics, tiles, metalwork, woodwork, and so on by a host of craftsmen whose work requires a Betjeman to do them justice.[42]

The Ultramontanes wanted miracles, and they got them officially at Lourdes, La Salette, Knock, and Fatima. Not surprisingly in the resulting emotionally charged atmosphere of sentimental piety, they apparently got them in Lancashire too. Teresa Helena Higginson, born at Holywell, in 1844, was brought up in a devout Catholic family frequently visited by Barberi and Faber. She worked as a teacher at Bootle, Clitheroe, Newchurch, Orrell, Osbaldestone, St Helens, Wigan, and elsewhere. She practised extreme mortification, not only fasting but also wearing thorns and barbed wire. She frequently went into ecstatic trance, and rumours of diabolic attacks, divine revelations, and supernatural manifestations—stigmata and miraculous communions—surrounded her. She declared herself entrusted with a divine mission to encourage devotion to the Sacred Head of Jesus as the seat of the divine wisdom. She died in Devon, but was buried at Neston on the Wirral.[43]

Fin de siècle Catholic Lancashire found its expression in the poetry of Hopkins and Thompson. Hopkins was trained as a Jesuit at Stonyhurst and then taught there before serving as a curate at St Joseph's, Leigh, and at St Francis Xavier's, Liverpool. He felt 'born to deal with them [the Lancastrians]. Religion ... enters very deep'. Although his poems were not published until 1918, after his death, it was in Lancashire that he wrote *At A Wedding March*, *Felix Randal*, *Spring and Fall*, and *Ribblesdale*, the last in praise of its 'sweet landscape'. Francis Thompson, born in Preston in 1859, was brought up in Ashton-under-Lyne, and educated at Ushaw and Manchester University, where he became addicted to laudanum, and then fled to London. His *Poems* were published in 1893, and his collected works in 1913, after his death in 1907. He remained devoted to Lancashire and the Church, to 'my own red roses' and 'the beauty of Thy house'.[44]

Transformed by the Industrial Revolution, by Irish immigration, and by Ultramontanism, Catholic Lancashire entered the 20th century as a peculiar combination of isolated provincialism and exotic cosmopolitanism. Its people left their factories and their terraced streets to kneel in Gothic churches, lit by stained glass and candle light, as amidst clouds of incense, to the sound of Latin chant the priest performed his daily miracle.

Notes

1. J. F. Supple-Green, *The Catholic Revival in Yorkshire*, 1850-1900 (1990); E. I. Watkin, *Roman Catholicism in England from the Reformation to 1850* (1957), pp.180-1; G. Connolly, 'The Transubstantiation of Myth', *JEH*, vol.35 (1) (1984).
2. Walton, pp.198-324.
3. P. Hughes, 'The English Catholics in 1850' in G.A. Beck (ed.), *The English Catholics 1850-1950* (1950), pp.42-85.
4. *CE*, vol.9, pp.314-5, vol.13, pp.399-400.
5. Walton, p.252; D. Gwynn, 'The Irish Immigration' in Beck, *English Catholics*, pp.264-90.
6. Walton, pp.252-54, 261-62; E.D.Steele, 'The Irish Presence in the North of England', *NH*, vol.12 (1976); F. Neal, *Sectarian Violence: The Liverpool Experience, 1819-1914* (1988); Neal, 'A Criminal Profile of the Liverpool Irish', *THSLC*, vol.140 (1991).
7. Steele, *NH*, vol.12, pp.239-40.
8. E. E. Y. Hales, *The Catholic Church in the Modern World* (1958), pp.168-78; Gwynn, *English Catholics*, pp.264-90; Steele, *NH*, vol.12, pp. 221-41; Plumb, *Found Worthy* (1986), p.1.
9. W. J. Lowe, 'The Lancashire Irish and the Catholic Church, 1846-71: the social dimension', *Irish Historical Studies*, vol.20 (78) (1976); Lowe, *The Irish in Mid-Victorian Lancashire* (1989); T. McGrath, 'The Tridentine Evolution of Modern Irish Catholicism, 1563-1962', *RH*, vol.20 (4) (1991).
10. Steele, *NH*, vol.12, p.236.
11. Burke, p.88; Steele, *NH*, vol.12, pp.230-1; Plumb, *Found Worthy*, p.92.
12. Burke, p.167; Steele, *NH*, vol.12, p.224.
13. J. Dunleavy, *Haslingden Catholics 1815-1965* (1987); Bolton, p.176.
14. Walton, p.262; Burke, p.243.
15. Vidler, pp.146-56; Hilton, 'Acton: Liberal Catholic Historian', *Worcestershire Recusant*, vol.42 (1983).
16. Vidler, pp.179-89.
17. G. Albion, 'The Restoration of the Hierarchy' in Beck, *English Catholics*, pp.86-115; Bolton, p.130; M. V. Sweeney, 'Diocesan Organisation and Administration' in Beck, *English Catholics*, p.148.
18. Sweeney, *English Catholics*, pp.117, 148; J. D. Holmes, *More Roman than Rome* (1978), pp. 86-7; Ward, *Sequel*, vol.2, pp. 289-90.
19. Plumb, *Arundel to Zabi*; P. H. Doyle, 'Bishop Goss and the Gentry', *NWCH*, vol.12I (1985).
20. Doyle, 'Bishop Goss of Liverpool (1856-1872) and the Importance of Being English' in S. Mews (ed.), *Religion and National Identity* (Studies in Church History, vol.18, 1982): Holmes, pp.121-3.
21. Hales, pp.122-30; Burke, pp.144-7, 201.
22. McLeod, p.36.
23. S. J. Curtis, *History of Education in Great Britain* (1963), pp.184-339.
24. Ward, *Sequel*, vol.1, p.195-98, vol.2, pp.146-58; M. Whitehead, 'Briefly, and in confidence', *RH*, vol.20 (4) (1991).
25. Conlon, pp.48-53, 62-74.
26. CE, vol.9, pp.314-15, vol.13, pp.399-409.
27. McLeod, p.49; E. Cruise, 'Development of the Religious Orders' in Beck, *English Catholics*, pp.442-74; W. J. Battersby, 'Educational Work of the Religious Orders of Women' in Beck, *English Catholics*, pp.337-66; S. O'Brien, '10,000 Nuns', *Catholic Archives*, vol.9 (1989); O'Brien, 'Terra Incognita', *Past and Present*, vol.121 (1988).
28. The Foundations of the Sisters of Notre Dame (1895).
29. O'Brien, *Past and Present*, vol.121, pp.124-8.
30. Battersby, 'Secondary Education for Boys' in Beck, *English Catholics*, pp.322-36; Whitehead, 'Charles Januarius Acton (1803-1847) and the Liverpool Beginnings of English Catholic Secondary Day-School Education' in Hilton, *Loveable West*.
31. S. Forster, 'The English Seminary, Bruges', *NWCH*, vol.12 (1985); Bolton, p.313; Burke, p.72; *Upholland Centenary* (1983); Plumb, *Found Worthy*, pp.iii, vi.

32. D. Attwater, *The Catholic Encyclopaedic Dictionary* (1931), p.346; Ward, *Sequel*, vol.2, p.178; Plumb, 'Some Religious Orders in the North West', *NWCH*, vol.16 (1989).

33. Plumb, *Found Worthy*, p.111; C. Bennett, *Father Nugent of Liverpool* (1949); Burke, passim; J. Davies, 'The Catholic Community and Social Welfare Provision', *NWCH*, vol.18 (1991).

34. Plumb, *Arundel to Zabi*; Holmes, pp.199-246; O. P. Rafferty, 'The English Jesuit College, Manchester, 1875', *RH*, vol.20 (2) (1990).

35. Davies, 'Parish Charity', *NWCH*, vol.17 (1990); L. Warren, 'Hard Times in Catholic Preston' in Hilton, *Catholic Englishmen*.

36. J. Dunleavy, 'The Emergence of the New Laity in Nineteenth-Century England: John Yates', *NWCH*, vol.14 (1987).

37. Plumb, *Arundel to Zabi*; Dunleavy, 'Schools To-day, Home Rule To-morrow', *NWCH*, vol.16 (1989); P. Hughes, 'The Coming Century' in Beck, *English Catholics*, pp.38-9.

38. Haile and Bonney, pp.304-10, 353-55; Holmes, *More Roman than Rome*, pp.69-71; Ward, *Sequel*, vol.1, pp.82-121, vol.2, pp. 255-72; Plumb, 'A Victorian Monk-Musician', *Ampleforth Journal*, vol.79 (2) (1974).

39. S. Fielding, 'The Catholic Whit-Walk in Manchester and Salford 1890-1939', *Manchester Region History Review*, I (1) (1987).

40. Holmes, *More Roman than Rome*, pp.69-71.

41. Attwater, *Catholic Encylopaedic Dictionary*, pp.354-5.

42. K. Clark, *The Gothic Revival* (1964), pp.106-33; R. Dixon and S. Muthesius, *Victorian Architecture* (London, 1985), pp.182-92, 236-39; Little, pp.66-164; Pevsner, *Lancs: South*, pp.32-4, 40-2, 106, 154, 221, 250, 307, 326, 331, 404; Pevsner, *Lancs: North*, pp.31-2, 56, 122, 150, 155, 199-200.

43. Plumb, 'Teresa Helena Higginson (1844-1905)', *NWCH*, vol.18 (1991).

44. J. McDermott (ed.), *Hopkins in Lancashire* (1989); McDermott (ed.), *Francis Thompson: Selected Writings* (1987).

Chapter VIII

Indian Summer, 1918-65

In the middle of the 20th century Catholic Lancashire possessed a self-confidence, which it had not known since its ascendancy under James II, and a real security, which it had not had since the Reformation. It had an autonomous hierarchy, its population was growing, and it was making a successful attempt to provide a formal Catholic education for all its numerous children. Within its self-imposed ghetto a warm sub-culture fermented and expanded.

In his sermon 'The Second Spring', preached at the first provincial synod of Westminster in 1852, Newman had characterised English Catholic history in a form which has acquired widespread acceptance within and without the Catholic community: 'The English Church was, and the English Church was not, and the English Church is once again ... It is the coming in of a Second Spring...'. He looked back to a time when there was 'No longer the Catholic Church in the country; nay, no longer a Catholic community ... not a sect, not even an interest, not a body, however small, representative of the Great Communion abroad,—but a mere handful of individuals... Here a set of poor Irishmen ... There, perhaps an elderly person ... of good family, and a "Roman Catholic"'. Newman was, of course, right about the hierarchy, but as an Oxford convert he neglected the survival and growth of the Lancashire Catholic community. Nevertheless, his view of English Catholic history became the authorised version.[1]

For the pioneering historian of Catholic Lancashire, a native Lancastrian Catholic, Dom F. O. Blundell, OSB, writing in 1938, it had been 'the Catholic army, for years fighting a retiring action, it is true, but only awaiting the dawn of emancipation ... to carry everthing before them ... so that the Catholic church in Lancashire to-day enjoys a fervour in numbers and in the spirit of religion, which is equalled nowhere else'. Similarly in the foreword to a collection of historical essays published to mark the centenary of the restoration of the hierarchy, Cardinal Griffin, Archbishop of Westminster, contrasted 'the small numbers and meagre resources' of 1850 with the position in 1950 when Catholics were 'a real force'. Again, Bishop Marshall of Salford in the preface to the centennial history of his diocese declared that 'to see something of the power, the beauty, and the prestige of Catholic life in a great metropolis like Manchester, let him [the reader] come to the Whit Friday procession and he will witness a public demonstration of religious faith and piety that probably has no rival anywhere in the land'.[2]

As Protestantism declined a Triumphalist Catholicism stood face to face with infidelity and prepared itself for the conversion of England. It was inspired and directed by an Ultramontane papacy which emphasised Catholic devotion to the Eucharist and to the Blessed Virgin Mary. Pope Pius X (1903-1914), who had encouraged frequent communion and reduced the age at which children could make their first communion, was canonised in 1954 by Pope Pius XII (1939-1958), who in 1953 also reduced the eucharistic fast, permitted evening Mass, and in 1950 defined the dogma of the Assumption of the Blessed Virgin Mary. If the mid-19th century was a second spring, then, viewed from the colder climate of the end of this century, the mid-20th century looks like an Indian summer.[3]

This Triumphalism was reflected in the development of ecclesiastical organisation. In 1908 the English hierarchy had been freed from its dependence on the Vatican missionary congregation of Propaganda. In 1918 a new code of canon law was introduced which elevated the local churches, hitherto missions, into parishes. The rector of a parish was appointed for life and was irremovable save by due process of canon law. However, the bishops used the need to keep parishes free for priests serving as forces chaplains during World War II to appoint mere adminstrators removable at episcopal will, a device which continued to be used after the war was over. Moreover, the laity were given no share in parochial government and the very idea that they should have one could be dismissed as counter-productive by the historian of ecclesiastical organisation: 'It is probably as well then that parish councils did not exist when the missions were built up, since it is doubtful whether any of the parishes would have been founded at all'.[4]

In 1911 the Northern province of Liverpool was created with the diocese of Liverpool elevated into an archdiocese under its bishop Thomas Whiteside (1894-1921), described by the Liberal politician Augustine Birrell (quoted by Plumb) as 'the mildest man who ever slit a throat'. The bishops of Salford, Leeds, Middlesbrough, Hexham and Newcastle became his suffragans. However, separate provincial synods did not replace the hierarchy of England and Wales meeting together regularly as a body.[5]

The Vatican still continued to interfere directly in diocesan organisation. The division of the large archdiocese of Liverpool into its largely urban southern and mainly rural northern parts had long been conjectured, but Archbishop Keating (1921-1928) was opposed to such a separation because of the expenses incurred by the expansion of Upholland College and the decision to build Liverpool Cathedral. Nevertheless, in 1924 the northern hundreds of Amounderness and Lonsdale were detached from Liverpool and joined with the counties of Cumberland and Westmorland, hitherto parts of Hexham and Newcastle, to form the diocese of Lancaster with the Preston-born Benedictine Thomas Wulfstan Pearson as its first bishop. Sixty-seven secular priests were transferred from Liverpool archdiocese and 15 from Hexham and Newcastle, reflecting the respective Catholic populations of the Lancastrian and Cumbrian parts of the new diocese.[6]

This ecclesiastical re-organisation marked real growth in the number of Catholics against a paradoxical background of economic decline and increased prosperity, whilst democracy was finally achieved. Universal adult male suffrage and limited female suffrage were enacted in 1918, followed by universal adult suffrage in 1928.[7]

The 20th century saw Lancashire lose its industrial primacy. The First World War disrupted its cotton industry, and it never really recovered from the loss of its foreign markets. Though it survived in a slimmed-down form, it was no longer 'King Cotton'. The two World Wars provided a boost for the coal, engineering, and chemical industries, but in peace time they all suffered depression, and coal in particular has suffered a fundamental decline. New industries, such as car assembly and aircraft construction, developed in the Liverpool-Manchester axis and around Preston, but cotton and coal, the staple industries of Lancashire's industrial pre-eminence, almost disappeared. There was unemployment, insecurity, and poverty.[8]

At a time when English Catholic thought was dominated by Belloc, the distress called forth an Utopian experiment. 'Getting back to the land' had been an element in the Socialist tradition, and it was the continual theme of the sermons of the Dominican Father Vincent McNabb who preached frequently to large crowds in Lancashire until his death in 1943. In 1935 the Catholic Land Association bought Priorswood Hall and its 119 acres in Parbold to establish a community of unemployed to live off the land. The Benedictine Dom Gregory Buisseret was appointed warden with a farmer, J. Pope, as bailiff. The community was inaugurated by Archbishop Downey in a ceremony attended by crowds from Wigan, St Helens, and Liverpool. However, a single farm could not solve the problem of regional unemployment, and the scheme was finally abandoned in 1950.[9]

The economic gloom was lightened by new cheap pleasures, such as cigarettes, cinemas, and greyhound racing, though the last two eventually gave way to television, whilst drink and sport retained their hold. This was the Lancashire of L. S. Lowry, Gracie Fields, George Formby, and Frank Randle cheerful in adversity. Moreover, the Second World War was followed by increased social spending by government, and in the 1960s and 1970s by economic subsidies to the region. Lancashire reverted to a poor, but subsidised, peripheral region in danger of becoming a vast museum of industrial archaeology. To add insult to injury local government reform detached Furness to Cumbria and Warrington to Cheshire, and divided the rest of the county into monstrosities called 'Lancashire', 'Merseyside' and 'Greater Manchester'. Its people remained insular and conservative, even in their attachment to the Labour Party. In such conditions Catholicism, the most conservative form of western Christianity, flourished.[10]

The consequences of this combination of economic decline and individual prosperity were exemplified in Holy Family parish, New Springs, Aspull, near Wigan. New Springs owed its growth to the coal and iron industries centred on the Kirkless Iron and Steel Works built in 1858. As a result the church of Our Lady of the Immaculate Conception was built in neighbouring Haigh in 1858, and a

Catholic school in 1861. Then in 1887 another Catholic school was opened in New Springs to forestall the opening of a board school which would have provided non-sectarian education. The Catholic school doubled as a chapel, which was served from Haigh until an independent mission was established in 1898. However, in 1930 the Kirkless Works was closed, and the pits followed, leaving only what Orwell described as a 'lunar landscape of slag-heaps'. The population of Aspull fell from 8,388 in 1901 to 6,522 in 1951, whilst the number of baptisms at Holy Family fell from 25 in 1900 to 13 in 1950. The building of new housing in New Springs resulted in an increase of population to 7,522 in 1971 and an increase in the number of baptisms at Holy Family to 20 in 1970. A new church was built in 1959 and a new school in 1972.[11]

Lancashire remained the dynamic centre of an expanding English Catholicism. In 1914 the total Catholic population of England and Wales was 1,860,000 and by 1939 it had grown to 2,360,000, an increase of 26 per cent. By 1965 it had grown to 3, 956,500, an increase of a further 67 per cent. The county continued to have the largest Catholic population. In 1921 the diocese of Liverpool contained 390,713, and Salford 293,400, a total of 684,119 that is 35.7 per cent of the 1,915,473 Catholics in England and Wales. By 1939 the industrial North-West, consisting of Lancashire and parts of Cheshire, contained some 820,000 Catholics, twice as many as the industrial North-East or Greater London and eight times as many as the industrial Midlands. By 1965 Liverpool diocese contained 518,000 Catholics, Salford 380,000, and Lancaster 132,000, a total of 1,030,000, that is 26 per cent of the 3,956,500 Catholics in England and Wales. The Lancashire Catholics were also a significant proportion of the county's population, 15 per cent in 1911 (when Catholics made up five per cent of the national population) and 15 per cent in 1961 (when Catholics made up six per cent of the national population).[12]

This largely natural growth was assisted by the provisions of canon law, which insisted that Catholic children be given a Catholic education, discouraged mixed marriages, required that any children of such marriages be brought up as Catholics, and encouraged the conversion of the non-Catholic partner. One result of this policy, as well as the Church's commitment to conversion, was a steady stream of converts. In 1921 the diocese of Liverpool received 1,502 converts, and Salford 970, a total of 2,472, and in 1960 Liverpool received 1,563, Salford 1,036, and Lancaster 651, a total of 3,250, an increase of 171 per cent. Some 3,000 converts per annum kept the Lancashire Catholic community constantly supplied with new blood.[13]

This growth was also partly caused by continual immigration. The Irish continued to come, though the rate of immigration slowed down. Those already settled were increasingly integrated into the Lancashire Catholic community by marriage and education. The Liverpool Irish, amongst others, volunteered in battalions to serve in the British army in the First World War. The Anglo-Irish war of 1919-1921 did not spill over into Lancashire, and when southern Ireland became independent in 1921 the Irish retained the right of free entry into Britain. The first high commissioner to represent Ireland in Britain was John Dulanty, the Mancunian child of Irish parents, who had been the Manchester representative on the executive of the United Irish League. He had also seen active service in France before being appointed deputy director of the ministry of munitions and establishment officer in the Treasury. Meanwhile the Lancashire Irish transferred their party political allegiance from the Irish Nationalists and the Liberals to Labour. When T. P. O'Connor retired in 1929 his Liverpool parliamentary seat went to Alderman Logan, the Irish Catholic leader of the local Labour Party. For Bill Naughton, born in Ireland and brought as a child to Bolton in 1914, the native Lancastrians seemed to belong to a different world, but to Don Howarth, a Methodist child in Burnley between the World Wars, the Irish and the English developed a common speech, habits, manners, and physique, indistinguishable except for the schools they attended, the churches they lived around, and the Catholic boys' habit of abandoning the Saturday morning game of football to go to confession. At the same time, Catholic Lancashire could seem a province of Ireland with its provincial capital at Liverpool.[14]

After the Second World War significant numbers of Catholics arrived in Lancashire from Europe. By 1965 there were German and Lithuanian congregations with their own chaplains in Manchester, an Italian chaplaincy in Rochdale, and Polish congregations in Manchester, Liverpool, Lancaster, Bolton, Blackburn, Rochdale, and Ashton-under-Lyne. Moreover, the Ukrainians, Byzantine rite Catholics, had parishes in Manchester, Bolton, Oldham, and Rochdale, under their apostolic exarchate headed by their own bishop. There were also Catholics amongst the immigrants from the West Indies, but as English-speaking Roman Catholics they did not form separate congregations.[15]

There was also considerable internal migration, partly spontaneous but largely the result of local government housing policy. Between the two World Wars, especially after the Housing Act of 1924, and after the Second World War there were massive programmes of re-housing, which usually involved uprooting urban working-class populations and moving them into new suburban housing estates. Such a programme could devastate a town-centre parish like St Mary's, Warrington, which lost half its population between 1934 and 1937. It could also transform a suburban parish like West Derby, a middle-class suburb of Liverpool, where the building of the Deysbrook housing estate after the Second World War doubled the population of St Paul's parish to over 4,000 Catholics. These changes took no more account of diocesan than of parish boundaries. In 1926 Manchester corporation purchased the Wythenshawe estate, and embarked on an ambitious long-term programme to re-house the population of its slums there, moving Mancunian Catholics out of the diocese of Salford and into the diocese of Shrewsbury. The Rev. Bernard Coleman, parish priest of St Hilda's, Northenden, made provision for them. He established the parish of SS John Fisher and Thomas More, Wythenshawe, in 1934, and this was followed by St Peter's in 1946, St Anthony's in 1953, St Elizabeth's in 1965, and Sacred Heart in 1967.[16]

The geographical extension and the continued increase in the Catholic population necessitated a massive programme of church building. In 1921 the diocese of Liverpool had 204 churches, chapels, mass-centres, etc, and Salford 146, a total of three hundred and fifty. By 1965 this number had more than doubled. Liverpool had 320, Salford, 283, and Lancaster 162, a total of seven hundred and sixty-five.[17]

In the inter-war years the prevailing style of ecclesiastical architecture was early Christian in both its Byzantine and Romanesque forms with its semi-circular arches and domes. The fashion was set by Westminster Cathedral opened in 1903, and followed by Gernson's Premonstratensian church of Corpus Christi, Miles Platting, Manchester (1906), Powell's St Mary's, Lowe House, St Helens (1924-30), Hill, Sandby, and Norris's St John the Baptist's, Rochdale (1924), Gilby's St Philip Neri's, Catherine Street, Liverpool (1925), and Brocklesby's St Oswald's, Ashton-in-Makerfield (1930). Pevsner dismissed the Italian Romanesque as a dead end, and described the Rochdale church as 'desperately reactionary' and the Ashton church as 'totally outdated', but from a post-Modern vantage-point it is Modernism which appears the dead end that all but some architects always knew it was. The Romanesque style was given a Modernist twist by Velarde who built St Matthew's, Clubmoor, Liverpool (1930), St Monica's, Bootle (1936), St Teresa's, Upholland (1952-57), and St Alexander's, Kirkdale, Liverpool (1955-57). Meanwhile only the crypt of Lutyens' 'Wrennaissance' (an English revival of Renaissance Classicism which drew inspiration from the example of Christopher Wren) Liverpool Cathedral, begun in 1933, was completed in 1940 as a complex of vaults. Interrupted by the war and then abandoned as too expensive, Lutyens' cathedral would have had the largest dome in the world, the final expression of Lancastrian Catholic Triumphalism. Apart from the crypt, the model survives in the Walker Art Gallery, Liverpool, as a reminder of what might have been.[18]

Towards the end of this period the International Modern style with its steel and concrete materials and its circular and polygonal plans appeared in Weightman and Bullen's circular St Mary's, Leyland (1959-64), one of the first signs that Lancastrian Catholicism was to attempt to come to terms with the modern world.[19]

As the Catholic population increased so did the number of priests but the ratio of priests to people was large and getting larger, compared with the national ratio. In 1921 the diocese of Liverpool had 322 seculars and 182 regulars, and Salford had 290 seculars and 85 regulars, a total of 879 or one priest for every 778 Catholics compared with a national ratio of one priest for every 482 Catholics. By 1965 the number of Lancashire's priests had almost doubled, but the ratio of priests to people was even larger. The archdiocese of Liverpool had 537 seculars and 176 regulars, the diocese of Salford 487 seculars and 118 regulars, and Lancaster 216 seculars and 66 regulars, a total of 1,600 or one priest for every 643 Catholics compared with a national ratio of one priest for every 506 Catholics.[20]

The bulk of the priests for Liverpool diocese and many of those for Salford and Lancaster were trained at St Joseph's College, Upholland. Founded in 1883 as the senior seminary for the Liverpool diocese it was emptied of students by the First World War. In 1919 the junior seminary was transferred from St Edward's, Liverpool, to Upholland, and Archbishop Keating decided that the senior seminary should be re-established there under the presidency of Mgr. Joseph Dean. A large Gothic collegiate chapel and new wings forming a great quadrangle were built between 1923 and 1930. It had accommodation for a hundred senior students and 150 junior students. It had a teaching staff of 20 professors. It was also staffed by nuns (the Sisters of Charity from 1918 to 1930, and the Sisters of the Sacred Heart of Jesus and Mary from 1930 to 1975) who supervised the largely resident domestic staff. During the Second World War it also temporarily housed the Beda College, the English seminary for mature students for the priesthood, evacuated from Rome. In the 1960s the increasing number of junior students led to the building of a second quadrangle, financed by selling off some of the works of art bequeathed to the college by its original architect, O'Byrne.[21]

Bishop Thomas Holland of Salford (1964-1983), who was a student there before the Second World War, remembered the discipline enforced on junior students by minor professors (not yet ordained teachers) with written impositions and by priest professors with the sanction of sending a student to be beaten on the hand by the prefect of discipline. He looked back with affection on men like Fr. Wilfrid Finessy (nicknamed 'pa Fin') who taught him Latin, and Fr Cuthbert Waring (nicknamed 'Cuddy') who taught him English, and all those professors who provided him with 'a harmonious pattern of the priesthood'.[22]

8 *St Joseph's College, Upholland. By permission of Aerofilms Limited.*

Anthony Kenny, subsequently master of Balliol College, Oxford, who was a student at Upholland after the Second World War, describes its isolation and its severe discipline. The students were roused at six in the morning, went to the chapel for meditation and Mass, breakfasted at 7.45, and started their studies at 8.35. After lunch there were more classes or games, then the rosary in the chapel, and then more study between 5.30 and 7 p.m.; supper was at 7.15, and the day ended with night prayers in the chapel at 9.15 followed by the great silence. There were two weeks holidays at Christmas and eight weeks in summer. There was expulsion for fraternisation between senior and junior students or with the maids. There were two silent retreats every year with hourly spiritual exercises such as sermons and prayers. The liturgy was sung in plainsong with polyphony for the offertory motet, and the holy week ceremonies were performed with great precision. There were annual performances of pantomimes and of Gilbert and Sullivan operas with women and love removed from the plots. The religious instruction in the junior classes was based on the *Catechism*, and a student's place in the college depended on his performance in Latin. The senior seminary enabled a student to get through a considerable amount of reading, almost as much as a traditional university course.[23]

In addition to training the clergy, massive resources were committed to educating the community's children in response to the state's erection of a national system of universal, free, compulsory secondary education. The dual system in education whereby the state financed its own schools and contributed towards the cost of denominational schools was established by Forster's Education Act of 1902, and, despite attempts to demolish it, remained intact as formal education was increasingly extended to older children. McKenna's Education Act of 1907 increased the powers of local authorities to build their own secondary schools, and created free scholarship places in fee-paying secondary schools. Fisher's Education Act of 1918 banned the employment of children under the age of 12, and fixed the age of compulsory schooling between five and fourteen. In 1926 the Hadow Report recommended a division at the age of 11 between primary and secondary education. The Education Act of 1936 arranged for the school-leaving age to be raised to 15 in 1939, and empowered local education authorities to make grants to denominational secondary schools. By 1939, therefore, parochial schools were educating all Catholic children to the age of 11 and the bulk of them up to 14, whilst some went at 11 as scholarship pupils to the grammar schools, including the few Catholic grammar schools. The Second World War held up the extension of the school-leaving age and led to the evacuation of children from the cities. Towards the end of the war Butler's Education Act of 1944 made provision for the school-leaving age to be raised to 15 in 1947 and later to sixteen. It contained the provision of local authority grants to denominational schools and of government grants for free places in fee-paying secondary schools. It also led to the setting up of the tripartite system of secondary education from the age of 11 with secondary modern, technical, and grammar schools. However, a few local authorities chose to establish comprehensive secondary schools, and these spread—St Gregory's and St Kevin's, Kirkby, led the way for Catholic schools—until in 1965 they replaced the tripartite system.[24]

The Catholic Church was concerned that Catholic children should be educated by Catholic teachers in Catholic schools, and Archbishop Richard Downey of Liverpool (1928-1953) in particular took up the cudgel. In Liverpool, where between the Wars the local Tory Party maintained its tradition of militant Protestantism and one-third of the local Labour councillors were Catholics, this was a particularly contentious issue, but the dual principle was maintained and applied. Nevertheless, the Catholic hierarchy failed to convince successive governments that since Catholics paid their taxes and rates they ought not to pay any more for Catholic education. Government and local authority grants covered only a fraction of the cost of Catholic education, and the Catholic community was saddled with a heavy burden of debt. However, despite the difficulties, a complete system of primary and secondary education was established in Lancashire, though the secondary schools which recruited children from several parishes tended to weaken the links between school and parish.[25]

The four Rs remained the basis of both primary and secondary modern education, and Latin retained its primacy in the grammar schools, though all introduced an increasing range of subjects. The school-day was punctuated by a pattern of prayer, and the 'Penny' *Catechism of Christian Doctrine* had to be learnt by heart. The *Catechism* covered faith by means of the apostles' creed, hope by means of the Our Father and Hail Mary, charity by means of the commandments, and then went on through the sacraments, the virtues, the rule of life, and the daily exercise. The minds of Catholics were engraved with its lapidary formularies all the way from 'God made me' and 'God made me to know Him, love Him, and serve Him in this world, and to be happy with Him for ever in the next' to 'After my night prayers I should observe due modesty in going to bed; occupy myself with the thoughts of death; and endeavour to compose myself to rest at the foot of the cross, and to give my last thoughts to my crucified Saviour'. This education was imparted by the ferocious discipline of constant caning, common to secular, Protestant, and Catholic schools in the period. By some it was considered as inevitable and natural, but it came increasingly to be regarded as wrong by pupils, teachers, and parents.[26]

The Catholic schools were largely dependent for Catholic teachers on the Catholic training colleges. By 1950 there were nine recognised by the Ministry of Education, most of them controlled by religious congregations of women. They included Notre Dame College, Mount Pleasant, Liverpool, with 220 students, and Sedgeley Park, Manchester, with 168 students, run by the Faithful Companions of Jesus. By 1965 De La Salle College, Hopwood Hall, Middleton, had been added to their number.[27]

The grammar schools sent an increasing number of students to the universities. By 1950 most of the universities were provided with part-time chaplains, but at Liverpool and Manchester were the only provincial universities with full-time chaplains. In 1922 the University Catholic Federation of Great Britain was set up, and in

1942 it was divided into the undergraduate Union of Catholic Students and the postgraduate Newman Association. In 1942 the Newman Association had only 20 members but by 1950 they had increased to 1,500. As these graduates entered the professions they provided the Catholic community with a new level of leadership whilst they weakened its social solidarity.[28]

The community continued to look to its bishops for leadership. These included men like Richard Downey, Archbishop of Liverpool from 1928 to 1953. Born in Ireland in 1881, he was brought as a child to Liverpool, educated at St Edward's, Upholland, and Rome. Ordained in 1907, he served as a member of the Catholic Missionary Society, preaching throughout England, until his appointment as vice-rector of Upholland in 1926. He laid the foundation stone of Liverpool Cathedral, and fought to defend and extend Catholic schools. Having laid the foundation stone of St Gregory's School, Weld Bank, Chorley, he collapsed, and died a few weeks later. He was supported by Thomas Henshaw, Bishop of Salford from 1925 to 1938. Born in Manchester in 1873, he was educated at Salford Catholic Grammar School, Lisbon, Ushaw, Paris, and Bonn, and ordained in 1899. He taught at Ushaw and St Bede's, Manchester, and served in various parishes before he became bishop. He and Downey led the opposition to the government proposal in 1930 to transfer denominational schools to local authority control, a plan that was, in Plumb's phrase, 'killed in Liverpool and buried in Manchester'. His interest in education led to the foundation of the De La Salle school at Pendleton, the Salesian school at Bolton, and the Marist school at Blackburn, and he was regarded as the second founder of St Bede's, Manchester. Thomas Wulfstan Pearson, O.S.B., was the first bishop of the diocese of Lancaster from 1924 until his death in 1938. Born in Preston in 1870, he was educated at Douay, entered Downside in 1887, and was ordained in 1897. He taught at Downside until appointed assistant priest to St Mary's, Liverpool, in 1912, and then was appointed prior of St Benedict's, Ealing, in 1916. His episcopate saw the Catholic population of his diocese increase from 88,536 in 1926 to 98,212 in 1936, an increase of 10 per cent, and the number of secular priests increase from eighty to 124, an increase of 55 per cent. His continual exhortation from the pulpit was for daily Mass and Communion: 'Is it not worth it?' The bishops, usually seen only at special events such as confirmations, were formidable but remote from the daily lives of the people.[29]

Immediate leadership was exercised by the parish priests, amongst whom were such heroic figures as Father Shee, the curé d'Ars (St John Vianney, the patron saint of parish priests) of Wigan. Henry Joseph Shee was born at Ainsdale in 1881, and educated at St Edward's, Upholland, Rome, and Paris. He was ordained in 1909, and served as a curate in Preston until in 1924 he became parish priest of St Joseph's in the Wallgate district of Wigan with its 'labyrinths of little brick houses blackened by smoke' described by Orwell and only a few hundred yards from the Wigan Pier, which Orwell could not find but is still there. At St Joseph's Father Shee received 7,000 converts, and was famous as a confessor. He rose at 5 a.m. and entered the confessional to be available to the mill-hands on their way to work. He heard confessions and distributed Holy Communion until 7 when he said Mass, and then went back to the confessional while his curates said their Masses. On Saturday he would enter the confessional at 2.30 p.m., while his curates went to watch Wigan Rugby League Football Club. He emerged at 5 for a cup of tea and then stayed in the confessional until 10 or even later during Lent. He loved personally to decorate the church for the forty hours exposition of the Blessed Sacrament. When he died in 1958 the streets were lined with crowds to see his funeral procession led by the chief constable and the town council.[30]

Nuns remained at the centre of Catholic education, and exercised a wider influence over parochial life. Sister Michael Joseph (Anne McCabe) of the Sisters of St Paul taught at St Marie's school, Southport, from 1915 to 1954. She also acted as sacristan, trained the altar boys, supervised the boys' club, and helped to found the men's club. She died in 1967, aged 79, after more than 50 years as a nun.[31]

The traditional leadership provided by the gentry was disappearing from the towns, though it lingered on in the countryside. In some cases families died out, but in others they left for more salubrious surroundings an environment they had helped to pollute with industry. In 1921 the Gerards, having presided over the exploitation of coal in much of the Wigan coalfield, left for Blakesmere in Hertfordshire, and Garswood Hall was demolished. Sir Francis Anderton, the last of the Andertons of Euxton, Chorley, took up residence in London, but he contributed to local Catholic funds until his death in 1950 when his body was buried in the family tomb at Euxton. The Brethertons, having made their money in trade and retired as gentry to Rainhill, married into the local gentry such as the Gerards and into the European aristocracy. Frederick Stapleton-Bretherton sold the Rainhill estates in 1920, leaving the house to become a Jesuit retreat house, and retired to Hampshire where he died in 1938, and the male line became extinct. Geoffrey Edward de Trafford succeeded to the estates at Croston in 1937. His twin brother had been killed in the First World War, and he himself had been wounded and gassed. When he died in 1960 he left the estate to the archdiocese of Liverpool, which sold it to the Ainscoughs. His sister Ermyntrude Frances Mary de Trafford, the last of the line, died in 1964. The hall was demolished but the family chapel was preserved for the local Catholic congregation. Similar stories could be told about families throughout Lancashire, but here and there the Catholic squires remained ensconced in or near their ancestral homes at the centre of the local congregations. The Reynolds of Woolton, having married into the Gillows of Leighton, still live at Leighton Hall, Yealand Conyers, in its romantically feudal landscape. Towneley Hall was sold to Burnley corporation in 1902, and is now a museum and art gallery, but the family continued to live nearby and to exercise local influence. In 1955 the Towneley heir, Simon Peter Edmund Cosmo William Koch de Gooreynd, assumed the Towneley name. He was appointed a justice of the peace in 1956, served as a county councillor from 1961 to 1964, and in 1976 was appointed lord lieutenant of Lancashire, and has maintained the family tradition of civilised scholarship by writing a book on 17th-century Venetian opera.[32]

An increasingly important rôle was taken by lay professionals, who had long played an important part in teaching. Teresa Mabel Miller graduated in 1926, and obtained her teaching diploma in 1927. She worked in Scotland and then at Padgate, before becoming head teacher at St Peter's school, Woolston, Warrington, a position she held until her retirement in 1968, when she received the papal *Bene Merenti* medal for her services.[33]

Meanwhile a working-class leadership was already being exerted in public affairs, largely through the Labour movement. Liverpool, where in 1929 one third of its Labour councillors were Catholics, and the Catholic Alderman Logan was elected M.P., was outstanding in the strength of its Catholic representation. In Southport Councillor T. Hampson was elected mayor in 1917. In Warrington Austin Matthew Crow was elected mayor in 1933. Perhaps the most outstanding was Joseph Gormley. Born in 1917, and educated at St Oswald's school, Ashton-in-Makerfield, he began work in the coal mines at the age of fourteen. He joined the Labour movement, became a local councillor, was elected to the national executive of the National Union of Mineworkers in 1957, became general secretary of the north west area of the N.U.M. in 1961, joined the national executive of the Labour Party in 1963, was elected president of the N.U.M. in 1971, and joined the general council of the Trades Union Congress in 1973. He retired from the N.U.M. leadership, and was created a life peer in 1982.[34]

Then there were the activists who sustained parochial life as house-keepers, sacristans, altar-servers, organists, choristers, and so on, and joined the societies dedicated to good works, such as the Saint Vincent de Paul Society, the Legion of Mary, the Young Christian Workers Movement, and the Catholic Women's League. For example, William McKenna was a founder member of the St Vincent de Paul Society in the parish of St Mary's, Ulverston in 1913, and continued to serve it until his death in 1965. They also included outstanding figures like Patrick Keegan (1916-90), born in Hindley, Wigan, who was a founder member of the Young Christian Workers in 1937, and rose to become not only its national president but also its first international president.[35]

Finally there were the ordinary parishioners in the pews, the faithful and the not so faithful. They included people like Bill Naughton's prayerful Irish mother and uncles, who nightly asked God for a happy death by which they meant not in Bolton but in Ireland. They also included Anthony Burgess's father who, having been rebuked by the priest at the start of Mass for absent-mindedly entering the church wearing his hat and smoking a cigarette, only attended Christmas Midnight Mass but on his death-bed sent for a priest.[36]

The devout remained predominantly women. When boys left school to go to work they also tended to stop attending Mass, though they might return on marriage to a Catholic girl. As John Carmel Heenan, Archbishop of Liverpool (1957-1963), put it, 'The Catholic men of Scotland Road [Liverpool] were ready to fight or die for their faith. They found it more difficult to go to Mass'.[37]

Some Catholics ceased to practise their religion, whilst still professing belief, but others abandoned both practice and belief. Anthony Burgess explains how, 'Loss of faith shows as a syndrome. Many symptoms come together and add up to it', so that he was 'slowly divested of the peel of faith'. Nevertheless, he points out how difficult it is to abandon Catholicism altogether, 'For Catholicism is, in a paradox, a bigger thing than the faith. It is a kind of nationality one is stuck with for ever'.[38]

Lancashire Catholics preserved their own sub-culture. They tried to be good neighbours. As Bishop Holland remembers, 'Neighbours dropped in and out. The sick were sure of a companion. The needy got the crucial loan—the half cup of sugar, a twist of tea, perhaps an egg, all scrupulously returned when the ship came home'. They continued to go on pilgrimage, with trains, motor-cars, and planes taking them further afield to Holywell, Walsingham, and Lourdes. Harold Rawcliffe, a parishioner of St Gregory's, Weld Bank, Chorley, was an outstanding pilgrim. He was a brancardier—one who assists the sick—at Lourdes, and he helped to organise the annual Liverpool Archdiocesan pilgrimage to Lourdes. He also designed and carved the statutes placed in 1953 on either side of the door of the Slipper Chapel at Walsingham. Jack Traynor of Liverpool became famous because of the cure at Lourdes in 1923 of the paralysis and epilepsy he had suffered since being wounded in the First World War. He returned to Liverpool and a job as a coal-heaver, and continued to go to Lourdes as a brancardier. It was a sub-culture lovingly described by the writers it produced: Bill Naughton in Bolton, John Farrimond in Hindley, near Wigan, and Anthony Burgess in Manchester. Catholics seemed obsessed with death, living in constant fear of hell and hope of heaven, continually praying and going to confession. They prayed to the saints and especially to the Blessed Virgin Mary. Above all they worshipped Christ, made present in bread and wine, sacrificed on the altar, consumed in communion, reverenced in the tabernacle, and adored in the monstrance. Naughton remembers, 'The altar ... radiant with bright candles and the Host exposed in the setting of the golden monstrance ...'. Farrimond describes how 'The priest was somehow God, the way the altar was God, and the church was God, and the communion bread was God'. Burgess explains 'That Christ was really present on the altar, disguised as unleavened bread and sweet red wine...'. The patrician David Mathew wrote the elegy of this urban Catholicism: 'In the bedrooms mild sunlight would strike the oleographs of the Sacred Heart; the engines whistled and the smoke from the factory chimneys moved over slowly above the walls of sidings and the mean house fronts; the soot was flaking from the worn rose brick'.[39]

This local Catholic community was seen in its most complete form in Chorley between the Wars, when in 1938 there were 9,000 Catholics, one-third of its total population of twenty-seven thousand. Set where the River Yarrow enters the Lancashire plain under Winter Hill, the western bastion of the Pennines which dominates south Lancashire, it was an industrial town of mill chimneys and church towers. It includes the old chapel of Slate Delf, and the parishes of St Gregory's, Weld Bank, founded in 1774, Sacred Heart in 1876, St Joseph's in 1910, St Anselm's in 1953, and the town-centre parish of St Mary's founded in 1847. St Mary's church was built in 1853 by Joseph Hansom, and restored in 1910 by Canon Thomas Stanislaus Crank, who removed the galleries and installed the stained glass, the stations of the cross, the marble altar-rails and the silver sanctuary lamp. In the 1930s it had a flourishing Catholic Young Men's society with a hall for billiards and dancing, and gardens, bowling-green, and swimming-pool. However, the parish's proudest boast was that it was the most Catholic parish in the archdiocese if not in the world. It made the highest contributions to the ecclesiastical education fund and the other diocesan charities, and it had the highest proportion of Sunday Mass-attendance to baptised Catholics, and the highest proportion of communions to communicants, 100,000 communions per annum for 1,500 communicants. If love of God and neighbour can be quantified, then St Mary's, Chorley, had the most.[40]

Not a million miles away Hilary Mantel's fictional village of Featherhoughton lay amongst the moors looking towards Liverpool, Wigan, and Manchester, 'the black heart of the industrial north'. There, about 1956 the parish priest explained to his bishop, 'These people aren't Christians. These people are heathens and Catholics' and 'They play football with human heads'.[41]

In 1950 George Andrew Beck,[42] the editor of the collection of essays commemorating the restoration of the hierarchy (he was at the time coadjutor bishop of Brentwood, and was to become bishop of Salford [1955-1964] and archbishop of Liverpool [1964-1976]) surveyed the prospects for English Catholicism. He looked back on a century of numerical and institutional growth, especially in education, but there were signs that the former was not as great as it could or should have been. Whilst the birth/marriage ratio for the national population had declined during the 20th century to 2.0 children per marriage by 1950, it had also declined for the Catholic population to just below the 2.6 needed to enable the population to replace itself. As a result, although the percentage of Catholics in the total population might remain the same, a decline in the total numbers of Catholics was a possibility. However, he asserted that:

> The day of doctrine is returning ... The intellectual security born of certitude, the fruit of 'the faith of Christ and the sacraments of the faith' will be perhaps the most powerful argument for Catholicism in the years which lie immediately ahead of us.[43]

To make the Church more effective in reaching the modern world, Pope John XXIII summoned the Second Vatican Council in 1961. The Council met in 1962, and closed in 1965. For Catholics nothing would be quite the same again.[44]

Notes

1. J. H. Newman, *Sermons Preached on Various Occasions* (1913), pp.163-83; Connolly, 'The Transubstantiation of Myth', *JEH*, vol.35 (1) (1984); Bossy, *Community*, p.297; Holmes, *More Roman than Rome*, pp.249-57.

2. Blundell, vol.2, p.235; B. Griffin, 'Foreword' in Beck, *English Catholics*, p.v; H. V. Marshall, 'Preface' in *Bolton*, p.8.

3. A. Freemantle, *The Papal Encyclicals* (1963), pp.196, 299; B. Sharratt, 'English Roman Catholicism in the 1960s' in A. Hastings (ed.), *Bishops and Writers* (1977), p.153; D. Gwynn, 'Growth of the Catholic Community' in Beck, *English Catholics*, pp.410-41.

4. M. V. Sweeney, 'Diocesan Organisation and Administration' in Beck, *English Catholics*, p.136.

5. Plumb, *Arundel to Zabi*.

6. Plumb, 'The Founding Fathers of Lancaster Diocese' in Hilton, *Catholic Englishmen*.

7. M. Bentley, 'Social Change' in C. Haigh, (ed.), *The Cambridge Historical Encyclopedia of Great Britain and Ireland* (hereafter CHE)(1985), pp.327-36.

8. Walton, pp.325-54.

9. A. Hastings, 'Some Reflections on the English Catholicism of the late 1930s' in Hastings, *Bishops and Writers*, pp.107-25; K. G. Schmude, *Hilaire Belloc* (1978); W. Parking, *The Friars Preacher in Lancashire* (1991), p.71; Plumb, *Our Lady and All Saints*, Parbold (1984), p.25.

10. Walton, pp.355-59; F. Musgrove, *The North of England* (1990), pp.298-319; Bentley, *CHE*, pp.327-36; Bagley, pp.62-6; B. Jones, *Homo Northwestus* (1992), pp.70-72.

11. G. Orwell, *The Road to Wigan Pier* (1962), pp.94-5; Hilton, 'Holy Family, New Springs', *NWCH*, vol.15 (1988).

12. D.Gwynn, 'Growth of the Catholic Community' in Beck, *English Catholics*, pp.410-441; *Catholic Directory 1965* (hereafter *CD*)(1965), p.771; *CD* 1921 (1921), p.591; *CD* 1961 (1961), p.726.

13. Hastings, *Bishops and Writers*, pp.127-58; *CD* 1921, p.572; *CD* 1961, p.726.

14. Gwynn , *English Catholics*, pp.265-89; B. Naughton, *On The Pig's Back* (1988), p.171; D. Howarth, *Figures in a Bygone Landscape* (1991)(hereafer Howarth), pp.150-51; Burgess, *Urgent Copy* (1973), p.296.

15. Bagley, pp.62-63; *CD* 1965, pp.470, 553-4.

16. Plumb, *Our Glorious Chapter* (1977), p.31; L. Hanley, *The History of St Paul's, West Derby* (1979); E. M. Abbott, *History of the Diocese of Shrewsbury* (1986), pp.114-8.

17. *CD* 1921, p.591; *CD* 1965, p.771.

18. A. Service, *Edwardian Architecture* (1977), pp.74-87; Little, pp.165-222; Pevsner, *Lancs: South*, pp.50-1, 66-7, 93, 180, 191-3, 216, 228. 300, 375, 384; Pevsner, *Lancs: North*, pp.35, 235-6, 253.

19. Pevsner, *Lancs: North*, pp. 36, 167.

20. *CD* 1921, p.591; *CD* 1965, p.771.

21. *Upholland Centenary*; Blundell, vol.2, p.87, Hilton, 'Upholland College Archives', *Catholic Archives*, vol.9.

22. T. Holland, *For Better and for Worse* (1989) (hereafter Holland), pp.15-9.

23. A. Kenny, *A Path from Rome* (1985), pp.23-41.

24. Hickey, pp.172-73; A. C. F. Beales, 'The Struggle for the Schools' in Beck, *English Catholics*, pp.365-409; Curtis, *History of Education*, pp.322-409; R. Pedley, *The Comprehensive School* (1963), pp.32-80.

25. J. Davies, 'Rome on the Rates', *NWCH*, vol.18 (1991); Beck, *The Cost of Catholic Schools* (no date).

26. *The Catechism of Christian Doctrine* (1904); Naughton, *On the Pig's Back*, pp.137, 142-43; Holland, p.7; Howarth, pp.113-18; Burgess, *Little Wilson and Big God*, pp.59-60.

27. Battersby, *English Catholics*, p.357; *CD* 1965, p.581.

28. H. O. Everett, 'Catholics and the Universities' in Beck, *English Catholics*, pp.290-321; Hickey, p.162.

29. Plumb, *Arundel to Zabi*; Bolton, pp.133-4; Plumb, 'The Founding Fathers of the Lancaster Diocese' in Hilton, *Catholic Englishmen*.

30.   J. Brown, 'God's Priest', *Christian Order*, vol.21 (8/9) (1980); Orwell, *Road to Wigan Pier*, p.45.

31.   M. Aldred, *St Marie on the Sands* (1991), p.35.

32.   Giblin, *NWCH*, vol.9, pp.15-16, 17, p.10; T. C. Gillett, *The Weld Bank Story* (1974), p.101; F. Ramsden, *A History of the de Trafford Family* (1986); Hilton, *Yealand*, p.10; Blundell, vol.1, pp.30-31; *Who's Who 1991* (1991).

33.   Plumb, *SS Peter and Michael*, Woolston (1985), p.27.

34.   Davies, *NWCH*, vol.18, 16-17; Gwynn, *English Catholics*, p.288; Aldred, *St Marie on the Sands*, p.28; Plumb, *Our Glorious Chapter*, p.31; *Who's Who 1991*.

35.   J. Bennett, 'The Care of the Poor' in Beck, *English Catholics*, p.583; T. G. Ward and L. Warren, *The Manor Mission of Low Furness* (1979), p.49; *Catholic Pictorial*, 18 March 1990.

36.   Naughton, *On the Pig's Back*, pp.117, 151; Burgess, *Little Wilson and Big God*, pp.51, 192.

37.   Mathew, p.277; H. Mantel, *Fludd* (1989), p.33; McLeod, pp.28-35; J. C. Heenan, *A Crown of Thorns* (1974), 237.

38.   Burgess, *Little Wilson and Big God*, pp.138, 141, 148.

39.   McLeod, p.126; Gillett, *Weld Bank Story*, pp.103-4; Holland, pp.238-9; Hilton, 'Holy Ground' in Hilton, *Loveable West*, pp.7-14; N. C. Hypher, *Lourdes* (1982), pp.17; J. McDermott, 'John Farrimond, Novelist', *NWCH*, vol.13 (1986); Burgess, *The Piano Players* (1986), passim; Burgess, *Any Old Iron* (1989), passim; Holland, pp.238-9; Naughton, *Saintly Billy* (1989), p.88; J. Farrimond, *Kill Me A Priest* (1965), p.181; Burgess, *Little Wilson and Big God*, p.85; Mathew, p.276.

40.   Blundell, vol.2, pp.91-111; *CD* 1965, pp.260-61.

41.   Mantel, *Fludd*, pp.11, 22, 24.

42.   Plumb, *Arundel to Zabi*.

43.   Beck, 'To-Day and To-Morrow' in Beck, *English Catholics*, pp.585-614.

44.   Abbott, W. M.(ed.), *The Documents of Vatican II* (1966)(hereafter Abbott, *Vatican II*).

Chapter IX

Renewal, 1965-91

No history of Catholic Lancashire would be complete without some account of the developments which have followed the Second Vatican Council. However, such an account is fraught with peculiar difficulties. The consequences of the Council have not yet worked themselves out, and, if historical periods have any meaning, this period has not ended. The verdict of history is not yet in. The developments arouse profound commitment or intense aversion, and are, therefore, essentially controversial. The statistics have been compiled by different means within shifting boundaries and definitions, and are often merely estimates. Unofficial words and actions have largely escaped record or, at least, are scattered in ephemeral publications. There is a temptation to rely on one's own memory for a period one has lived through, but one's memory is suspect. I have therefore provided only information for which I can cite written evidence. Moreover, *Tempora mutantur, et nos mutamur in illis*—the times change, and we change with them, so that my own verdict remains doubtful. I have, therefore, tried, whilst not hiding my own opinions, to provide a balanced summing up so that the reader can draw his or her own conclusions.[1]

Since the Council, Catholic Lancashire has been called upon to adopt essential re-orientations, officially described as 'renewal'. Pope John XXIII's (1958-1963) watchword was 'aggiorniamento', 'bringing up-to-date'. The Council was announced in 1959, convoked in 1961, opened in 1962 by Pope John XXIII, and closed by Pope Paul VI in 1965. The conciliar documents make up a tome of over 700 pages, the most cited and least read book in the Church, an oracle which authorises any innovation. Nevertheless, the decrees have been summarised. The Church was to be seen as the People of God. This concept involved an increased emphasis on the Eucharist, expressed in a new liturgy. It also involved a new emphasis on Scripture, on religious pluralism, and on ecumenism, and a new concern with justice and peace. The changes were implemented by Pope Paul VI (1963-1978), and consolidated by his successors John Paul I (1978) and John Paul II (1978-). Most practising Catholics seem to have responded to these changes with enthusiasm, but there has been a significant decrease in the number of practising Catholics in Lancashire.[2]

Despite its attempt to meet the modern world, Lancastrian Catholicism is at last falling victim to the secular trend, to which Protestantism has already succumbed. Lancashire continued the difficult process of adjustment to a post-industrial economy and its paradoxical consequences of economic decline and social affluence. The economic decline of this peripheral region was apparently exacerbated by Britain's entry into the European economic community in 1973, which was completed by the end of 1992. The 'Swinging Sixties' heralded permissiveness, leisure increased, and consumer goods became widely available. Redevelopment and university expansion ripped the hearts out of the county's two great cities, destroying their communities, and condemning the poor to tower-blocks. The family decreased in size and stability, as women asserted their rights, and youth assumed its own identity, while the gap widened between high and popular culture. Catholicism was not immune to these pressures. By the 1980s in the archdiocese of Liverpool 17 per cent of the children baptised were either the children of one-parent families or were born out of wedlock, and in inner-city Liverpool this figure was as high as 40 per cent. It was in these circumstances that the conciliar renewal was attempted.[3]

The first-fruit was in Biblical studies. The impetus given to the study of Scripture by Pius XII's encyclical *Divino Afflante Spiritu* of 1945 was confirmed by the conciliar constitution on Divine Revelation (*Dei Verbum*). The Rev. Alexander Jones, head of divinity at Christ's College, Liverpool, from 1964 to his death in 1970, was the general editor of the English version of the *Jerusalem Bible*, which on its publication in 1966 replaced the Douay and Knox versions for English Catholics. Jones set out the purpose of his version in his 'Foreword'. It was to respond to 'the two principal dangers facing Christianity to-day ... the reduction of Christianity to the status of a relic ... [and] its rejection as a mythology ...'. He aimed to produce a translation in 'the language we use to-day' with notes 'neither sectarian nor superficial'. The 'Introduction to the Pentateuch' summarised the story of the people of God and its message for the individual soul: 'it breaks with the old way of life, it suffers a time of testing, it emerges purified'. This was to be the fate of Catholic Lancashire, though it is not yet clear whether it will survive this purification. He insisted that the Judaeo-Christian religion 'is a historical religion: it is based on a divine revelation made to definite individuals at definite times, and in definite circumstances...', but in the 'Introduction to the Synoptic Gospels' he came to the curious conclusion that 'The three Synoptics may not be history books but they do set out to give us historical fact'. It is the nature of these facts that lies at the heart of the matter.[4]

The dogmatic constitution on the Church (*Lumen Gentium*) with its concept of the people of God was, as Archbishop Worlock of Liverpool puts it, 'The platform upon which all Conciliar teaching would rest'. It re-affirmed the doctrinal infallibility of the Church, embodied in councils and in the papacy, it defined the doctrine of episcopal collegiality, and it emphasised the apostolate of the laity. There is an awareness of the need to avoid the clericalisation of the laity and a recognition that the laity best fulfil their apostolate in their family, their work, and their community, rather than in ecclesiastical activity. The revised canon law provided for diocesan pastoral councils which were to be composed of priests, religious and especially lay people, and in 1980 a National Pastoral Congress was held in Liverpool. These councils remain only consultative rather than deliberative, but there seems to be a lack of any machinery for ensuring that their members are representative. For Archbishop Worlock the Church 'is not a democracy ruled by majority vote', a clear statement of the Ultramontane position in contrast to the Cisalpine appeal to the tradition of ecclesiastical election and representative consultation. The rights of election and representation have legal force in the Anglican Church with which Archbishop Worlock has such good relations. In 1982 Pope John Paul II visited his Lancastrian people, and received the adulation of the crowds. Modern communications, especially television and aircraft, have increased the Ultramontane cult of the papal personality. Some things have not changed.[5]

Whilst much else changed, nostalgic expression was given to that Lancashire Catholic tribalism which Archbishop Worlock recognised in his Pastoral Plan on arriving in his archdiocese in 1976: 'the "faith of our fathers" always to be preserved'. Anthony Burgess embodied and expressed that tribalism. Born John Burgess Wilson in Manchester in 1917, he was, like most Lancashire Catholics, of English recusant and Irish immigrant descent. His relatives included Patrick Dwyer, Archbishop of Birmingham. Educated at the Xaverian College in Manchester, he lost his faith while still at school. His Catholicism remains, he writes in *You've Had Your Time* (1990), 'a nostalgic culture with very little faith in it'. His massive oeuvre expresses a Roman vision in a Lancashire accent, and returns continually to the exploration of Catholic Lancashire and Catholic theology. In *Abba Abba* (1979) his alter ego Joseph Joachim Wilson, a Mancunian Catholic of English, Irish, and Italian descent, educated at St Bede's College and Manchester University, translates the blasphemous sonnets of the Roman dialect poet Belli into 'English with a Manchester accent'. His theme is:

> You look incredulous, my friend. But know
> That faith, though buffeted, must never fail.[6]

Ecumenism and the concern for justice and peace have gone hand in hand in Liverpool, where the Roman Catholic Archbishop Worlock and the Anglican Bishop Sheppard have formed a partnership called, according to them, 'Fish and Chips— always together and never out of the newspapers', which also includes the leaders of the Nonconformist churches. This partnership extends to shared Catholic and Anglican churches at Hough Green, near Widnes, and Warrington New Town.[7]

This ecumenical Christian leadership has been concerned to improve the economic and social conditions of the whole community, and ready to intervene in politics in order to do so. Archbishop Worlock and his fellow Christian leaders have tried to bring justice and peace to a community deprived by unemployment, aggravated by conflict in local government, and erupting into riots. The churches are also active in practical work to help the community. In 1985 there were a hundred Church-sponsored schemes in Merseyside, mainly funded by the Manpower Services Commission, employing 273 full-time, 1,123 part-time, and 547 voluntary workers.[8]

For the ordinary Catholic in the pew the most obvious change has been the reform of the liturgy. The consititution on the Sacred Liturgy (*Sacrosanctum Concilium*) called for its revision 'to meet the circumstances and needs of modern times'. In doing so it insisted that 'The rites should be distinguished by a noble simplicity'. A wider use was to be made of Scripture, the use of the vernacular was to be extended, 'though the use of the Latin language is to be preserved in the Latin rites', and 'full and active participation by all the people is the aim to be considered before all else'. Accordingly, in 1964 the vernacular was introduced for the proper and common of the Mass (the readings from Scripture and the prayers of the people), and the ceremonial of the liturgy was simplified. However, in 1970 a new Roman Missal was issued which permitted the whole of the liturgy to be celebrated in the vernacular, greatly extended the Scriptural readings, and introduced three more eucharistic prayers. The priest was called upon to celebrate Mass facing the people and given liberty to address the congregation extemporaneously. Priests were permitted and encouraged to concelebrate. The permanent diaconate was revived. Lay readers and lay ministers of the eucharist were introduced. The reception of holy communion standing and in the hand was permitted. Sanctuaries were re-ordered: the high altar was removed from the east wall to become free standing, and communion rails were removed. The eucharistic fast was reduced to one hour, and the days of fasting and abstinence were reduced to Ash Wednesday and Good Friday. These changes were marked by a semantic shift in the meaning of the verb 'to celebrate' from 'duly perform' to 'enjoy', for instance in Haring's writings, and the Mass, weddings, and even funerals were celebrated in this new sense. Meanwhile devotions such as Benediction, the Stations of the Cross, and the Rosary declined, and charismatics introduced hand-waving and shouting. The hymn sandwich, punctuating the Mass with hymn-singing, became the normal liturgical form, and several new hymns became popular, such as Estelle White's 'Walk with me oh my Lord', and tunes such as Carey Landry's 'Abba, Father', often performed *adagio* to guitar accompaniment. I have to break my self-denying ordinance on anecdotes by citing the bride who wanted for a wedding hymn 'This is my body broken for you' and the bereaved who requested for a cremation 'So light up the fire. Let the flame burn'.[9]

These changes could be presented as the continuation of a long tradition of liturgical innovation, but the cumulative effect amounts, in E. Mathews's phrase to 'quite basic changes in our liturgy'. They involved the attempt to make the liturgy contemporary and to restore it to its primitive purity, an approach previously condemned by Pius XII in the encyclical *Mediator Dei*.[10]

The new liturgy won widespread and positive support from priests and people, partly because it was introduced gradually to a Church which prided itself on obedience, and partly because of its obvious advantages. It is intelligible, it provides a wide range of Scripture, it offers a new range of ministry to the laity, and it encourages the oral participation of the congregation. As the Rev. Bernard Eager, parish priest of St Catherine's, Lowton, near Warrington, put it:

One of the most important things that ever happened was the removal of the altar rail ... Because ... the barrier had gone, the priest had said 'You can come up here. You too can lead the prayers'.[11]

However, even its proponents admit that in practice the new liturgy suffers from, in Kavanagh's words, an 'untranscendental blandness', an 'aggressive educationalism', a middle-class 'elitism', and a clerical 'individualism' which makes it the 'plaything' and the 'casualty' of the celebrant. For others in the Church and for some who have left it, the new liturgy for these very reasons is, in Burgess's words, 'a disgrace'.[12]

The architecture of the period expressed and, under the influence of the liturgical movement, anticipated the new liturgy. Pevsner was an exponent of the International Modern style with its use of steel, concrete, and glass, but he was discerning in his criticism of the new churches: 'Their hyperbolic paraboloid roofs, jabbing at you, their irregular plans, their abstract concrete patterns attack you ... the best ... are the ones which allow contemplation and concentration, i.e. which keep quiet'. Such churches included Weightman and Bullen's Christ's College Chapel, Childwall, Liverpool (1964-66), their St Ambrose's, Speke, Liverpool (1959-61), and their St Margaret Mary's, Knotty Ash, Liverpool (1962-64); Desmond Williams and Associates' St Augustine's, Chorlton-on-Medlock, Manchester (1967); and Gibberd's De La Salle College Chapel, Hopwood (1963-65), a rehearsal for his Liverpool Cathedral. Sir Frederick Gibberd's Metropolitan Cathedral of Christ the King (1959-67) is a circle surrounded by eight chapels, with a conical roof rising to a tapering lantern tower. This International Modern style symbolised post-conciliar Catholicism.[13]

For defenders of the New Rite, such as Kavanagh, the celebration of the Old Rite or the use of Latin in the New Rite 'compromises the quality, not to say the deeply traditional Catholicity' of the New Rite. Nevertheless, liturgical pluralism permitted the survival of the Old Rite. The introduction of the New Rite in 1964 saw the formation of the Latin Mass Society to preserve the Old Rite (the so-called Tridentine Rite because it was fixed by, not introduced by, the Council of Trent). In 1971 Cardinal Heenan secured a papal indult permitting with episcopal approval the occasional celebration in England of the Old Rite. In 1988 the regular celebration of the Old Rite with episcopal approval was permitted and extended to other countries. The Old Rite was, therefore, celebrated continually, and in 1990 arrangements were made for its regular celebration at St Mary's, Highfield Street, Liverpool. The Old Rite was promptly attacked by Fr. Eager: '... the Parish Priest in his vestments, at the altar, talking in Latin the people behind him, cut off by the altar rail ... There wasn't much Liturgy at all really. There was Ritual'. It was, however, just this sense of immemorial prescription which appealed to those nostalgic for the Old Rite, for it enshrined the sacred. As Kenny remembers, 'Every word, movement, and gesture of the priest at Mass was carefully prescribed'.[14]

Liturgical changes reflected theological changes. *Lex orandi, lex credendi*, as the old adage says, 'The law of praying is the law of believing'. Bernard Sharratt (a

9 *The Metropolitan Cathedral, Liverpool. By permission of* The Catholic Pictorial.

native of Liverpool, an alumnus of Upholland, and the editor of the theological journal *Slant*) points out that 'since meaning and language cannot be finally separated' the introduction of the vernacular raised questions about the nature of Scripture and of the Eucharist. As Bishops Sheppard and Worlock note, 'Even to claim that people have faith is to invite the question, "What sort of faith? What kind of God do they have faith in?"'. Pope John XXIII could draw a distinction between 'The substance of the ancient doctrine of the deposit of the faith ... and the way in which it is presented'. Others have been less clear about this distinction. As the Right Rev. Thomas Holland, former Bishop of Salford (1964-88), complains: 'Liberation came on all fronts! Dutch catechism for dogma, jeans in the liturgy ... The authentic guidance of Vatican II encountered unforeseen rivals. A new breed of theologians ... We Bishops should have kept a closer watch on the ramparts'.[15]

This confusion was compounded in Catholic education, and nowhere else was this more apparent than in the seminaries, as priests abandoned their priesthood and the supply of new vocations began to dry up. In 1975 the Liverpool senior seminary at Upholland, which had trained 500 priests since 1930, was amalgamated with Ushaw. The junior seminary, to which was added the Lancaster junior seminary from Underley Hall, remained at Upholland with 20 staff and 150 boys. In 1976 the Northern Institute, with four priests and a nun, was established at Upholland to provide adult Catholic education. Between 1981 and 1983 it provided 50 residential courses attended by over 1,000 people, and another 1,200 people attended one-day courses, while 3,000 people attended courses there provided by organisations other than the institute. However, both the junior seminary and the institute have been wound down. The college, with its library, its buildings, and its grounds is in need of finance and of a purpose, if it is not to become a stranded whale beached on its ridge above Wigan.[16]

There have also been amalgamations and closures of Catholic teacher-training colleges. In Liverpool, Notre Dame college was amalgamated with Christ's College, and with the Anglican St Katherine's College formed the Liverpool Institute of Higher Education. By 1991 the other Catholic Lancashire colleges of further education had closed.[17]

Catholic schools have had to respond to changes in government policy as well as the progress of renewal. In 1965 the Labour government required local authorities to re-organise secondary schools as comprehensives, though in 1970 the Conservative government cancelled this requirement. Nevertheless, under the leadership of George Andrew Beck, successively Bishop of Salford (1955-64) and Archbishop of Liverpool (1964-76), and long the educational spokesman of the English hierarchy, Catholic education responded to the changing demands made on it by central and local government. By 1990 direct grant, grammar, and secondary modern schools had been virtually replaced by comprehensive schools, whilst Catholic independent schools in the region declined in numbers. The conciliar declaration on Christian Education (*Gravissimum Educationis*) insists on the Church's rôle in education. This claim was elaborated in a succession of Vatican documents. In 1971 a General Catechetical Directory called for new modes of expressing the faith, and led to the abandonment of the *Catechism* in favour of catechetical experiment. As Bishop Holland points out, 'Open-ended discussion was one of the educational fads of the day; indoctrination was a dirty word ... But there supremely "Truth is great and must prevail!" Open-ends must close'. Other documents issued by the Vatican have emphasised the importance of the school as a Christian community. Catholic schools have a declared commitment to care for the individual and the community, but they remain authoritarian institutions.[18]

The schools manifested the decline in the population of Catholic Lancashire. In 1965 in the three Lancashire dioceses there was a total of 837 schools and a total of 226,853 pupils. By 1990 these totals had fallen to 648 schools and 186,619 pupils. The schools' population had therefore fallen by 40,234 pupils, a decline of 17.7 per cent.[19]

The numerical decline of Catholic Lancashire was general and pronounced, despite an apparent growth in the total Catholic population of England and Wales from 3,956,500 in 1965 to 4,305,608 in 1990, an increase of 349,108, that is 0.8 per cent. Bishop Holland describes it as 'a phenomenon which continues to perplex and disturb me. Many of our Salford diocesan statistics began to go down steadily from 1962—the year the council began. Births, Baptisms, Converts, Confessions, Mass attendance, Easter Duties and the rest. The only increase was in Holy Communions'. The decline in the number of priests was marked. In 1965 the three Lancashire dioceses had a combined total of 1,600 priests or one priest per 643 Catholics. In 1990 the three dioceses had a total of 1,195 priests or one priest per 787 Catholics. There had, therefore, been a loss of 407 priests, that is 25.3 per cent. The decline in the total Catholic population of Lancashire was less pronounced. In 1965 the estimated Catholic population of the Lancashire dioceses was 1,030,000 or 26 per cent of the total English and Welsh Catholics. In 1990 their estimated Catholic population was 941,265 or only 21 per cent of the total English and Welsh Catholics, a fall of 88,735 or 8.6 per cent. The decline in population was reflected in a decline in churches and chapels from a total of 767 in the Lancashire dioceses in 1965 to 697 in 1990, a decrease of 70, that is 9 per cent. The decline in Catholic marriages was more marked. In 1963 (the last year available to the 1965 *Catholic Directory*) there was a total of 9,771 Catholic marriages in the Lancashire dioceses. In 1989 there were 5,554 Catholic marriages, a decline of 4,217, that is 43 per cent. The decline in the number of marriages and a relaxation in the restrictions on mixed marriages help to account for the disastrous decline in the number of converts. In 1963 there was a total of 3,089 conversions in the Lancashire dioceses. In 1989 there were 668, a decline of 78 per cent. The decline in the number of marriages, together with perhaps a popular repudiation of papal teaching on contraception, probably accounts for the disastrous decline in the numbers of infant baptisms. In 1963 there was a total of 32,576 baptisms in the Lancashire dioceses. In 1989 there were 16,688, a fall of 15,888, that is 48.7 per cent. These figures were also reflected in the fall in Mass attendance in England and Wales from 42 per cent in 1975 to 31 per cent in 1989. The only statistic to increase over this period was the number of convents from a total of 190 in the Lancashire dioceses in 1965 to 205 in 1990, an increase of 15, that is 7.8 per cent, but this is probably accounted for by the proliferation of smaller communities rather than an increase in the number of nuns. Taken over all, these figures indicate that Catholic Lancashire is withering away.[20]

The interpretation of these statistics is unavoidably controversial. It is possible to explain them away as the result of a regional decline in population. Archbishop Worlock noted in 1988 that 'In 1975 the numbers from the archdiocese were 550,000 (now, through emigration, 515,000)'. His press secretary, the Rev. P. F. Thompson, argues that the statistics are not necessarily accurate, and, though he accepts that the population of the archdiocese fell from 536,754 in 1980 to 496,194 in 1990, and that attendance at Mass fell from 183,578 or 30 per cent of Catholics in 1980 to 126,882 or 26 per cent of Catholics in 1990, he also points out that in the same decade the population of Merseyside fell by 100,000, though it is not clear how this would affect the percentage of Catholics attending Mass. However the bulk of the emigration from Merseyside seems to have been confined to the region, that is it went no further than the neighbouring administrative counties of Lancashire, Greater Manchester and Cheshire. Thus between 1965 and 1990 the Catholic population of the diocese of Shrewsbury, which covers Cheshire and Shropshire, increased from 178,000 to 198,526, that is by 20,526 or 11.5 per cent. Certainly the population of the North-West (the administrative counties of Lancashire, Greater Manchester, Merseyside, and Cheshire) fell from 6,407,000 in 1971 to 6,379,700 in 1989, a decline of 27,300, that is 0.42 per cent, compared with the 8.6 per cent by which the Catholic population fell. In other words, the decline of the Catholic population was 20 times greater than the decline of the regional population. Even if the population of Shrewsbury diocese is added to the population of the Lancashire dioceses, then between 1965 and 1990 their combined totals fell from 1,208,000 to 1,139,791, a decline of 68,203, that is 5.6 per cent, still much larger than the regional fall in population. If the decline cannot be explained away, perhaps it can be explained.[21]

The fundamental reason for the decline is the accelerating process of secularisation. As Augustine Harris, formerly auxiliary bishop in Liverpool, (quoted by Archbishop Worlock) put it 'As the external pressures ease off, because Catholics feel themselves fully accepted into the wider community, the religious practice drops off'. Western society has come to accept Nietzsche's proclamation that 'God is dead', because as Weber put it 'The world is disenchanted' (quoted by McLeod), as it becomes increasingly difficult to believe in divine supernatural intervention in the universe. Bishops Sheppard and Worlock recount 'a famous answer ... given to an inquiry into religious attitudes. In response to the question "Do you believe in a God who can change the course of events on earth?" the reply was given: "No. Just the ordinary one."' However, Catholic Lancashire had hitherto resisted the secular trend. Why then did it so suddenly collapse in the aftermath of the Second Vatican Council?[22]

It can be argued that, although the collapse was inevitable, the conciliar renewal has mitigated its worst consequences. The growth of secularisation was apparent before the Council, and, Ultramontanism having failed to defeat it, the Council was called to deal with the secular trend. The conciliar reforms have, therefore, ensured the survival of Catholicism. Indeed, the National Pastoral Congress argued that 'the teachings of Vatican II are not being sufficiently implemented', and that proper implementation would result in improvement. Meanwhile, those Catholics who remain are more informed and more committed. For them, according to Archbishop Worlock, 'the whole process of renewal has been a most exciting experience'.[23]

It can also be argued that the conciliar renewal has precipitated the collapse of Catholicism. Ultramontanism had defied the secular trend, and the conciliar renewal amounted to a surrender to secularisation. Some, like Bishop Holland, argue that 'The blame, however, rests not with the Council but with the rogue interpreters who crashed in with their own wishful thinking to make the occasion a supremely severe testing time for many of the faithful'. Others like Anthony Burgess go further: 'I asked the Church ... to consider Christ's statement, "By their fruits shall ye know them". If Pope John XXIII had been so saintly, why was Catholicism falling to pieces?'. As Sharratt points out, with the introduction of the New Liturgy 'it was suddenly easier and perhaps unavoidable to ask whether one really *understood* what it all *meant*' (his italics). As Archbishop Worlock is aware 'Move the loyal adherent from his customary surroundings or demolish those surroundings, and he can be confused, if not actually lost. For he can no longer recognise the externals of what has commanded his loyalty'. Catholicism has a capacity for amnesia, for abandoning positions and then assuming they were never held, that has helped it to survive. Nevertheless, the wholesale adoption of the liturgical programme of the Protestant Reformation—'In making the change,' writes Hastings, 'the Church effectively admitted that on these points the Reformers had been in the right'—amounted to a disjunction which affected the Church's credibility.[24]

Partly mitigated and partly aggravated by the conciliar renewal, the long-postponed decline of Lancastrian Catholicism has at last followed the collapse of Lancastrian industrial supremacy. Catholic Lancashire was in Gilbert's words 'a midwife of the new, urbanised industrial society, not an offspring'. Despite the conciliar attempt to place the Church at the centre of that society, it has become a marginalised sub-culture.[25]

The two Reformations—the Protestant Reformation and the Catholic Counter-Reformation —sought to replace the medieval, communal belief in religion as magic with a modern, personal belief in religion as salvation. Inspired by the university-educated clergy, the Reformation tried to create a literate and devout laity. In 1559 it seemed that the Protestant Reformation was to have its own way in England, but by the 17th century the Counter-Reformation had re-created a Catholic community in Lancashire. That community expanded with the Industrial Revolution and Irish immigration, and, as the Protestant Reformation became a spent force, Catholic Lancashire stood alone against the secular tendency of industrial society. The Second Vatican Council replaced the emphasis on personal salvation with a concern for interpersonal relationships and social justice, but it also renewed the call for total personal commitment. However, the final triumph of the Reformation was insufficient to prevent the final triumph of the Enlightenment, and, though a decade of evangelisation was proclaimed for the 1990s, Catholic Lancashire began to wither away.[26]

Notes

1. Vidler, pp.270-273; P. Hebblethwaite, *The Runaway Church* (1978); Hastings (ed.), *Modern Catholicism* (1991); Abbott, *Vatican II*; Hilton, 'Twenty Years On', *NWCH*, vol.13 (1986).

2. Vidler, pp.270-273; Abbott, *Vatican II*; Hastings, 'Catholic History from Vatican I to John Paul II' in Hastings, *Modern Catholicism*; Hastings, 'The Key Texts' in Hastings, *Modern Catholicism*; D. Sheppard and D. Worlock, *Better Together* (1988) (hereafter Sheppard and Worlock), pp.10-14.

3. Gilbert, pp.205-207; P. Buckland, 'Ireland and the British Government' in Haigh, *CHE*; B. Supple, 'The Economy' in Haigh, *CHE*; M. Bentley, 'Social Change' in Haigh, *CHE*; G. Sutherland, 'Culture' in Haigh, *CHE*; Sheppard and Worlock, pp.ix, 69, 195-198; Holland, pp.239-240.

4. Fremantle, *Papal Encyclicals*, pp.275-286; Abbott, *Vatican II*, pp.107-132; R. Murray, 'Revelation' in Hastings, *Modern Catholicism*; Plumb, *Found Worthy*, p. 75; Kenny, *Path from Rome*, pp.113-5; A. Jones (ed.), *The Jerusalem Bible* (1966), p.v, 'Old Testament', pp.12-4, 'New Testament', p.9; Burgess, *Homage to Qwert Yuiop*, pp.30-2; McLeod, pp.98-9; Chadwick, *Secularization of the European Mind*, pp.189-228.

5. Sheppard and Worlock, pp.13-14, 111, 118, 121-122, 131, 239-240; Abbott, *Vatican II*, pp. 9-106; *Congress Report* (1980); S. Neill, *Anglicanism* (1960), pp.435-440; Holland, pp.265-268.

6. Sheppard and Worlock, pp.44-5; Burgess, *Little Wilson and Big God*, pp.6-17, 22, 78-167; Burgess, *You've Had Your Time* (1990), p.370; Burgess, *Abba Abba* (1977), *passim*.

7. Sheppard and Worlock, pp.97-98, 222.

8. Sheppard and Worlock, *passim*.

9. Abbott, pp.133-182; T. Klauser, *A Short History of the Western Liturgy* (1979), pp.157-9; B. Haring, *Acting on the Word* (1975), p.194; E. Sands, 'Developing Parish Celebration', *Uniscript*, vol. 24 (1980); *Celebration Hymnal* (1977), no.340; D. Lundy, *Songs of the Spirit* (1978), no.85; P. Rowley, 'The Historical Search for Renewal', *Uniscript*, vol. 17 (1979); M. Hebblethwaite, 'Devotion' in Hastings, *Modern Catholicism*.

10. E. Mathews, 'More Than Just Words', *Uniscript*, vol. 24 (1980); Freemantle, *Papal Encyclicals*, pp.286-294.

11. *Catholic Pictorial*, 21 January 1990.

12. A. Kavanagh, 'Liturgy' in Hastings, *Modern Catholicism*; Burgess, *You've Had Your Time*, p.349.

13. Pevsner, *Lancs: South*, pp.51-2, 215, 230, 240, 306; Pevsner, *Lancs: North*, pp.35-6; Little, pp.195-228.

14. Kavanagh, *Modern Catholicism*, p.72; V. A. McClelland, 'Great Britain and Ireland' in Hastings, *Modern Catholicism*; *Catholic Pictorial*, 21 January 1990; Kenny, *Path from Rome*, p.99.

15. B. Sharratt, 'English Roman Catholicism in the 1960s' in Hastings, *Bishops and Writers*; Sheppard and Worlock, p.57; Abbott, *Vatican II*, p.715; Holland, pp.293-5.

16. M. Gaine, 'The State of the Priesthood' in Hastings, *Modern Catholicism; Upholland Centenary*; Hilton, *Catholic Archives*, vol.9; *Wigan Observer*, 28 November 1991.

17. Sheppard and Worlock, pp.103-4; *CD 1991* (1991), p.477.

18. Sutherland, *CHE*, pp.333-336; Plumb, *Arundel to Zabi*; *CD 1991*, p.522; *CD 1965*, p.772; *CD 1991*, p.522; Abbott, *Vatican II*, 634-55; McClelland, 'Education' in Hastings, *Modern Catholicism*; Holland, p.294; J. Callaghan and M. Cockett (eds.), *Are Our Schools Christian?: A Call to Pastoral Care* (1975).

19. *CD 1965* (London, 1965), p.773; *CD 1991*, p.522.

20. Holland, p.293; *CD 1965*, p.771; *CD 1991*, p.523; Sharratt, *Bishops and Writers*, pp.140-3; P. Brierley, *'Christian' England* (1991), p.32.

21. Sheppard and Worlock, p.60; P. F. Thompson, 'Liverpool Replies', *Christian Order*, vol.32 (10) (1991); T. Griffin, *Regional Trends*, vol. 26 (1991), pp.20; *CD 1965*, p.771; *CD 1991*, p.523.

22. McLeod, pp.98-102, 118-21; Sheppard and Worlock, p.57.

23. *Congress Report*, p.11; Sheppard and Worlock, p.77.

24. Holland, p.275; Burgess, *You've Had Your Time*, p.349; Sharratt, *Bishops and Writers*, pp.127, 138-9; Sheppard and Worlock, p.45; Hastings, *Modern Catholicism*, p.64.

25. Gilbert, p.207; McLeod, p.143.

26. J. McManners (ed.), *The Oxford Illustrated History of Christianity* (1992); J. Delumeau, *Catholicism between Luther and Voltaire* (1977); Brierley, *'Christian' England*, pp.9, 208.

Bibliography

Primary Sources

Manuscript Sources

Cheshire Record Office, Chester, Visitation Correction Book 1604, EDV 1/13
House of Lords Record Ofice, Westminster, Protestation Returns for the Hundreds of
  Amounderness, Leyland, Salford, and West Derby, 1642
Lancashire Record Office, DDKe 7/31(1)

Printed Primary Sources

Abbott, W. M. (ed.), *The Documents of Vatican II* (1966)
Adamson, J. H. (ed.), 'Popish Recusants at Broughton, Lancashire, 1676', *Recusant History*, vol.15 (3) (1980)
Beaumont, W. (ed.), *A Discourse of the Warr in Lancashire* (Chetham Society, new series, vol.62, 1864)
Beck, G. A., *The Cost of Catholic Schools* (n.d.)
Birrell, T. A. (ed.), *Robert Pugh, Blacklo's Cabal* (1970)
Blundell, M. (ed.), *Blundell's Diary and Letter Book, 1702-28* (1952)
Blundell, M. (ed.), *Cavalier: Letters of William Blundell to his Friends, 1620-95* (1934)
Brierley, P., *'Christian' England* (1991)
Burgess, A., *Abba Abba* (1977)
Burgess, A., *Any Old Iron* (1989)
Burgess, A., *Homage to Qwert Yuiop* (1987)
Burgess, A., *Little Wilson and Big God* (1987)
Burgess, A., *The Piano Players* (1986)
Burgess, A., *Urgent Copy* (1973)
Burgess, A., *You've Had Your Time* (1990)
Callaghan, J. and Cockett, M. (eds.), *Are Our Schools Christian?: A Call to Pastoral Care* (1975)
Caraman, C. P. (ed.), *The Hunted Priest: The Autobiography of John Gerard* (1959)
Catholic Directory 1921
Catholic Directory 1961
Catholic Directory 1965
Catholic Directory 1991
Catholic Pictorial
Celebration Hymnal (1977)
Congress Report (1980)
Dominicana (Catholic Record Society, vol.25, 1925)
Engels, F., *The Condition of the Working Class in England* (1987)
Estcourt, E. E. and Payne, J. O. (eds), *The English Catholics Nonjurors of 1715* (1885)
Farrimond, J., *Kill Me A Priest* (1965)

Foley, B. C.(ed.), 'Some Papers of a "Riding Priest", Thomas Roydon 1662-1741', *Recusant History*, vol.19 (4) (1989)

Foley, H.(ed.), *Records of the English Province of the Society of Jesus* (7 vols., 1977-83)

Franciscana (Catholic Record Society vol.24, 1923)

Freemantle, A. (ed.), *The Papal Encyclicals* (1963)

Gibson, T. E. (ed.), *Crosby Records* (1888)

Gillow, J. and Hewitson, A., *The Tyldesley Diary* (1973)

Griffin, T., *Regional Trends*, vol.26 (1991)

Halifax, *Complete Works* (1969)

Haring, B., *Acting on the Word* (1975)

Heenan, J. V., *A Crown of Thorns* (1974)

Historical Manuscripts Commission: Kenyon Manuscripts (1894)

Holland, T., *For Better and for Worse* (1989)

Holt, T. G. (ed.), *Thomas West: A Guide to the Lakes: A Selection* (1982)

Howarth, D., *Figures in a Bygone Landscape* (1991)

Jones, A. (ed.), *The Jerusalem Bible* (1966)

Kenny, A., *A Path from Rome* (1985)

Lancaster, J. A. (ed.), 'Returns of Papists for the Parishes of Bolton and Deane in the Diocese of Chester, October 1706', *North West Catholic History*, vol.18 (1991)

Law, T. G. (ed.), *A Catechisme or Christian Doctrine by Laurence Vaux* (Chetham Society, new series vol.4, 1885)

Lundy, D., *Songs of the Spirit* (1978)

Mantel, H., *Fludd* (1989)

Marx, K. and Engels, F., *The Communist Manifesto*

Mathews, E., 'More Than Just Words', *Uniscript*, vol.24 (1980)

Miscellanea (Catholic Record Society, vol.3, 1906)

Miscellanea (Catholic Record Society, vol.53, 1960)

McDermott, J. (ed.), *Francis Thompson: Selected Writings* (1987)

McDermott, J. (ed.), *Hopkins in Lancashire* (1989)

Mitchinson, A. J. (ed.), *The Return of the Papists for the Diocese of Chester, 1705* (1986)

Naughton, B., *On The Pig's Back* (1988)

Naughton, B., *Saintly Billy* (1989)

Newman, J. H., *Sermons Preached on Various Occasions* (1913)

Ormerod, G. (ed.), *Tracts relating to the Military Proceedings in Lancashire during the Great Civil Warr* (Chetham Society, vol.2, 1844)

Rhodes, W. E. (ed.), 'The Apostolical Life of Ambrose Barlow', *Chetham Miscellanies* (Chetham Society, new series, vol.2, 1909)

Rock, D., *Hierurgia* (2vols., 1833)

Rowley, P., 'The Historical Search for Renewal', *Uniscript*, vol.17 (1979)

Royalist Composition Papers (Record Society of Lancashire and Cheshire, vol.24, 1891, vol.36, 1898. vol.95, 1941, vol.96, 1942)

Sands, E., 'Developing Parish Celebration', *Uniscript*, vol.24 (1980)

Sheppard, D. and Worlock, D., *Better Together* (1988)

Tait, J. (ed.), *Lancashire Quarter Sessions Rolls* (Chetham Society, new series, vol.77, 1917)

The Catechism of Christian Doctrine (1904)

The Registers of Estates of Lancashire Papists (Record Society of Lancashire and Cheshire, vol.98, 1961, vol.108, 1970, vol.117, 1977)

Thompson, P., 'Liverpool Replies', *Christian Order*, vol.32 (10) (1991), pp.488-92

Tierney, M. A. (ed.), *Dodd's Church History of England* (5 vols., 1839-49)

Trappes-Lomax, R. (ed.), *Lancashire Registers VI* (Catholic Record Society, vol.36, 1936)

Tyson, M. and Guppy, H. (eds), *The French Journals of Mrs Thrale and Doctor Johnson* (1932)

Whyte, J. H., 'The Vicars Apostolics' Returns of 1773', *Recusant History*, vol.9 (4) (1968), pp.205-14

Wigan Observer

Worrall, E. S.(ed), *Returns of Papists 1767* (2vols., 1980-9)

Yates, W., *A Map of the County of Lancashire, 1786* (1967)

Secondary Sources

Abbott, E. M., *History of the Diocese of Shrewsbury* (1986)

Aldred, M., *St Marie on the Sands, Southport* (1991)

Alger, B., 'An Optimist's Will and Convent Life', *North West Catholic History*, vol.2 (1) (1970)

Alger, B., 'The Priest and Informer Hitchmough', *North West Catholic History*, vol.1 (1) (2) (1969)

Anderson, D., *The Orrell Coalfield* (1975)

Anderson, D., Lane, J. and France, A. A., *The Standish Collieries, Wigan, Lancashire, 1635-1953* (1984)

Anstruther, G., 'Lancashire Clergy in 1639', *Recusant History*, vol.4 (1) (1957)

Anstruther, G., *The Seminary Priests* (4 vols, 1968-77)

Anstruther, G., *Vaux of Harrowden* (1953)

Armitage, P., 'Catholicism and Educational Control in North-East Lancashire in the Reign of Elizabeth I', *North West Catholic History*, vol.13 (1986)

Ashton, R., *The English Civil War* (1978)

Attwater, D., *The Catholic Encyclopaedic Dictionary* (1931)

Aveling, H., 'Catholic Recusancy in York' (Catholic Record Society monograph vol.2, 1970)

Aveling, H., 'The Catholic Recusants of the West Riding of Yorkshire', *Proceedings of the Leeds Philosophical and Literary Society, Literary and Historical Section*, vol.10 (6) (1963)

Bagley, J. J., *A History of Lancashire* (1961)

Bagley, J. J., *Lancashire Diarists* (1975)

Bagley, J. J. and Lewis, A. S., *Lancashire at War: Cavaliers and Roundheads, 1642-1661* (1977)

Bamber, J., 'Yealand Bi-centenary and Restoration of the Chapel', *North West Catholic History*, vol.10 (1983)

Beales, A. C. F., *Education Under Penalty* (1963)

Beaumont, W., *The Jacobite Trials at Manchester in 1694* (Chetham Society, old series, vol.28, 1853)

Beck, G. A. (ed.), *The English Catholics 1850-1950* (1950)

Bellenger, D. A., *English and Welsh Priests 1558-1800* (1984)

Bellenger, D. A., *The French Exiled Clergy* (1986)

Bennett, C., *Father Nugent of Liverpool* (1949)

Bentley, A., 'Lancashire Missions: Crossbrook', *North West Catholic History*, vol.1 (2) (1969)

Birt, H. N., *Obit Book of the English Benedictines* (1913)

Blackwood, B. G., 'Parties and issues in the Civil War in Lancashire', *Transactions of the Historic Society of Lancashire and Cheshire*, vol.132 (1983)

Blackwood, B. G., 'Plebeian Catholics in Later Stuart Lancashire', *Northern History*, vol.25 (1989)

Blackwood, B. G., 'Plebeian Catholics in the 1640s and 1650s', *Recusant History*, vol.118 (10) (1986)

Blackwood, B. G., *The Lancashire Gentry and the Great Rebellion* (Chetham Society, 3rd series, vol.25, 1978)

Blundell, F. O., *Old Catholic Lancashire* (3vols., 1915-39)

Bolton, C. A., *Salford Diocese and its Catholic Past* (1950)

Bossy, J., *The English Catholic Community, 1570-1850* (1975)

Bossy, J., *Christianity in the West* (1985)

Bossy, J. and Jupp, P. (eds.), *Essays Presented to Michael Roberts* (1976)

Broxap, E., *The Great Civil War in Lancashire* (1910)

Brooks, L., *Faith Never Lost* (1982)

Brown, J., 'God's Priest', *Christian Order*, vol.21 (8/9) (1980)

Bull, S., *The Civil War in Lancashire* (1991)

Burke's Landed Gentry (1964)

Burke's Peerage and Baronetage (1980)

Burke, T., *Catholic History of Liverpool* (1910)

Cartmel, J., *Blessed John Rigby* (1958)

Catholic Encyclopedia (15vols., 1906-14)

Chadwick, O., *The Secularization of the European Mind in the Nineteenth Century* (1990)

Champ, J. F., 'St Martin's Parish, Birmingham, in 1767', *Recusant History*, vol.15 (5) (1981)

Chinnici, J. P., *The English Catholic Enlightenment* (1980)

Clark, K., *The Gothic Revival* (1964)

Collins, H. C., *Lancashire Plain and Seaboard* (1953)

Conlon, M., *St Alban's, Blackburn* (1973)

Connolly, G., 'The Catholic Church and the First Manchester and Salford Trade Unions in the Age of the Industrial Revolution', *Transactions of the Lancashire and Cheshire Antiquarian Society*, vol.83 (1985)

Connolly, G., 'The Transubstantiation of Myth', *Journal of Ecclesiastical History*, vol.35 (1) (1984)

Connolly, G., '"With more than ordinary devotion to God": The Secular Missioner of the North in the Evangelical Age of the English Mission', *North West Catholic History*, vol.10 (1983)

Cragg, G. R., *The Church in the Age of Reason* (1970)

Crook, J. M., *The Greek Revival* (1972)

Coverdale, P., 'Ralph Standish Howard's Wooing of Lady Catherine Petre', *Essex Recusant*, vol.22 (1980)

Curtis, S., *History of Education in Great Britain* (1963)

David, C., *St Winefride's Well* (1971)

Davies, G., *The Early Stuarts* (1959)

Davies, J., 'Parish Charity', *North West Catholic History*, vol.17 (1990)

Davies, J., 'Rome on the Rates', *North West Catholic History*, vol.18 (1991)

Davies, J., 'The Catholic Community and Social Welfare Provision', *North West Catholic History*, vol.18 (1991)

Delumeau, J., *Catholicism between Luther and Voltaire* (1977)

Dickens, A. G., *The English Reformation* (1967)

Dictionary of National Biography (21vols., 1907-17)

Dixon, R. and Muthesius, S., *Victorian Architecture* (1985)

Doyle, P., 'Bishop Goss and the Gentry', *North West Catholic History*, vol.12 (1985)

Duffy, E. (ed.), *Challoner and his Church* (1981)

Duffy, E., *The Stripping of the Altars, Traditional Religion in England, c.1400-c.1580* (1992)

Dunleavy, J., *Haslingden Catholics 1815-1965* (1987)

Dunleavy, J., 'Schools To-day, Home Rule To-morrow', *North West Catholic History*, vol.16 (1989)

Dunleavy, 'The Emergence of the New Laity in Nineteenth-Century England: John Yates', *North West Catholic History*, vol.14 (1987)

Dykes, G., *Chowbent 1784* (n.d.)

Elliott, J. H., *Europe Divided, 1559-1598* (1968)

English and Welsh Hierarchical Structure (1990)

Fairhurst, S., *St Wilfrid's Church, Standish* (1972)

Fallon, G. A., 'The Catholic Justices of Lancashire under James II', *North West Catholic History*, vol.VIII (1981)

Fallon, G. A., *The Roman Catholics in Standish* (1976)

Fielding, S., 'The Catholic Whit-Walk in Manchester and Salford 1890-1939', *Manchester Region History Review*, vol.1 (1) (1987)

Foley, B. C., *Ann Fenwick of Hornby* (1977)

Foley, B. C., *Some People of the Penal Times* (1991)

Foley, B. C., *The Eighty-Five Blessed Martyrs* (1987)

Foster, C. S., *The Catholic Church in Ingatestone* (1982)

Forster, S., 'The English Seminary, Bruges', *North West Catholic History*, vol.12 (1985)

Fox, C., *The Personality of Britain* (1959)

Giblin, J. F., The Gerard Family', *North West Catholic History*, vol.17 (1990)

Giblin, J. F., 'The History of Birchley Hall', *North West Catholic History*, vol.4 (1972)

Giblin, J. F., 'The Stapleton-Bretherton Family and the Mission of St Bartholomew's, Rainhill', *North West Catholic History*, vol.9 (1982)

Gilbert, A. D., *Religion and Society in Industrial England* (1976)

Gillett, T. C., *The Weld Bank Story* (1974)

Gillow, J., *Bibliographical Dictionary of English Catholics* (5vols., 1885-1902)

Gooch, L., 'Papists and Profits: The Catholics of Durham and Industrial Development', *Durham County Local History Society Bulletin*, vol.62 (1989)

Gratton, J. M.,'The Earl of Derby's Catholic Army', *Transactions of the Historic Society of Lancashire and Cheshire*, vol.137 (1988)

Gratton, J. M., 'The Military Career of Richard Lord Molyneux, c.1623-54', *Transactions of the Historic Society of Lancashire and Cheshire*, vol.134 (1985)

Green, B., *The English Benedictine Congregation* (1979)

Haigh, C., *Reformation and Resistance in Tudor Lancashire* (1975)

Haigh, C. (ed.), *The Cambridge Historical Encyclopedia of Great Britain and Ireland* (1985)

Haigh, C., 'The Continuity of Catholicism in the English Reformation', *Past and Present*, vol.93 (1981)

Haile, M. and Bonney, E., *Life and Letters of John Lingard* (1912)

Hales, E. E. Y., *Revolution and Papacy* (1960)

Hales, E. E. Y., *The Catholic Church in the Modern World* (1958)

Halevy, E., *History of the English People in the Nineteenth Century* (6 vols., 1926)

Hampson, N., *The Enlightenment* (1968)

Hanley, L., 'John Sadler', *North West Catholic History*, vol.7 (1981), pp.16-24

Hanley, L., *The History of St Paul's, West Derby* (1979)

Hastings, A. (ed.), *Bishops and Writers* (1977)

Hastings, A. (ed.), *Modern Catholicism* (1991)

Havran, M. J., *The Catholics in Caroline England* (1962)

Haydon, C. M., 'Samuel Peploe and Catholicism in Preston, 1714', *Recusant History*, vol.22 (1) (1990)

Hebblethwaite, P., *The Runaway Church* (1978)

Hemphill, B., *The Early Vicars Apostolic of England* (1954)

Hibbard, C., 'The Contribution of 1639: Court and Country Catholicism', *Recusant History*, vol.16 (1) (1982)

Hibbert, C., *The Grand Tour* (1987)

Hickey, J., *Urban Catholics* (1967)

Hilton, J. A., 'A Catholic Congregation in the Age of Revolution: St Benedict's, Hindley', *North West Catholic History*, vol.17 (1990)

Hilton. J. A., 'Acton: Liberal Catholic Historian', *Worcestershire Recusant*, vol.42 (1983)

Hilton, J. A. (ed.), *Catholic Englishmen* (1984)

Hilton, J. A., 'Dodd's Church History', *North West Catholic History*, vol.14 (1987)

Hilton, J. A., 'Holy Family, New Springs', *North West Catholic History*, vol.15 (1988)

Hilton, J. A., 'Post-Reformation Catholicism in Cheshire', *North West Catholic History*, vol.9 (1982)

Hilton, J. A., 'Post-Reformation Catholicism in Derbyshire', *Derbyshire Miscellany*, vol.11 (3) (1987)

Hilton, J. A., 'The Case of Wigan', *North West Catholic History*, vol.10 (1983)

Hilton, J. A., 'The Catholic Ascendancy in the North, 1685-88', *North West Catholic History*, vol.5 (1978)

Hilton, J. A., 'The Catholic North-East, 1640-1850', *Durham County Local History Society Bulletin*, vol.24 (1980)

Hilton, J. A., 'The Catholic Revival in Thurnham', *North West Catholic History*, vol.12 (1985)

Hilton, J. A., *The Catholic Revival in Yealand* (1982)

Hilton, J. A., 'The Cumbrian Catholics', *Northern History*, vol.16 (1980)

Hilton, J. A. (ed.), *The Loveable West* (1990)

Hilton, J. A., 'Twenty Years On', *North West Catholic History*, vol.13 (1986)

Hilton, J. A., 'Upholland College Archives', *Catholic Archives*, vol.9, (1989)

Hilton, J. A., 'Wigan Catholics and the Policies of James II', *North West Catholic History Society*, vol.1(3) (1969)

Hobsbawm, E. J., *Industry and Empire* (1969)

Hobsbawm, E. J., *The Age of Revolution* (1977)

Hole, C., *Witchcraft in Britain* (London, 1980)

Holmes, J. D., *More Roman Than Rome* (1978)

Holt, T. G., 'Father Thomas West', *North West Catholic History*, vol.6 (1978)

Houston, S. J., *James I* (1973)

Hughes, P., *The Reformation in England* (3 vols., 1963)

Hughes, P., *Rome and the Counter-Reformation in England* (1941)

Hypher, N. C., *Lourdes* (1982)

Jones, B., *Homo Northwestus* (1992)

Jones, M. and Underwood, M. G., *The King's Mother: Lady Margaret Beaufort, Countess of Richmond and Derby* (1992)

Jordan, W. K., *The Social Institutions of Lancashire* (Chetham Society, 3rd series, vol.11, 1962)

Kelly, B., *Historical Dictionary of English Catholic Missions* (1907)

Kenyon, J. P., *Stuart England* (1978)

Kirk, J., *Biographies of English Catholics* (1909)

Klauser, T., *A Short History of the Western Liturgy* (1979)

Lancashire Record Office, 'The Rev. John Barow of Claughton', *North West Catholic History*, vol.3 (1971)

Lannon, D., 'Rook Street Chapel, Manchester', *North West Catholic History*, vol.16 (1989)

Laslett, P., *The World we have lost* (1979)

Leatherbarrow, J. S., *The Lancashire Recusants* (Chetham Society, new series, vol.90, 1957)

Leys, M. D. R., *Catholics in England 1559-1829* (1961)

Little, B., *Catholic Churches Since 1623* (1966)

Lowe, W. J., *The Irish in Mid-Victorian Lancashire* (1989)

Lowe, W. J., 'The Lancashire Irish and the Catholic Church, 1846-71: the social dimension', *Irish Historical Studies*, vol.20 (78) (1976)

Lunn, D., *The English Benedictines, 1540-1688* (1980)

Lytham Hall (1981)

Marsh, V., *St Joseph's, Wrightington* (1969)

Mathew, D., *Catholicism in England* (1948)

Mathew, D., *The Jacobean Age* (1938)

McDermott, J., 'John Farrimond, Novelist', *North West Catholic History*, vol.13 (1986)

McGrath, T, G., 'The Tridentine Evolution of Modern Irish Catholicism, 1563-1962', *Recusant History*, vol.20 (4) (1991)

McLeod, H., *Religion and the People of Western Europe 1789-1970* (1981)

McManners, J., *The Oxford Illustrated History of Christianity* (1992)

Mews, S. (ed.), *Religion and National Identity* (Studies in Church History, vol.18, 1982)

Miller, J., *Popery and Politics in England 1660-88* (1973)

Milner, F., *J. M. W. Turner Paintings in Merseyside Collections*

Milward, P., *Religious Controversies of the Jacobean Age* (1978)

Mullet, '"To Dwell Together in Unity": the Search for Agreement in Preston Politics, 1660-90', *Transactions of the Historic Society of Lancashire and Cheshire*, vol.125 (1974)

Musgrove, F., *The North of England* (1990)

Neal, F., 'A Criminal Profile of the Liverpool Irish', *Transactions of the Historic Society of Lancashire and Cheshire*, vol.140 (1991)

Neal, F., *Sectarian Violence: The Liverpool Experience, 1819-1914* (Manchester, 1988)

Neill, S., *Anglicanism* (1960)

Newman, P. R., 'Aspects of the Civil War in Lancashire', *Transactions of the Lancashire and Cheshire Antiquarian Society*, vol.72 (1983)

Newman, P. R., 'Catholic Royalist Activists in the North, 1642-46', *Recusant History*, vol.14 (1) (1977)

Norman, E., *Roman Catholicism in England* (1985)

Norman, E., *The English Catholic Church in the Nineteenth Century* (1984)

O'Brien, S., '10,000 Nuns', *Catholic Archives*, vol.9 (1989)

O'Brien, S., 'Terra Incognita', *Past and Present*, vol.121 (1988)

O'Gorman, E., *The History of All Saints Church, Barton-upon-Irwell* (1988)

Parking, W., *The Friars Preacher in Lancashire* (1991)

Pelling, H., *A History of British Trade Unionism* (1963)

Petrie, C., *The Jacobite Movement* (2 vols, 1948-50)

Pevsner, N., *The Buildings of England: Lancashire, The Industrial and Commercial South* (1969)

Pevsner, N., *The Buildings of England: Lancashire, The Rural North* (1969)

Plumb, B., 'A Victorian Monk-Musician', *Ampleforth Journal*, vol.79 (2) (1974)

Plumb, B., *Arundel to Zabi: A Biographical Dictionary of the Catholic Bishops of England and Wales* (1987)

Plumb, B., *Found Worthy* (1986)

Plumb, B., *Our Glorious Chapter* (1977)

Plumb, B., *Our Lady and All Saints, Parbold* (1984)

Plumb, B., *SS Peter and Michael, Woolston* (1985)

Plumb, B., 'Some Religious Orders in the North West', *North West Catholic History*, vol.16 (1989)

Plumb, B., 'Teresa Helena Higginson (1844-1905)', *North West Catholic History*, vol.18 (1991)

Plumb, B., *The Warrington Mission* (1978)

Porteus, T. C., 'New Light on the Lancashire Plot, 1692-4', *Transactions of the Lancashire and Cheshire Antiquarian Society*, vol.50 (1936)

Rackham, O., *The History of the Countryside* (1987)

Ramsden, F., *A History of the de Trafford Family* (1986)

Reid, R., *The Peterloo Massacre* (1989)

Reid, S., *The Finest Knight in England* (1979)

Richardson, R. C., *Puritanism in North-West England* (1972)

Rowse, A. L, *The England of Elizabeth* (1950)

Rowse, A. L, *The Expansion of Elizabethan England* (1955)

Scarisbrick, J. J., *The Reformation and the English People* (1984)

Schmude, K. G., *Hilaire Belloc* (1978)

Scott, G., 'A Benedictine Conspirator: Henry Joseph Johnston (c.1656-1723)', *Recusant History*, vol.20 (1) (1990)

Scott, G., '"The Times are Fast Approaching": Bishop Charles Walmesley OSB (1722-97) as Prophet', *Journal of Ecclesiastical History*, vol.36 (4) (1985)

Service, A., *Edwardian Architecture* (1977)

Shanes, E., *Turner's England* (1990)

Singleton, F. J., *Mowbreck Hall and the Willows* (1983)

Singleton, F. J., 'Recusancy in the Fylde', *North West Catholic History*, vol.13 (1986)

Smith, A. G. R. (ed.), *The Reign of James VI and I* (1973)

Smith, W. V., 'The Rev. Simon George Bordley, Schoolmaster', *Recusant History*, vol.13 (4) (1976)

Steele, E. D., 'The Irish Presence in the North of England', *Northern History*, vol.12 (1976)

Stonor, R. J., *Liverpool's Hidden Story* (1957)

Supple-Green, J. F., *The Catholic Revival in Yorkshire, 1850-1900* (1990)

Taylor, H.,'The Ancient Crosses of Lancashire: The Hundred of West Derby', *Transactions of the Lancashire and Cheshire Antiquarian Society*, vol.19 (1901)

The Foundations of the Sisters of Notre Dame (1895)

Thomas, K., *Religion and the Decline of Magic* (1978)

Upholland Centenary (1983)

Vaughan, F. J., 'Bishop Leyburn and His Confirmation Register of 1687', *Northern Catholic History*, vol.12 (1980)

Victoria County History of Lancaster (8 vols., 1966)

Vidler, A., *The Church in an Age of Revolution* (1974)

Walker, F., *Historical Geography of South West Lancashire before the Industrial Revolution* (Chetham Society, new series, vol.113, 1939)

Walton, J. K., *Lancashire: A Social History, 1558-1939* (1987)

Ward, B., *The Dawn of the Catholic Revival in England* (2 vols., 1909)

Ward, B., *The Sequel to Catholic Emancipation* (2 vols., 1915)

Ward, T. G. and Warren, L., *The Manor Mission of Low Furness* (1979)

Ware, S. H., *The State of the Parties in Lancashire before the Rebellion of 1715* (Chetham Society, vol.5, 1845)

Wark, K. R., *Elizabethan Recusancy in Cheshire* (Chetham Society, 3rd series, vol.19, 1971)

Watkin, E. I., *Roman Catholicism in England from the Reformation to 1850* (1957)

Warren, L., *A Short History of St Wilfrid's Church, Preston* (1972)

Webster, C., 'Richard Towneley, 1629-1707, and the Towneley Group', *Transactions of the Historic Society of Lancashire and Cheshire*, vol.118 (1966)

Werly, J. M., 'The Irish in Manchester, 1832-49', *Irish Historical Studies*, vol.18 (71)(1973)

Whitehead, M., 'Briefly, and in confidence', *Recusant History*, vol.20 (4) (1991)

Whitehead, M., *Peter Newby* (1980)

Williams, J. A., 'The Distribution of Catholic Chaplaincies in the Early Eighteenth Century', *Recusant History*, vol.12 (1)

Williams, M. E., *The Venerable English College, Rome* (1979)

Wise, M. J., *Ordnance Survey Atlas of Great Britain* (1980)

Index